# PLOUGHSHARES

*Fall 1994 · Vol. 20, Nos. 2 & 3*

GUEST EDITOR
Rosellen Brown

EXECUTIVE DIRECTOR
DeWitt Henry

EDITOR
Don Lee

POETRY EDITOR
David Daniel

ASSISTANT EDITOR
Jessica Dineen

EDITORIAL ASSISTANT
Jodee Stanley

FOUNDING PUBLISHER
Peter O'Malley

PLOUGHSHARES, a journal of new writing, is guest-edited serially by prominent writers who explore different and personal visions, aesthetics, and literary circles. PLOUGHSHARES is published in April, August, and December at Emerson College, 100 Beacon Street, Boston, MA 02116-1596. Telephone: (617) 578-8753. Phone-a-Poem: (617) 578-8754.

INTERNS: Angela Pogany, Joanna Yas, Katherine Reed Ives, and Matt Jones. POETRY READERS: Renee Rooks, Bethany Daniel, Susan Rich, Tom Laughlin, Jason Rogers, Mary-Margaret Mulligan, Rachel Piccione, Karen Voelker, and Linda Russo. FICTION READERS: Billie Lydia Porter, Michael Rainho, Stephanie Booth, Jodee Stanley, Esther Crain, Karen Wise, Tanja Brull, Christine Flanagan, Lee Harrington, David Rowell, Maryanne O'Hara, Barbara Lewis, Holly LeCraw Howe, Sara Nielsen Gambrill, Kim Reynolds, and Elizabeth Rourke. PHONE-A-POEM COORDINATOR: Joyce Peseroff.

SUBSCRIPTIONS (ISSN 0048-4474): $19/domestic and $24/international for individuals; $22/domestic and $27/international for institutions. See last page for order form.

UPCOMING: Winter 1994-95, Vol. 20, No. 4, a special staff-edited poetry and fiction issue, will appear in December 1994 (editorially complete). Spring 1995, Vol. 21, No. 1, a fiction and poetry issue edited by Gary Soto, will appear in April 1995. Fall 1995, Vol. 21, Nos. 2&3, a fiction issue edited by Ann Beattie, will appear in August 1995.

SUBMISSIONS: Please see back of issue for detailed submission policies.

BACK ISSUES are available from the publisher. Write or call for abstracts and a price list. Microfilms of back issues may be obtained from University Microfilms. PLOUGHSHARES is also available as a CD-ROM full-text product from UMI and Information Access Company. INDEXED in M.L.A. Bibliography, American Humanities Index, Index of American Periodical Verse, Book Review Index. Self-index through Volume 6 available from the publisher; annual supplements appear in the fourth number of each subsequent volume. All rights for individual works revert to the authors upon publication.

DISTRIBUTED by Bernhard DeBoer (113 E. Centre St., Nutley, NJ 07110), Fine Print Distributors (6448 Highway 290 East, Austin, TX 78723), Ingram Periodicals (1226 Heil Quaker Blvd., La Vergne, TN 37086), and L-S Distributors (130 East Grand Ave., South San Francisco, CA 94080). PRINTED in the United States of America on recycled paper by Edwards Brothers.

PLOUGHSHARES receives additional support from the Lannan Foundation, the National Endowment for the Arts, and the Massachusetts Cultural Council. The opinions expressed in this magazine do not necessarily reflect those of Emerson College, the editors, the staff, the trustees, or the supporting organizations.

# CONTENTS

*Ploughshares · Fall 1994*

# Introduction

I knew an editor once—alas, an editor whose magazine commanded a good deal of national attention—who hated to publish fiction unless he could be assured that it was "true," that it "had happened." Having restricted his interest to the documentary, one must assume his list of approved works could not have included the monumental pillars of literature, which, by his lights, would have to seem fudged, faked, frivolous.

The "personal essay," the "nonfiction narrative," presents itself, if not as precisely true, then as an emanation of an identifiable speaking voice making statements for which it takes responsibility. Is there something philistine about wanting to locate the "actual" source of a story, an argument, a complaint? Does the essay make fiction look unmoored and arbitrary? Do those who prefer it, with their utilitarian respect for "the genuine," have some corresponding suspicion or lack of need for the "made up," the "merely dreamed"?

Those, of course, are loaded questions.

The essay, in fact, by virtue of its finely inflected voice, admits to being every bit as much an imaginative construction as a short story. It must use some, if not all, of the techniques of fiction: plot, characterization, physical atmosphere, thematic complexity, stylistic appropriateness, psychological open-endedness. Further, it proceeds by creating for its "I" an "eye," a persona through whose unique vision, experience or information will be filtered, perhaps distorted, perhaps questioned, and that persona will cast a shadow as dense and ambiguous as that of an imaginary protagonist. *The self* is surely a created character.

Perhaps the boniness, the lack of juice, in minimalist writing has contributed to our current passion for the testimony of a full-blooded essayist's voice. Or it may be that the coolness of a post-modern world whose ironies and moral relativism keep us on shifting ground leads us to want to hear the opinions and interpretations of discursive writing. One way or another, readers, these days, seem to yearn for *assertion.*

With a few exceptions, it's been a long time since we've allowed our novelists to lecture us with all their wisdom showing ("Miss Brooke had that kind of beauty which seems to be thrown into relief by poor dress"). My students, typical of their generation, call such unabashed *sententiae,* when they're found in contemporary fiction, "pushy" and "didactic." They resist writing that dares interpret the world so forthrightly, as if, all certainties having been deconstructed and destabilized, those are outdated parental voices, shamelessly patriarchal (even if it's Jane Austen who's doing the pronouncing). We think ourselves not in the mood to be enlightened by our stories; rather, we'd like to assemble our opinions, do-it-yourself, out of the shards of experience that come to us "objectively" and without comment—the text as stage or screen or television play. And so, in fiction, there is no one left to tell us much.

Enter the essay, because we still have a sneaking need for authority. We really do want our authors smart, we want the benefit of their engagement and analysis, though perhaps we like those best cut with some vulnerability. And the useful information larded into some essays makes us feel virtuously employed. Like a nation of sleepers who set foreign-language tapes to murmuring beneath our pillows, we don't want to lose a few hours of possible self-improvement.

There's been great pleasure for me in assembling an issue of *Ploughshares*—the first devoted entirely to nonfiction—that includes considerations of intimate personal history, science, travel, the acquisition of language, religion, politics, food, pop culture, birth and dying, war, sex, friendship, and a little professional attention to literary matters as well. The manner in which these "subjects" come under scrutiny ranges from the traditional "well-made" construction to a few looser, associative flights that laugh in the earnest face of the (extended) five-paragraph theme.

Interestingly, part of the pleasure, as well as the difficulty, of assembling this collection has been the surprisingly high quality of the submissions. At the very least, most essays are engaging if only at the literal level—the voyeur in us will find almost any story worth listening to, up to a point. Mediocre essays, I can swear after months of reading, are never as boring as mediocre fiction because, even in the hands of the inept, the lives we actually live or witness are more interesting than the ones most of us can (or dare to) invent from scratch. Thinly imagined fiction is dead because, too often, it is blighted at conception by the clumsy utility of its "message," or by the banality of its shape and its language. Essays can be badly written and banal, too, but (to mix metaphors wantonly) the wildly unpredictable movements of real event and outcome tend to poke through and make a lively choreography.

Better yet, the essayist need not claim to comprehend or speak from *within* experience the way the fiction writer must. The speaker is on a journey of discovery, often unasked for and unplanned, and though he or she has witnessed enough to introduce us to a character or a landscape, a quandary or a memory, the complex delight of the essayist's voice is that it can admit to bewilderment without losing its authority. The essayist is an explorer, whereas the fiction writer is a landed inhabitant, or, confident at make-believe, the ventriloquial voice of one.

I will admit, however, that I am more uncertain than ever of what elevates a particular writer's personal testimony into an embodiment of something more general that makes the intimacy of memoir, which is reflexive, into an essay worthy of a public stage. Many of the works I did not choose for publication were fascinating, but somehow, though I was not searching for the overtly didactic, they didn't seem to me sufficiently emblematic. However emotionally informative, they were finally sui generis. They did not vault some invisible wall to come down hard where others might feel themselves implicated. Every editor will draw that line in a different place, I'm sure. Even this editor felt her standards on this question wobble and contradict themselves.

*Ploughshares* issues usually organize themselves around a theme—recent years have brought us everything from ecstasy to a reconsideration of race. For this first voyage into nonfiction, it seemed sufficient to concentrate on the multiplicity of available subjects and forms. Nonetheless, a few thematic clusters have presented themselves uninvited, and I've bowed to them by virtue of my own interests and obsessions: One, reiterated again and again, is a search for home, a return from some kind of exile or confusion about where the writer's "true west" lies.

Another, surely inescapable today, is a questioning of "expected" responses: a doctor's refusal to keep his emotional needs separate from his patients'; a young woman's discovery that the politically correct words are not the ones that leap to her lips when they "ought to"; a sister's acquiescence to her own as well as her brother's sexual curiosity when every conventional judgment—the shaken finger of external authority—would tell her that she should see herself as a victim. A boy, in 1946, encounters the Japanese—*a* Japanese—as human; a writer from Yugoslavia escapes, bitterly, from his warring native languages into English; a child, rescued from Hitler's Germany, identifies more deeply with a hanged man than with his executioner.

Enumerated by "theme," all that sounds very grim. But the invigorating fact is that I feel I've been giving my ear to a chorus of highly individual and independent singers and have pulled out a few clear voices, almost arbitrarily, from among them. I am grateful to these essayists for complicating "truth" so unpredictably, for roughing up its edges and fingering its contradictory textures so deftly that, were he to open these pages—an unlikely possibility—I'm sure my old friend, the editor-in-search-of-the-real, in his irritable reaching after (documentable) fact, would find his thick head spinning.

*The photograph on the cover has been "doctored," manipulated by the artist. He has refracted reality through the visual equivalent of a voice and a whole new reality has emerged, with its own claims on our imagination. I see this little girl about to set sail in the basket of a balloon, dreaming wistfully above the earth and all those distant adult figures. Whether she is leaving home or, like Alice or Dorothy, returning to the familiar, she exists as we see her only through the mediation of the artist who created this poignant moment. (In literal fact, the child is in an iron lung; she comes to us from the era before the vanquishing of polio. Some things we need to know, others we don't.)*

*Here is a new actuality, imagined out of raw fact: The photographer as essayist.*

## Relics of Summer

The fonts in all the churches are dry. I run my fingers through the dusty scallops of marble: not a drop for my hot forehead. The Tuscan July heat is invasive to the body but not to the stone churches that hold onto the dampness of winter, releasing a gray coolness slowly throughout the summer. I have a feeling, walking into one then another, that I walk into palpable silence. A lid seems to descend on our voices, or a large damp hand. In the vast church of San Biago below Montepulciano, there is an airy quiet as you enter. Right under the dome, you can stand in one spot and speak or clap your hands, and far up against the inner cup of the dome an eerie echo sends the sound rapidly back. The quality of the sound is not like the hello across a lake but a sharp, repeated return. Your voice flattened, otherworldly. It is hard to think a mocking angel isn't hovering against the frescoes, though more likely a pigeon rests there.

Since I have been spending summers in Cortona, the major shock and joy is how at home I feel. But not just at home, *returned* to that primal first awareness of home. I feel at home because dusty trucks park at intersections and sell watermelons. The same thump to test for ripeness. The boy holds up a rusty iron scale with discs of different sizes to counterweigh the striped Sugar Baby. His arm muscle jumps up like Popeye's and the breeze brings me a whiff of his scent of dry grasses, onions, and dirt. In big storms, lightning drives a jagged stake into the ground and hailstones bounce in the yard, bringing back the smell of ozone to me from Georgia days when I'd gather a bowlful the size of Ping-Pong balls and put them in the freezer.

Sunday is cemetery day here, and though our small-town Southern plots are austere compared to these lavish displays of flowers on almost every grave, we, too, made Sunday pilgrimages to Evergreen with glads or zinnias. I sat in the back seat, balancing the cool teal vase between my knees while my mother complained that Hazel never turned her hand to pick one stem and it was *her* own mother lying there, not just a mother-in-law. Gathered around Anselmo Arnaldo, 1904–1982, perhaps these families are saying, as mine did, thank God the old goat's lying here rather than still driving us crazy.

Sweltering nights, the air comes close to body temp., and shifting constellations of fireflies compete with stars. Mosquito nights, grabbing at air, the mosquito caught in my hair. Long days when I can taste the sun. I move through this foreign house I've acquired as though my real ancestors left their presences in these rooms. As though this were the place I always came home to.

Living near a small town again certainly is part of it. And living again with nature. (A student of mine from Los Angeles visited. When I walked him out to the end of the point for the wide-angle view of lake, chestnut forests, Apennines, olive groves, and valleys, he was unprepared. He stood silently, the first time I'd known he could, and finally said, "It's, uh, like nature.") Right, nature: clouds swarm in from over the lake and thunder cracks along my backbone, booms like waves boom far out at sea. I write in my notebook: "The dishwasher was struck. We heard the sizzle. But isn't it good, the gigantic storm, the flood of terror they felt beside fires in the cave? The thunder shakes me like a kitten the big cat has picked up by the neck. I ricochet home, heat lightning; I'm lying on the ground 4,000 miles from here, letting rain soak through me."

Rain flays the grapes. Nature: what's ripe, will the driveway wash away, when to dig potatoes, how much water is in the irrigation well? Early life reconnects. I go out to get wood; a black scorpion scuttles over my hand and suddenly I remember the furry tarantulas in the shower at Lakemont, the shriek when my barefooted mother stepped on one and felt it crunch then squash up soft as a banana between her toes.

Is it the spill of free days? I dream my mother rinses my tangle of hair with a bowl of rainwater.

Sweet time, exaggerated days, getting up at dawn because when the midsummer sun tops the crests across the valley, the first rays hit me in the face like they strike some rock at Stonehenge on the solstice. To be fully awake when the sky turns rose-streaked coral and scarves of fog drift across the valley and the wild canaries sing. In Georgia, my father and I used to get up to walk the beach at sunrise. At home in San Francisco what wakes me is the alarm at seven, or the car-pool horn blowing for the child downstairs, or the recycle truck with its crashing cascade of glass. I love the city and never have felt really at home there.

I was drawn to the surface of Italy for its perched towns, the food, language, and art. I was pulled also to its sense of lived life, the coexistence of times that somehow gives an aura of timelessness—I toast the Etruscan wall above us with my coffee every morning—all the big abstracts that act out in everything from the aggression on the *autostrada* to the late afternoon stroll through the piazza. I cast my lot here for a few short months a year because I know my curiosity for the layered culture of the country is inexhaustible. But the main umbilical I feel is totally unexpected, elides logic, and it reaches to me through the church.

To my surprise I have bought a ceramic Mary with a small cup for home use of holy water. As a fallen-away Methodist, then a fallen-away Episcopalian, my holy water, I suppose, is a sham. However, I have taken it from the spring I discovered near the house, a hidden natural well where a deep pool of clear water collects in a declivity of white stone. This looks like holy water to me. It must have been the house's original source. Or it's older than the house—medieval, Roman, Etruscan. Though some interior juggling is going on, I do not expect to emerge as a Catholic, or even as a believer. I am essentially pagan by birth. Southern populism was boiled into my blood early; the idea of a pope with the last word gives me hives. "Idolatrous," our minister called the worship of Mary and the saints. "Mackerel snapper," my classmates teased Andy Evans, the lone Catholic in our school. Briefly, in college, I was drawn to the romance of the mass, especially the three a.m. fishermen's mass in St. Louis's Cathedral in New Orleans. I lost interest in the whole show when my good friend, a New Orleans Catholic, told me in complete seriousness that mortal sin began if you kissed longer than ten seconds. A ten-second French kiss was okay but a dry twenty-second kiss would land you in trouble. Though I still like rituals, even empty ones, what magnetizes me here feels more radical.

Now I love the quick mass in tiny upper Cortona churches,

where the same sounds have provided a still point for the residents for almost eight hundred years. When a black Labrador wandered in, the priest interrupted his holy spiel to shout, "For the love of God, somebody get that dog out of here." If I stop in on a weekday morning, I sit there alone, enjoying the country Baroque. I think: *Here I am.* I love the parade of relics through the streets, with gold-robed priests traveling along in a billow of incense, their way prepared by children in white, scattering the streets with petals of broom, rose, daisy. In the noon heat, I almost hallucinate. What's in the gold box held aloft with banners—a splinter from the cradle? Never mind we thought Jesus was born in a lowly manger; this is the splinter of the true cradle. Or am I confused? It's a splinter of the true cross. It is on its way through the streets, brought out into the air one day a year. And suddenly I think, What did that hymn mean, *cleft for me,* rising years ago, perpendicular from the white board church in Georgia?

In my South, there were signs on trees that said "Repent." Halfway up a skinny pine, up beyond the tin trough that caught the resin, hung a warning, "Jesus is coming." Here, when I turn on the car radio, a lulling voice implores Mary to intercede for us in purgatory. In a nearby town, one church has as its relic a phial of Holy Milk. As my student would say, That's from, like, Mary.

On the terrace at noon, I'm tanning my legs as I read about early martyrs and medieval saints. I'm drawn to the martyred San Lorenzo, who was put on a grill for his troublesome faith and seared until he reportedly said, "Turn me over, I'm done on this side," and thereby became the favorite saint of chefs. The virginal young women martyrs all were raped, stabbed, tortured, or locked away because of their devotion to Christ. Sometimes the hand of God reached down and swept one away, like Ursula, who did not wish to marry the barbarian Conan. With her ten thousand virgins (all avoiding men?), God miraculously lifted them in boats and sailed them across the unfriendly skies, depositing them in Rome, where they bathed in lime-scented water and formed a sacred order. Stunning, the prevalence of the miracle. In the middle ages, some of the venerated women found the foreskin of Jesus materialized in their mouths. I don't know if there exists a relic of that. (Would it look like a chewed rubber band? A dried wad of bubble gum?) The foreskin stops me for a good ten minutes and I stare out at the bees swarming the *tigli* trees, trying to imagine that event happening, and not just once. The moment of recognition, what she said, what the reaction was—a boggling speculation. Somehow, I'd never heard of these kinkier saints in America, although someone once sent me a box of new books, each one about a saint's life. When I called the bookstore, they told me my benefactor wished to remain anonymous. Now I read on and find that some had "holy anorexia" and lived on the wafer alone. If a saint's bones were dug up, a flowery fragrance filled the town. After San Francesco preached to the birds, they flew up into the shape of a cross then separated into the four directions. The saints would eat the pus and lice of the poor to show their humility; in turn, the faithful liked to drink the bath water of a holy person. If, after death, a saint's heart was cut out, perhaps an image of the holy family carved in a ruby would be found inside. *Oh*, I realize, *here's where they put their awe. I understand that.*

I understand because this everyday wildness and wonder come back so naturally from the miracle-hungry South. They almost seem like memories somehow, the vertebrae of the virgin, the toenail of San Marco. My favorite, the breath of San Giuseppe, foster father of Christ. I imagine an opaque-green glass bottle with a ground stopper, the swift exhaling of air if it were opened. At home when I was small, our seamstress kept her jar of gallstones on the window sill above her Singer. Marking my hem, her mouth full of pins, she'd say, "Lord, I don't want to go through nothing like that again. Now you turn round. Those things won't even dissolve in gasoline." Her talisman against sickness. Emblems and omens.

Santa Dorotea immured in her cell for two years, against a high walled pit in the dank cathedral. Communion through a grate and a diet of bread and gruel. I hated visiting Miss Tibby, who treated the corns on my mother's little toes, shaving yellow curls of skin off with a vegetable peeler, then rubbing her feet with thick lotion that smelled like crank case oil and Ovaltine. The bare bulb lit not only my mother's foot on a cushion but also a coffin where Miss Tibby slept at night so there would be no surprises later.

In high school my friends and I parked a block away and

secretly peered in the windows of the Holy Rollers, who spoke in tongues, sometimes screaming with a frightening ecstatic look on their faces and falling to the floor writhing and jerking. We were profane, smothering our laughter at the surely sexual fervor and the contorted postures. Later we'd sit in the car, Jeff smoking, and watch them file out of the peeling church, looking as normal as anyone. In Naples, the phial of San Gennaro's congealed blood liquifies once a year. There's also a crucifix that used to grow one long hair of Jesus that would have to be barbered once a year. That one seems particularly close to Southern sensibilities.

In the U.S., I think there is no *sanctioned* place to put such fixated strangeness, so it just jumps out when it has to. Driving through the South last spring, I stopped near Metter, Georgia, for a barbecue sandwich. After the sweet salty pork and iced tea, I was directed out back to the bathroom by the owner; pork-bellied, sweating over his pit, he merely nodded toward the rear. No sign at all that as I opened the screen door I would encounter two moulting ostriches. How they came to be in that out-of-the-way town in South Georgia and what iconographical necessity led the family to gaze on and house these dusty creatures are philosophical gifts I've been given to ponder in nights of insomnia.

Growing up in the God-fearing, faith-healing, end-of-the-world-is-at-hand South gave me many chances to visit snake collections beside gas stations when my parents stopped to fill up; to drive past roadside religious ceremonies in which snakes were ecstatically "handled"; to see tumble-down wonders of the world exhibits—reliquaries of sorts—in the towns bordering the swamps. I know a box of black cat's bones makes a powerful conjure. And that a bracelet of dimes can ward it off. I was used to cages of baby alligators crawling on the back of the mother of all, a fourteen-foot beauty who opened her jaws wide enough that I could have stood in them. The sagging chicken-wire fences couldn't save you if those sleeping logs rose up and decided to take off after you—alligators can run twenty-five miles an hour. Albino deer covered with ticks that leapt on my hand when I petted their mossy noses, a stuffed painter (panther) with green marbles for eyes, a thirty-foot tapeworm in a jar. The owner explains that it was taken from the throat of his seventeen-year-old niece when the doctor lured it out of her stomach with a clove of garlic on a toothpick. They waited until it showed its head, lured it out farther, then grabbed, chopped off its head with a straight razor while hauling the thing out of Darleen's stomach like a rope out of the river.

Wonders. Miracles. In cities, we're less and less capable of the imagination for the super real, ground down as we are by reality. In rural areas, close to the stars and groves, we're still willing to give it a whirl. So I recover the cobra, too, so much more impressive with his flattened head than rattlesnakes, whose skins paper the office of the owner of the Eighth Wonder of the World, where we have stopped for gas at the Georgia border. We are close to Jasper, Florida, where my mother and father were married in the middle of the night. I am amazed, despite my mother's warning that the owners are carnival people and it is not worth seeing and I have exactly ten minutes or they will go on to White Springs without me. The slight thrill at the possibility of being left behind on this curve of road lined with moss-draped oaks, the trailer like a silver bullet set up on concrete blocks, a woman glimpsed inside, washing her hair over a tin bowl and the radio blaring "I'm So Lonesome I Could Die." I knew then and still know that the man with the phosphorescent glow-in-the-dark torch tattooed on his back and the full-blown roses tattooed on his biceps believed his wonders were real. I follow him to the bamboo hut where the cobra from darkest Calcutta rises to the song made by blowing on a comb covered with cellophane. The cobra mesmerizes the mangy dog thumping his tail in the doorway. The peacock gives a powerful he-haw, shakes himself into full regalia, the blues in his fan of feathers more intense than my own or my mother's eyes, and, as everyone knows, we have the purest sky-blue eyes. The peacock's eyes looked exactly like the snake's. The owner's wife comes out of the trailer with a boa constrictor casually draped around her neck. She checks on another snake, to whom she has fed a large rat without even cutting it up. The rat was simply disappearing, like a fist into a sweater sleeve. I buy a Nehi and an oatmeal cookie sandwich, run out to the Oldsmobile vibrating in the heat. My father scratches off; gravel spumes behind us. "What have you got?" My mother turns around.

"Just a cold drink and this." I hold up the large cookie.

"Those things have lard in the middle. That's not icing—that's pure T lard with enough powdered sugar to make your teeth ache."

I don't believe her but when I break open the cookie, it is crawling with maggots. I quickly throw it out the window. "What did you see in that awful gyp joint?"

"Nothing," I answer.

Growing up, I absorbed the Southern obsession with place, and place can seem to me somehow an extension of the self. If I am made of red clay and black river water and white sand and moss, that seems natural to me.

However, living as a grown woman in San Francisco, I never have that belonging sensation. The white city with its clean light on the water, the pure, heart-stopping coast, and the Marin hills with the soft contours of sleeping giants under blankets of green—I am the awed tourist, delighted to have made this brief escape, which is my adult life. My house is just one of thousands; my life could be just another story in the naked city. My feet feel only a friendly connection with concrete and my eye looks with insouciance at the scissors point of the Transamerica pyramid and jagged skyline I can see from my dining-room window. Everyone seems to have cracked the door two inches to see who's there. I see you through my two inches; you see me through yours. We are monumentally self-reliant.

I never tire of going into Italian churches. The vaulted arches and triptychs, yes. But each one also has its characteristic blue dust smell, the smell of time. The codified annunciations, nativities, and the crucifixions dominate all churches. At the core, these all struggle with the mystery of the two elementals—birth and death. We are frangible. In the side altars, the high arches, the glass manuscript cases in the crypts, the shadowed curves of the apse, these archetypal concerns and the dreamland of religious fervor lock horns with the painterly subject matter in individualized ways. I'm drawn to a bizarre painting that practically leaps off the wall. In a dark, high panel close to the ceiling in San Gimignano, there's Eve rising boldly out of supine Adam's open side. Not the *whoosh* of instantaneous creation I've imagined from reading Genesis, when she appeared as easily as "Let there be Light." This is graphic, someone's passion to be *present* at the miracle. As graphic as the wondrous cobra of Calcutta spiraling up in the humid air of South Georgia before my very eyes. Adam is meat. The vision grabs the viewer like the glow-in-the-dark torch. Now hear this, loud and clear. In Orvieto's Duomo, Signorelli's humans, just restored to their flesh on Judgment Day, stand grandly and luxuriously beside the grinning skeletons they were, just moments before. Parts of the body still glow with the aura of the bare bone, a gauzy white light emanating from the firm, new flesh in its glory. A strange turn—we're used to thinking of the decay of the flesh; here's the dream of rejuvenation. Flitting around in the same arena of that cathedral are depictions of hell, green-headed devils with snaky genitals. The damned are twisted, poked, jabbed, while one voluptuous blonde (no doubt what *her* sins were) flies away on the back of a devil with stunted, unaerodynamic wings. Clearly we are in someone's head, midnight imaginings of the descent, the fall, the upward turn. The paintings can be sublime, but there is a comic-book aspect to much church painting, a wordless progression of blunt narrative very close to fire-and-brimstone fundamentalists who still hold forth in the South. If there was more than one word, Repent, hanging on those Southern pines, it was bound to be Doomsday.

Wandering around in churches, I see over and over San Sebastiano pierced with arrows, martyred Sant' Agata holding out her breasts on a plate like two over-easy eggs, Sant' Agnese kneeling piously while a lovely youth stabs her in the neck. Almost every church has its locked relic box like a miniature mausoleum and what does this mean? Thorn from the crown. Finger digits of San Lorenzo. The talismans that say to the viewers, "Hold on, like these, have faith." Standing in the dim crypt in a country church where a handful of dust has been venerated for several hundred years, I see that even today, toward the end of the century, the case is remembered with fresh carnations. I uncover my second realization: *This is where they put their memories and wants.* Besides functioning as vast cultural repositories, these churches map intimate human needs. How familial they begin to seem (and how far away from the historical church, the bloody history of the Papacy): the coarse robe of San Francesco, another phial of Mary's, this one filled with tears. I see them like the locket I had, with a curl of light-brown hair, no one remembered whose, the box of rose petals on the closet shelf behind the blue Milk of Magnesia bottle and the letters tied with frayed ribbon, the translucent white rock from Half Moon Bay. *Never forget.* As I wax the floor tiles and wring out the mop, I can think of Santa Zita of Lucca, saint of housekeeping, as was Willie Bell Smith in my family's house. Basket maker, beggar, funeral director, dysentery sufferer, notary, speleologist—everyone has a paradigm. *I once was lost but now I'm found.* The medieval notion that the world reflects the mind of God has tilted in my mind. Instead, the church I perceive is a relief map of the *human* mind. A thoroughly secular interpretation: that *we* have created the church out of our longing, memory, out of craving, and out of the folds of our private wonders.

If I have a sore throat from drinking orange juice when I know I'm allergic to it, the saint is there in his monumental church at Montepulciano, that town that sounds like six plucked strings on the cello. San Biago is a transubstantiated metaphor and a handful of dust in a wrought box. Its small keyhole reminds us of what we most want to be reminded of: *You are not out there alone.* San Biago focuses my thoughts and throws me beyond the scratchy rawness of my own throat. *Pray for me, Biago, you are taking me farther than I go.* When the TV is out of whack and the buttons won't improve the picture, nor will slapping the side soundly, Santa Chiara is out here somewhere in saintland. *Chiara,* clear. She was clairvoyant and from there is only a skip and jump to *receiver* to patron saint of telecommunications. So practical for such a transcendent girl. A statue of her on top of the TV won't hurt a thing. Next year on July 31, the wedding ring of Mary will be displayed in the *duomo* in Perugia. The history says it was "piously stolen"—isn't that an oxymoron?—from a church in Chiusi. Without a shred of literal belief, I, for one, will be there.

At the top of the stairs, I touch the spring water in my ceramic Mary with my fingertip and make a circle on my forehead. When I was baptized, the Methodist minister dipped a rose in a silver bowl of water and sprinkled my hair. I always wished I'd been baptized standing knee-deep in the muddy-brown Alapaha, held under until the last moment of breath then raised to the singing congregation. My spring water in Mary's cup is not transformed to wash away my sins or those of the world. She always seems like *Mary*, the name of my favorite aunt, rather than Santa Maria. Mary simply became a friend, friend of mothers who suffered their children's pain, friend of children who watched their mothers suffer. She's hanging over almost every cash register, bank teller, shot giver, bread baker, in this town and I've grown used to her presence. The English writer Tim Parks says that without her ubiquitous image to remind you that all will go on as before, "you might imagine that what was happening to you here and now was unique and desperately important.... I find myself wondering if the Madonna doesn't have some quality in common with the moon." Yes. My unblessed water soothes. I pause at the top of the stairs and repeat the lovely word *acqua*. Years ago, the baby learned to say *"acqua"* on the lakeshore at Princeton, under a canopy of trees blooming madly with pink pom-poms. *"Acqua, acqua,"* she shouted, scooping up water and letting it rain on her head. *Acqua* sounds closer to the sparkle and fall, closer to wetness and discovery. Her voice still reverberates but now I touch my little finger as I remember. The gold signet ring, a family treasure, slipped off in the grass that day and was not to be found. *Water of life. Intimacy of memory.*

*Intimacy.* The feeling of touching the earth as Eve touched it, when nothing separated her.

In paintings, the hilltop town rests in the palm of Mary's hand or under the shelter of her blue cloak. I can walk every street of my Georgia town in my mind. I knew the forks in the pecan trees, the glut of water in the culverts, the hog pear in the alley. Often the Tuscan perched villages seem like large castles—extended homes with streets narrow as corridors and the *piazze* the public-reception rooms teeming with visitors. The village churches have an attitude of privacy; the pressed-lace altar cloths and droopy scarlet dahlias in a jar could be in family chapels; the individual houses, just suites in the big house. I expand, as when my grandparents' house, my aunt's, my friends', the walls of home, were as familiar to me as the lines in my own palm. I like the twisted streets up to the convent where I may leave a bit of lace to be mended on a Catherine wheel, spin it in to the invisible nun, whose sisters have mended lace in this great arm of the castle for four hundred years. I do not glimpse even the half-moons of her nails or the shadow of her habit. Outside, two women who must have known each other all their lives sit in old wooden chairs between their doorways and knit. The stony street slopes abruptly down to the town wall. Beyond that stretches the broad valley floor. Here comes a miniature Fiat up this ridiculous steep street no car possibly should climb. Crazy. My father would drive through swollen streams that flooded sudden dips in the dirt roads. I was thrilled. While he laughed and blew the horn, water rose around the car windows. Or was the water really that high?

We can return to live in these great houses, unbar the gates, simply turn an immense iron key in the lock, and push open the door.

# The Mistake Game

I spoke to my daughter, Anya, in complete sentences when she was a conceptee and I listened for a response in her earliest cries. Some books recommended baby talk, and that was my wife, Moira's, language with Anya, but I preferred plain English. Why offer her ears a blurry target?

When it didn't drive me over the edge, her cry intrigued me. She had only one word to express every need and fantasy, from the inner world to the outer. Once, in the depths of their despair, certain Jewish kabbalists in medieval Europe made a similar cry, a magical name of God of enormous length—a thousand Hebrew letters jumbled together for pages. Properly intoned this jumbo word—blessing or curse—promised magical powers. This dream was shared by white and black magicians, Jewish and Christian, throughout the middle ages up to the renaissance. But their ancient predecessors, mystics less entranced by literacy, found God immediate in their own breath. They yowled the primal vowels A-E-I-O-U, rapidly "aah-eh-eee—ohh—oooh," producing the lost name of YHWH, known only to the High Priest in the Holy of Holies. I heard a latter-day kabbalist perform this once at a poetry reading in New York. His chant was very like the full-throated, unconsonanted cry of the baby.

For most of us, language is utilitarian, but a baby in the house restores a sense of poetry. Like the early Romantic Jean Jacques Rousseau, I came to believe that "the first invention of speech is due not to need, but passion."

Later, Rousseau theorized, as agriculture develops, needs multiply, and "affairs become complicated": "language changes its character. It becomes more regular and less passionate. It substitutes ideas for feelings. It no longer speaks to the heart, but to reason. Language becomes more exact and clearer, but more prolix, duller and colder."

Rousseau wrote in an age of happy speculation before our science of linguistics, also "exact and clearer...prolix, duller and colder," took over the field he opened. The first order of business was to dismiss unanswerable questions. When the Linguistic Society of Paris was founded in 1866, its bylaws forbade discussion of the origin of language.

Logically, we can never know precisely how speech began, for its invention is hidden in silence. Or could I hear its traces in a crib? With Anya's first cries, I gained entree into the subject, not as a scientist, but as an amateur and a father. I listened for the speech in Anya's cry, for if ontogeny recapitulates phylogeny, as the old dictum goes, I was delighting in the growth and development of human language compressed from millennia to thirty months.

In her very first days, she learned to modulate her cries. Very quickly a parent learns the difference between the absolute pitch of "I'm in deep shit" and the warble that simply declares discontent, or the more subtle mewling of "A little more milk would be just dandy." The baby is a practical philosopher: she knows her cry works. It speaks worlds—and moves them.

Need or passion? Clearly her cry was both, all-encompassing, a formless chaos of spirit and matter, energy and need, light and darkness mixed.

Then consonants come to divide the primal vowel, to separate firmament from fundament, and night from day. The hour of cooing is first light. One morning, when Anya was about six months old, I lay awake, watching the minute hand move, dreading the hour of breakfast and work. I heard from her nursery a distinct burbling. She was shaping it into syllables, "bu-bu-bu-bu-*bo*."

She repeated the sounds, singer and listener, delighted and delighting. After that, I made it my business to wake early, just to hear her song. It was like a fountain bubbling from the depths of the earth with perfect clarity: bu-bu-bu-bu-*bo*.

If the vowels are nature, the consonants are culture, all cultures, for the infant speaks Urdu, Swahili, and something that resembles very much the glossolalia in a Free Will Baptist church, where I heard an old man on the altar produce "a-ka-ka-la-ka" for fifteen minutes, slapping his knees hard for punctuation. He said it was Japanese.

The baby speaks in tongues, too, her early morning Pentecost is a descent of the spirit, an entry into a more human language. At first she rehearses these new consonants for her own entertainment. It takes a while for this solipsistic cooing to evolve into genuine babbling. But after a time, I thought I heard inflections of my Baltimorese and Moira's softer North Carolina drawl. Anya was rehearsing the characteristic songs of her tribe.

That these patterns of stress and pitch are more primary than actual vocabulary or pronunciation can be illustrated by listening to distraught speech. The wrong syllables get emphasized: we hear severe "dis-stress": Please pass *the* su*gar*. We feel the emotion in the underlying music—we know something is wrong.

Yet there's also the clear legato of well-being, though the music of language is often lost to us because we are intent on words, not sounds. We forget that the stresses and intonations of every sentence we utter are not only expressive, but sometimes beautiful in themselves. Our needs have multiplied more than Rousseau dreamed: legalese, bureaucratese, computerese; languages frozen shut, with clauses stiff as ice; all need—no passion.

Some parents can't get excited about a child's babble until the first words roll out. The competitive urge is enormous and in our culture we love anything we can count: "My child can say ten words." This stress on acquiring vocabulary overlooks a greater achievement: the melodies a baby can babble by the time she gets around to inserting *Dada* or *car-car* into the tune. Actually, the first words emerge singularly from the flow—like rocks jutting from a stream, around which melodies continue to swirl. A toddler's musical abilities outpace her vocabulary by far and this is as it should be.

Still, when Anya first spoke words, not sounds, I admit Moira and I were proud. Anya's first word uttered in Baton Rouge was recorded dutifully in her baby album. "Ball" seemed to have universal application: my head was a ball, so was a head of lettuce in the A&P.

After "ball" came "No"; after "No," "Mama" and "Dada." I remember her sitting in the corner of the bedroom going, "Mama, Dada, Mama, Dada," looking left then right as if trying to place these important nouns properly in the universe.

By January, when she was sixteen months, she could say ball, bird, bottle, tee-tee (TV), bow-wow (dog), door, book, Mama, Ieeovu (I love you), car, bapu (apple), Dada, bath, bye-bye.

With this tiny vocabulary, Anya could already play what the philosopher Ludwig Wittgenstein calls a "language game."

"Ball," I said, and Anya motored off to her room, and returned with the ball. "Good," I said. "Car." She raced off and brought her toy car. "Anya," I said. She puzzled for a minute, then laughed. I couldn't help myself: I had to tease her a little.

Our language game had an ancient lineage, going back to St. Augustine, as Wittgenstein notes in the opening of his *Philosophical Investigations*: "When they [my elders] named some object, and accordingly moved towards something, I saw this and I grasped that the thing was called by the sound they uttered when they meant to point it out. Their intention was shewn by their bodily movements, as it were the natural language of all peoples: the expressions of the face, the play of the eyes, the movement of other parts of the body, and the tone of voice which expresses our state of mind in seeking, having, rejecting or avoiding something. Thus, as I heard words repeatedly used in their proper places in various sentences, I gradually learnt to understand what objects they signified; and after I had trained my mouth to form these signs, I used them to express my own desires."

Augustine writes as if all the words he learns were like nouns, whose meaning came to him ostensively, that is, by pointing. The concept seems simple enough: you say apple and point to an apple. But observing Anya learn to talk I share a sense Wittgenstein develops that the obvious is not obvious.

For one thing, Anya's first words included "Ieeovu"—I love you—clearly passion and not at all the name of a thing pointed to. "No" was also not ostensive. It not only does not point to a thing, it negates things, and therefore seems to imply a whole concept of thingness. Yet "No" was her second word. If "ball" represented the universe, "not-*ball*," or "No," was its shadow.

How does a child learn language? Augustine suggests gestures: "the natural language of all peoples: the expressions of the face, the play of the eyes, the movement of other parts of the body, and the tone of voice," but how do you point to "no" or "I love you"? For that matter, as Wittgenstein asks, how do you point to pointing?

For instance, if I point to a dog and say "bow-wow," how does the child know which way to follow my finger? For Wittgenstein to ask such a question seems absurd, but when you realize there is no particular answer—beyond "convention"—you reel in the chaos of the child. She doesn't have conventions yet. She's sorting sounds and words and categories without a clue.

When he was about two, one of Anya's playmates, Carl, shook his head no when he clearly meant yes. "Do you want some ice cream?" his father asked him. The boy shook his head and smiled. Should Stan give Carl the ice cream or not? He didn't want to teach him that shaking his head meant yes. But he didn't want to frustrate the boy either.

Whoever studies the child's use of the word "No" will see immediately a hole in Augustine's argument. "No" has never been the name of anything. Language cannot merely be ostensive, or strictly utilitarian. It's more as Rousseau has it: the terrible fury and poetry of *No* carries all the charge of an emerging personality.

Anya's *No* came when she was about one and a half, both a blessing and a curse. Her tantrums had a story line. She could shout *No* while she pushed her cereal bowl off the table. Yet her language also gave her parents an advantage. For language bonds in both directions, and her acquiring it allowed us to do terrible parental things, like manipulate and deceive.

Apart from the metaphysical "No" and the lovely "Ieeovu," most of Anya's basic vocabulary was ostensive and arose out of gestures that are very here and now. For her, almost magically, the word was the thing named, and problems emerged whenever words named things that weren't present. This came most clear to me one afternoon when Anya and I were driving home from the hardware store and the child went stark, raving cranky. Already at eighteen months she could concentrate on television for an hour at a time, a talent we found somewhat disturbing, but which some of our friends assured us was remarkable.

Her favorite television show was *The Muppet Hour*. Hoping to distract her, I said, "When we get home, after dinner, you can watch the Muppets."

"Muppets," Anya said, from the back seat.

"Yes," I said. "The Muppets will be on at six."

"Muppets," she repeated sharply.

"At six." Unfortunately, the hour was four.

"Muppets, muppets, muppets..." She let it rip, syllables ratcheting into a scream. My mistake. Muppets meant *Muppets now*.

I was trapped at close quarters with an outraged infant—there is no howl like the howl of outrage. Seemingly, I had deceived her with her most precious acquisition, the word. Once we got home, she ran to the set, still bawling, and pointed indignantly at the empty screen. There was something wonderful in that gesture, in her face—this was not only frustration, but the kind of righteous anger adults have when they feel they have been tricked. I turned the set on and spun through the channels, hoping to demonstrate, in vain, the existence of time, the nonexistence of Muppets.

Yet despite the moral risks, as her ability to speak in sentences developed our second fall in Baton Rouge, I often used language to distract her. One morning, she spotted a piece of chocolate on the breakfast table. Her oatmeal lost its savor. "I want candy," she said. "Candy, candy candy." Who taught her that word?

"Oh yes," I answered, "you can certainly have the candy"— though I had no intention of giving it to her and while I was talking was secretly palming it, an old magician's sleight that came in handy. "But before you have *it*"—another trick of the trade is to veil the object of desire with a pronoun—"wouldn't you like some *apple juice* first?" She nodded her head, and as her tears dried, I made a long ceremony of finding the bottle—"Oh, here it is"—and getting the glass, narrating the whole time: "The glass is on the top shelf, Anya, isn't it pretty, I think it has *Bert* and *Ernie* on it—is that *Bert*?" and I gave her the glass to inspect. She said, "No, that's *Ernie*." "Oh," I said, slowly pouring the juice. "Here you go—the *juice*," and by this time, she'd forgotten all about the chocolate.

This cowardly technique often seemed preferable to the head-to-head confrontation, and Moira and I, without being aware of it, fell into this pattern as Anya entered the terrible twos.

But who were we fooling?

I am sure if I had more moral fiber I would have faced some of these issues straight on, and not divagated my child's desires down so many trickling paths. But the chicanery worked.

Children are mirrors, and the great moral lesson they teach, sooner or later, is that they will do as they were done to. They have the annoying habit of always witnessing our most embarrassing errors and bouncing them right back to us. In that light, I could not entirely applaud my method of dealing with what I considered her unreasonable desires.

I was using her own gifts against her, but for her own good. Yet I don't know if I was entirely wrong to avoid confrontations with my child. If I wanted to dress Anya for nursery school, so I could get my own day started, this wasn't a moral issue. What is moral or immoral about a kid kicking like mad and refusing to let me slip a sock on her when I have exactly a minute to get her out of the house so I can make a nine o'clock class? She wasn't being bad. Her refusal around age two came from her need to express herself. She—*Anya*—was the person who did not put her sock on when I asked her. As she wriggled and screamed, all her being was invested in this. How could I possibly match her in will? I have seen parents who force their children to knuckle under in every confrontation because they view each challenge as a threat to their overall authority. I suppose there are lock breakers for every lock, but I didn't want to break Anya.

She was fighting for her life, in a way. On my side, I had patience and guile. True, sometimes, there was no other way: grab her foot and stuff the sock on and let her answer the indignity with a cloudburst tantrum. But if I could distract her with mere words, wasn't that preferable? "No, you don't have to put your sock on right now," I'd say. "It's okay. Here, sit down in my lap. Let's look at the tee-tee." And while she relaxed, I'd slip the sock on without her noticing. With baby's attention, the rule was, Divide and conquer.

With two verbal maniacs all to herself, she acquired adult habits of conversation early. Her pronunciation was flawless. She quickly outgrew baby words and often her vocabulary outstripped other developments. Sometimes she astonished us with her early pronouncements: "I had a good time at the restaurant. *Actually,* I made pee-pee in the booster."

Or, listening to jazz on the radio, "That piano has a clown in it."

Other parents sometimes became anxious around Anya because of her rapid development. Seething with pride, we tried to downplay it. Anyway, I could see things to admire in other kids besides their ability to produce sentences. They had means of communication just as effective as Anya's. Undistracted by the lies of language, they may have established a more primal relation to their own desires.

Once, when they were both about two, Carl, the head-shaker, stayed with us one weekend while Stan and Molly went on a trip. Though he could barely speak, it was a pleasure how well he could communicate.

That Saturday morning, the children woke early to watch cartoons. I turned them on and crawled back into bed.

We must have overslept, because about ten, I woke to the sound of Carl toddling into our bedroom, holding an empty cereal bowl which he'd grabbed off the kitchen table. (Anya had forsaken her stomach for Smurfs.) Carl didn't say a word, but I got the messages: Breakfast. Feed me. Now.

I called him Harpo after that. Carl, I decided, was deliberately avoiding speech. He was a second-born child, and wisely seeing that he couldn't compete with his parents and older sister, he refined ostensive language to sheer wordless pointing, like the Zen master who defined Buddha by pointing at the moon. Hadn't Wittgenstein himself written, "Whereof one cannot speak, thereof one must be silent?"

In our house, speech and bantering were the rule between Moira, me, and Anya. Classically we speak of a mother tongue and father time, which seems to imply that the child learns her language exclusively from the mother—and learns the demands of the world from father. I know that's exactly how I conceived it as a boy. I wonder which was the greater aberration, the rigid apportioning of gender roles in my parents' generation, or the more fluid arrangements today.

With both of us working full time, teaching and writing, Moira and I became nearly interchangeable as parents. We couldn't afford to divide child-rearing responsibilities into neat categories. Anyway, teaching a child to speak is so natural and successful an enterprise, it was more game than chore.

Anya and I invented our own talking games as soon as Anya could talk. These were far more complex than Wittgenstein's "language games"—they were for pleasure only, and turned the world upside down. The most important one was "the mistake game."

"I woke up this morning and brushed my face, then I washed my teeth with soap. Was that a mistake?"

"Yes," she answered. "You should brush your teeth and wash your face with soap."

"Oh, I see. Then I put on my shoes and tied my socks. Was that a mistake?"

"Yes, Daddy. You should put on your socks and tie your shoes."

"I see."

I don't know how it started, exactly. The mistake game flew out of nowhere, a time-filler at meals, a distraction while getting her dressed. The game mixed logic with the absurd, inflicting my sensibility on Anya. It also gave her a taste of role reversal, a chance, for once, to correct her illogical father.

It's wrong to tease children overmuch. I've been guilty of it, going too far with the game, taking advantage of their sweet willingness to believe what an adult says.

A few times I drove Anya into screaming fits with my silly wordplay, forgetting she was still a child, in spite of her complex sentences and adult vocabulary. Other times, she'd laugh so hard we had to stop for fear of choking her.

"You're not Mommy, are you?" I'd say.

"No."

"I'm not Mommy either, am I?"

"Right." She'd nod her head sagely, knowing a new game was afoot.

"Well, if I'm 'not-Mommy,' and you're 'not-Mommy,' I must be you because we're both 'not-Mommy.'"

She'd splutter and laugh. "No, you're Daddy."

"I though you said I was not-Mommy..."

Soon "not-Mommy" replaced the mistake game, hilarious to her and to me, too.

Teasing is a father's game of distance and closeness, a verbal shadowboxing or peekaboo. I'm here, I'm not here; I mean it, I don't. Whether the teasing heals or hurts probably depends on how secure the child is in that difficult quality, her father's love.

The hardest thing to learn in any language is irony. When I lived in Mexico for six months, I mastered Spanish vocabulary and grammar, but never learned when a declarative sentence was intended in its opposite sense. I drank in every word like a child.

Young children have absolutely no taste for irony. It shakes a child's bare grasp of language. Teasing Anya was a big mistake—an adult game she was not ready to play.

Once, at the dinner table, carried away by the spirit of absurdity, I said, "You know, Anya, we've been feeding you all these years, and you still haven't gotten any bigger." The remark was true enough, by the way. Anya reached thirty pounds by her second year and stayed there, getting taller, like a round piece of clay pinched thinner.

As soon as the words slipped out, Anya turned red and threw her fork down on the floor. "That's not funny," she shouted, slid out of her chair, and ran out of the kitchen. Despite our mistake game, she was still a language fundamentalist and I had violated her sense of fair play. I hadn't meant to be cruel, just forgotten that she took my joke quite literally. If I didn't want to damage the bond between us, I had to be very careful not to import adult irony into her world.

A father witnesses crucial developments in his children they themselves would otherwise never be conscious of. In two and a half years, Anya moved from "bu-bu-bu-*bo*" to "Actually, I made pee-pee in the booster" to the serrated edge of adult irony. She progressed from vowels to consonants to melodies to words, phrases, and sentences: I can't help thinking that somewhere within her story is a clue to the broader historical question about the evolution of language and consciousness.

But that is probably my delusion. History, and time itself, is an adult deception. Young children know every when is now, every tense is present. "Did you have a nice day at Carl's?" I once asked Anya when she was barely two. "Gapes," she answered positively, and while I tried to puzzle out who gaped at what, she pointed to green grapes in a bowl. The past is a wispy illusion, but "gapes" are sweet.

## Why My Uncle Was Late for Breakfast

While he was the governor of Leeds Prison, my uncle Bourke was late for breakfast twice. Usually he'd finished eating by quarter past eight, and by eight-thirty he was walking down the avenue of horse chestnuts which led from our front door to the main road; there he caught the No. 16 Wingate tram to his prison office. But on those two mornings when he was late, he'd already left the house before any of us were up, and by the time he was driven back by a prison guard in an official car with *H.M. Prison* painted in gold on the side, we were halfway through breakfast. He came into the dining room and sat down at the breakfast table in his usual place, and as usual he unfolded his napkin from its silver ring while my aunt Helen poured him tea. But he said "Good morning" without looking at us, and then he went upstairs to bed before he'd either drunk the tea or eaten his breakfast; on one of these two occasions what he rejected was a boiled egg—a rare treat, this being wartime.

Still, his lack of appetite was perhaps understandable. My uncle Bourke had gone out so early and been driven back late for breakfast because he was an official witness whenever one of the prisoners at Leeds Prison was being hanged.

I should add here that he was not really my uncle—just a member of the English family to whom my sister, Ruth, and I had been sent when things in Karlsruhe got unpleasant for our own. That had been in the spring of 1939. I was seven, Ruth was thirteen. Our German neighbors had taken a dislike to us—well, you know the story—and had provided us, and all our friends and relatives and all our friends' and relatives' friends and relatives, with special papers which documented our distinction and difference from themselves. A nameless menace seeped from the dividing line between us and them. Children on the street called out jokes at me I didn't understand and my best friend, Ursula, no longer played with me. Her mother wouldn't even open the front gate to let me in when I went to her house to ask why. My other friends—the ones I began to play with, lacking Ursula—were leaving Karlsruhe. The first to go left with their parents; later, one by one, they went by themselves.

Ursula's father had recently started wearing black outfits with shining metal buttons, as did the men who processed our new certificates of difference and who stood guard at the *Hauptbahnhof* to make sure that everyone stepping onto the trains possessed the correct permits for doing so. These uniforms were rather like the uniforms of the guards at Leeds Prison, and I was puzzled as to how I should feel about the two hangings there. I'd been told, of course, that the men who were hanged had committed murder: I think in both cases it was their wives whom they had killed, in ways which—although these were naturally never discussed—were understood to be unacceptable. But since I knew it was possible, and even quite likely, that I was closer to the two men being hanged than to the men in uniform who were doing the hanging, I was reluctant to reach any conclusion about whose side I was on. I could see that it would be easy for someone to decide carelessly for some casual reason or other to put a noose around my neck, too—or perhaps whoever put it there would have deep and cogent reasons which out of ignorance I failed to grasp.

When my sister, Ruth, and I first came to live in the governor's house, it was full of people. There were, to begin with, the four Harveys themselves—Aunt Helen, Uncle Bourke, and their daughters, Valerie and Diana. There were also other people who came and went; or who occasionally, like Ruth and me, came and stayed. Robin and Dickon, for instance, and Joy and Beechie, who normally lived in India, where their father was a bishop; they had been brought to England for the Duration by their rather sporadic mother so that Robin and Dickon could read Virgil at Marlborough. When it turned out that the Duration was going to be years rather than months, they all went back to India again. A boy named Michael also spent many holidays with us: his mother was a well-known actress and therefore assumed to lead an irregular life not good for a growing boy. Dozens of other visitors drifted through—young men recovering from wounds or home on leave;

young women getting over the deaths of fathers or fiancés. Some were relatives, some were godchildren, some merely the relatives of godchildren or the godchildren of relatives: diverse in age, sex, and marital status, they were all, ruthlessly, of one class, with titles twinkling in their genealogies, at regular and discreetly separated intervals, like sequins. This was true also of the older guests, the assorted aunts and uncles, whose imaginatively varied afflictions ranged from paralysis, amputations, deafness, arthritis, and chronic malaria to the benign and total dottiness favored by several of Uncle Bourke's siblings. There was a tea planter from Ceylon, a bush pilot from Kenya, a sheep rancher from Perth, and a beer baron from Belfast.

There were, at the very beginning, also servants: a cook, a gardener, and three maids, who changed their uniforms after lunch from starched pastel cotton, with big white caps and aprons, to starched black cotton, with little white caps and aprons. There had once been a nanny for Valerie and Diana, but they were now too old to have any use for her and she had gone off to instill manners into the children of the Irish beer baron, with whom she often came to visit. She was referred to as just plain Nanny—or sometimes Nanny Webb; but she was never Miss Webb or Mrs. Webb or just plain Elizabeth Ann. The cook was called, simply, Cook. Like animated objects in a children's book, people were stripped down to one essential quality and labeled accordingly. In the case of servants and prison staff, these identifying epithets were usually very straightforward—nothing more than a specific function or, in cases of duplication, a specific function and a last name; but the rest of us acquired nicknames of folkloric proportions: my sister, Ruth, for instance, was "Chyfe," because that was how she had once announced the arrival of the chief officer of the prison. I, after six weeks in bed with a combination of measles and whooping cough, became "Granny."

It was a world deliciously simplified; its daily ritual was casual, its repetitions ancient and well-worn. The grown-ups dressed for dinner, but did not bother to dress particularly well; while we children, which is to say all of us under twelve, had our bowls of soup and our cups of cocoa brought to the nursery by the upstairs maid, who then departed to draw our nightly bath. With history behind it, servants around it, and money under it, life at the governor's house of Leeds Prison looked so much like the Natural Order that to question it—whom did it exploit? what were its uses?—would have been, and still is, unthinkable.

Perhaps it was rationing that leveled everything; perhaps it was the blackout, or the camaraderie of battle, or simply the inevitable democracy of death delivered by bombs dropped from so high they could not distinguish rank or riches. Whatever it was, the class structure and social inequality which had survived and flourished through many wars in centuries past failed to survive this one. After Dunkirk, by the summer of 1940, it was easy to see that the pre-war world of easy privilege had vanished.

The first sign of its going was perhaps that the governor's house became suddenly understaffed. The gardener was called up and Cook, who happened to be his wife, went into factory work. The maids joined the Land Army and their replacements defected to other, even more bellicose lines of work. Since there were now no servants, the attic rooms which had been their mysterious habitat were turned into guest rooms. Extra beds were needed, in any case, since a fresh tide of visitors, most of them in uniform and bearing tins of meat and packets of butter to supplement our rations, lapped at our door each day. Uncle Bourke—who had had an earlier military calling in the Indian Cavalry—converted his battle expertise into three nights a week as an air-raid warden. Meanwhile I peeled potatoes, made pastry, and diced carrots for Aunt Helen, who now, of course, cooked the meals. She spent the greater part of each morning bicycling down to the greengrocer's, the fishmonger's, and the baker's to queue up for whatever was available that one didn't need coupons for. Once upon a time we had all gathered for morning prayers around the big bed where Aunt Helen and Uncle Bourke slept: we had reassured God each morning before breakfast that we believed in only one of him, and had then gone on to ask him to give us this day our daily bread. Now that our daily bread took so much longer to come by than it used to, we no longer had the time to follow protocol when we applied for it.

The war cut a sharp line for us between what was necessary and what was merely customary. Though Leeds was a city so hidden in fog that bombers could rarely find it, there were occasionally air raids, always at night; for a few months, when we all went down to the cellar and waited for the all-clear to sound, my aunt Helen, who always got dressed properly and did her hair after waking the rest of us, brought her box of heirloom jewelry with her. After a while, though she still got dressed, she left the heirlooms upstairs. And in the end she came down in her dressing gown, like everyone else, until somewhere around the beginning of 1942 when—deciding that we might as well die in our beds as be buried alive in the cellar—we all just turned over when the siren sounded and went to sleep again. But as we became more careless and began to take war as a matter of course, as the normal state of existence, we also discovered that we were filled with odd hungers, as if to make up for some unknown deprivation. We were assailed by exotic cravings for meat or fruit, for instance, or love, I suppose, or music. In my own case, it was a passion for mimesis which drove me, an unassuageable thirst for theater, films, playacting, reading. I daydreamed myself into fictional roles until I was roused by the voice of reality, usually that of Aunt Helen telling me to take the dogs for a walk.

To some degree, luckily, there was a social, and a socially acceptable, outlet for this mimetic compulsion in many of the games we played—played almost constantly—which were often little more than make-believe systems echoing the reality in which my uncle Bourke made his living: prisons and punishments were ubiquitous, though unlike the penal system he administered, which arguably had at least some reference to logic and to the actual present, our games were by and large complete anachronisms in which winning or losing were entirely and even emphatically unrelated to whether you deserved to win or lose. *Here comes a candle to light you to bed*, we sang. *And here comes a chopper to chop off your head.* If the last line coincided with your passage through, there was no avoiding the executioner: creative dawdling or running like mad only made things messy. For Hangman, we drew the outlines of wooden scaffolds and put nooses round our own necks; we threw dice to rise without effort or to fall without fault into serpent-filled dungeons in Snakes and Ladders. In Draughts and Chess there was, it's true, some room for intellect; but we tended to overlook this and blundered about the board taking prisoners and then holding them up for ransom at random. We preferred Monopoly, anyway, where we could gamble our way through London real estate priced to a strictly prewar market, and gladly went to Gaol ("Do not pass GO. Do not collect £200") for errors unpunished since the French Revolution. Though the rules of play and penalty were many and intricate in every card game we played, their very titles—*Double Demon, Saint Helena's*—evoked the histrionic and Gothic.

Our favorite game was Kickapeg—I have no idea why it was called that. It was a species of Hide and Seek which went on interminably, since after the person who was "It" had discovered where people were hiding and routed them out onto the first-floor front landing, which was always our designated "prison," any of the still-undiscovered players could set the prisoners free by touching them. It was usually impossible to finish rounding up all ten or twelve players hidden about the twelve-room house (not counting the attic) when as soon as your back was turned they all escaped and hid themselves again. The job was made even harder by the fact that the prisoners were supposed to keep their potential rescuers informed of the whereabouts of poor Kickapeg—as we called the "It" person—by shouting out a constant schedule of his movements, as far as these could be followed from the first-floor landing.

Kickapeg also must have been based on an antique and long-forgotten model, but unlike our other games whose patterns echoed a world gone by, our modifications had made it oddly contemporary—even perhaps futuristic. It described a sort of gentle chaos—an endless dance of bringing people together only to have them constantly disperse and fall apart again—which in retrospect I am tempted to see as a prefiguration of late-twentieth-century law enforcement—or perhaps even late-twentieth-century social life. All that endless and aimless finding and gathering on the first-floor landing! All that endless and aimless scurrying away, each of us back to his own snug, isolated hiding place!

As we got older and more experienced, some of us began to take books and flashlights with us to our favorite spots (one of mine was a very cozy nook in the back of the pillow cupboard next to the hot-water heater) so we could read between our short bouts of prison duty. When it was time for tea or time for bed, or when frustration at finding the prison emptied of its prisoners yet again drove a teenage Kickapeg to fury or a younger one to tears, Aunt Helen stopped the games and we all sat down for Horlick's and bread and butter—or for whatever meal it was now time to eat.

In a way, I wonder if Kickapeg was really a game at all. There was something natural and quite unforced about it. There was no competition, there was no winning or losing to it, and despite the general idea that one person was supposed to find everyone, and everyone was then supposed to try to get lost again, there were also no real rules. It was just something we did: a sort of demonstration of a centripetal impulse in eternal opposition to a centrifugal one. Without knowing it, we may have discovered a benign archetype of entropy—which was certainly a force we could see at work in the world around us.

During the summer of 1945, we moved to Dartmoor. The famous maximum security prison there was in the process of becoming a minimum security Borstal and First Offenders prison, and my uncle Bourke, who had been recognized as a reform-minded governor, was asked to oversee the transformation. The war in Europe was over; the war in Asia, soon to be over also, did not affect us much. I remember that spring and summer as lit with poignant brilliance; it was as if after a long submersion underwater, we had suddenly breached the surface to breathe the free, bright air. I felt I was in love—with Robin, who had come back from India to go to Oxford, but also with the whole world, which had opened itself in glorious anarchy all around me.

In 1945 Dartmoor Prison was also liberated to grace for a few brief years—though it reverted, soon enough, to its dour duties of imprisoning men for life—and it was almost beautiful. Built in 1812 to house French and American naval prisoners of war, it looked like a Georgian country estate with inexplicably high walls. It was perched on the edge of the moors, surveying a vast drama of unalloyed bleakness in one direction and, in the other direction, the little town of Princetown, a village still lit by gaslight, which seemed to exist in an earlier century. Now that the war in Europe was over and there was no need for blackout anymore, every evening the Borstal boys (in brown uniforms) and the First Offenders (in green uniforms) lit the gas jets of the streetlights one by one, so that magically the town began to glitter against the twilight and shine in counterpoint to the distant stars.

The prisoners did other chores as well: they collected rubbish, delivered milk, ran the prison farm which provided us with much of our food. A few of them were allowed to come to church on Sundays, and sat in the first few rows of pews at Vespers. Now and then, those soon to be released were given passes, and walked among us like proper men. Several—the ones, of course, whom I remember—were extraordinarily good-looking, and I yearned to assist them in daring escapes. I sent them psychic prayers to flee in my direction so that I could provide them with Uncle Bourke's shirts and as much of my allowance as they were willing to take from me.

They did escape now and then, without my help; barricades would be set up across the roads to check the passing cars for hidden Borstal boys. None of them stayed away long. The moor in those days was cold and pathless, inhabited only by the ghosts of ancient tribes and of those who had perished there. After falling into bogs and walking in circles, the prisoners were delighted to come back to the comforts of civilization, even as these were embodied in a prison cell.

Since the prison was a tourist landmark, the weekends would bring sightseers on bicycles or by way of the bus, or even—as petrol became more and more available—in cars which had driven them all the way from Plymouth and Exeter. They stared at the stone walls, which hid the prisoners working in the fields, as if they were witnessing a moment of historical importance, though in fact, of course, they could see nothing at all. One Saturday, driving to Tavistock to shop for shoes, Aunt Helen and I saw a big blond woman in kelly-green trousers trying to climb the prison wall to see into the garden. Aunt Helen stopped the car and rolled down the window. "Excuse me, madam!" she shouted, and the big blonde slithered half a yard downward in surprise. "You must be looking for your husband," my aunt Helen called, loud enough for all the other sightseers to hear. "He is most likely in the wing we reserve for our more desperate prisoners. You should inquire at the front gate, where they will happily assist you." And she rolled up the window again and drove on.

But though my aunt Helen could still be secure and brutal in keeping up the proprieties, I had the sense that they were not as rigidly set in the firmament as they had once been. It was partly, I suppose, because the war was finished, and with it had vanished the simple faith that everything our side did was good and everything their side did was bad. In the United States this was taken care of quite simply by crowning Communism as the new villain almost immediately. But in England the release from daily pressures of danger and emergency was so sudden that it created a sort of vacuum—or at least something one sensed as a vacuum. The laws of conduct seemed to have changed almost overnight: not merely were they more relaxed and more ambiguous than war allowed, but they were seen suddenly to be—to have always been—far from absolute. They could, it appeared, be broken; they had, perhaps, been broken all along.

When we were children we had felt so secure in the knowledge that evil was contained in its prison cell—guarded by Uncle Bourke—that we could play out crime and punishment in our games without a thought of danger. Our make-believe may have been patterned on the raw material of the world around us; and the world around us certainly patterned itself, in turn, on the violent fantasies of childhood. Still, the two had remained discrete, a yin-yang circle whose two halves never blurred. Now I saw the opposite sides as having, somehow, fused. Perhaps this had happened because we had all grown up; or perhaps it had happened because the world had not. But in any case, though the war had been won, order had not been restored. Instead, one huge and global enemy defeated had been replaced by a horde of private evils crawling around the earth. There was nothing to put a stop to them; no one displayed much interest in putting a stop to them. I began to notice them in unexpected places. I had the sense that they were closing in on me.

In Leeds, I had waited for the paper each evening to see how Monty was doing in the desert. Now that Monty had won the day,

I read the morning news for other things. A local story particularly fascinated me. A man was being tried for the murder of two little boys, his foster-children, one of whom had been found tied and gagged, drowned in a well shaft. The other was discovered later, in a locked cupboard, beaten to death. I was the first to seize the paper before breakfast and read every word of evidence and argument printed, compelled towards these dark revelations of hideous behavior by a mysterious appetite. The story filled me with confusion and escalating terror; my incomprehension was so overwhelming that it was close to exaltation. What had the little boys gone through, being tortured so? How had the man felt, doing it? Why had he done such things and no one noticed him? It was like looking into hell.

I was the only one left at home now. Valerie and Diana were in boarding school, my sister was at Leeds University. Lacking them, even the visitors had gone away. In due time I went away, too, and in the spring of 1946, my sister and I landed in New York.

My mother was living with relatives in Great Neck at the time, studying to pass her State Boards so as to be able to practice medicine again. I was installed next door to her, with another German Jewish family whose two young children I was supposed to help take care of. Everyone at our end of Nirvana Avenue—the end near the high school to which I walked each morning—had been uprooted. Everyone spoke German to each other or—when they spoke to me, to their children or to their American neighbors—spoke English with a German accent. Fragments of their past—paintings, books, Meissen bowls, silver coffee pots, embroidered bed linens, and Persian carpets—decorated their current existence as if to comment on its insufficiencies. In fact, the houses on Nirvana Avenue, even at the high school end, were all quite large and new, with half-acres of lawn in the back studded with ornamental fruit trees. Even so, the memorabilia they enclosed were too much for them. I remember there was a record, *The Lament of the Dachshund*, that the people on Nirvana Avenue used to play sometimes. Its chorus was: *Ich war einmal ein grosser Bernadiner* ("I used to be a big St. Bernard, once") / *Over there, over there, over there!*

In my class, there was a girl whose hair grew down to her eyebrows and covered the place where her nose and forehead met: it was whispered that she had been experimented on in the camps, injected with alien hormones and tampered with in other ways. There was also a pair from Holland, a brother and sister, blond, long-legged, arrogant, who had spent their entire childhoods in an attic—where they were luckier than Anne Frank, of whom we had not yet heard. A friend of my mother's, a gentile woman who had been married to a Jew, had been an inmate at several camps where, as a doctor, she had been treated relatively well: for a while she had supervised the arrival of new inmates, and had divided the healthy from the unhealthy into two separate files. She was thin and spoke with a stutter, and her eyelids fluttered perpetually, as if she had to force them open with brute will power and against their better judgment.

No one talked much of how they had escaped; it was enough that they had, some only barely with their lives, their health ruined, their nights filled with unbearable dreams, others—especially the ones who lived near us on Nirvana Avenue—with all of their money waiting for them in New York and most of their friends and relatives by their side, their lives merely ruffled, it seemed, by the brief inconvenience of resettlement.

Nevertheless, it was these apparently unscarred people who really frightened me: some invisible pressure seemed to have shattered the smooth surfaces of their character and left jagged edges to rub against. They lacked the social cover of benevolence and friendliness which other people throw over ordinary daily intercourse. It was as if they had been flayed to a state of rawness so irritating that it constantly demanded to be scratched and irritated more. Perhaps their uncomfortable self-laceration was related to the impulse of people who pinch themselves awake from nightmares—having fled and survived with so few visible wounds, they may have been in the constant process of proving to themselves that they were in fact still there—that escape and the memory of what they had escaped from had not been merely a bad dream.

And indeed, I suppose we were all just waking up. To a new dawn. In its way, to a new world. The rules of the game were changing—but now it was blatant, now it was impossible not to see, that there were people who had always failed to obey the old rules, anyway, and that they would not follow the new ones, either. Story by story, witness after witness, made that clear. Apparently there were many people—towns, nations, continents, filled with people like the man I had read about on Dartmoor, who had drowned one foster son and beaten the other to death— who did not accept the prescriptions for human behavior and who did not follow the normal definitions of human conduct. If there were so many, it became doubtful for whom the prescriptions had been written in the first place. Since they failed as true descriptions of human actions, their purpose was puzzling. Had they been created by good men as goals of conduct for which to aim? Or had they been created by evil men to keep the good men from acting against them?

I already knew about the camps, of course. There had been articles about their liberation in all the newspapers and there had been pictures of the living corpses which had come out and were now gathered into the shared homelessness of Europe. But the deeper horror, which these pieces merely adorned with obscene details, could manifest itself only as absence. The deeper horror therefore eluded us for a long time—and perhaps eludes us still. How long do you sit by the window waiting for someone to come before his not coming turns into the accepted fact which erases the expectation of its opposite? How long do you pity the displaced hundreds of thousands of the damned wandering through a world in ruins or shed compassion on the charred and mutilated survivors of Hiroshima before you recognize in the shadows beyond your vision, in the silence beyond your charity, the sum total of what is not there?

I am speaking, of course, not only of the dead, the millions who vanished into thin air at Auschwitz, who were shoveled as fertilizer into the fields of Russia, who evaporated in an instant at Nagasaki. I am speaking of a concept of humanity which— though it took us years even to acknowledge the fact which we still yearn to deny—had been erased overnight. It seems that the families on the high school end of Nirvana Avenue had escaped only temporarily, after all. The limits of anarchy were stretching to embrace us all again so that chaos might encircle the world.

We have all probably grown too used to fighting Armageddons

ever to say, even to ourselves: "This one is surely the last." But I think that most of us who lived on Nirvana Avenue in the late 1940's and early fifties have come to assume—and now accept the assumption almost placidly—that the forces of righteousness had sustained a major blow which may yet prove to be fatal. It was the price, perhaps, for winning the war.

At least I am sure now how I feel about hanging people. I think it is quite a bad idea—as, of course, is shooting them, or electrocuting them, or giving them kindly injections of deadly compounds. It is quite a bad idea because it necessarily puts the person doing the hanging, who should presumably be the one in the morally superior position, in the morally inferior position instead. I am convinced that this sort of paradox imposes an unnecessary strain on the fabric of society, which, given its fragility, should be spared such trauma. I understand now why my uncle Bourke, whose habits were unchanging and whose deportment was always cheerful and open, returned to the family breakfast table in such a queasy state. Only a wrenching dislocation, only a jolting glimpse of Pandemonium and the forces of darkness about to be loosed on the world, could have made a man like him late for breakfast and sent him slinking away, at eight-thirty in the morning, guilty to bed.

## Last Things

My sister and I step briskly out of the greengrocer to get away from the men behind us in line who have told us, in great detail, what they'd like to do to us, where they intend to put certain parts of their bodies. The clerk, kindly, rings their purchases up slowly, so Cyndy and I have a chance to hurry across the street, almost bumping into two men who are breaking raw eggs in their hands and leaning over to slip the viscous mess into their mouths.

One of those Manhattan nights, I think.

Earlier today, as Cyndy and I were taxiing away from Grand Central to her apartment in Chelsea, we were thrilled, saying: "New York. It's so great. Look at the dirt! Look at the guy peeing in the alley! I love it!" A joke, sure, but only partially. We'd just spent a claustrophobic weekend with our parents and other two siblings in the Berkshires. The occasion, I guess, was Cyndy's mastectomy last week.

Cyndy's nerves are pretty much gone in the right side of her body, so the operation didn't hurt as much as the lumpectomy she had two years ago, when she was twenty-one. Still, I can't help thinking, Wound, especially now that we're out with the crazies. And also, I'm thinking of my own toes, which are so black and blue with cold (a circulatory problem, I will learn later in the month) that I am having trouble walking. Indeed, at the moment, I feel more damaged than Cyndy appears to. We shuffle by the guys with the eggs, and I put my right arm around Cyndy's back—companionably, I think, because I want to restore the playful order that has reigned most of today, that was operative when we were at New York City Opera, and I was meeting Cyndy's co-workers and admiring the Mr. Potato Head doll she had placed over her desk, presumably to supervise her efforts as rehearsals coordinator. My arm has barely touched Cyndy's black coat (the coat I will someday wear) when she says, vicious as possible, "Don't you *dare* try to protect me."

I am quiet—my throat, for a minute, as pained as my toes—and then I say, my voice strangulated, half the words swallowed, "...not trying...protect you."

Cyndy is dead, of course. That is why I wear her black coat now. She died of breast cancer at age twenty-six, a fact which I find unbelievable, a fact that is (virtually) statistically impossible. When she was twenty-one, she was in the shower in her dorm room at the University of Pennsylvania. She was washing under her arm when she found the lump. She was not checking for breast cancer. What college girl does monthly exams on her own breasts? Laura, my twin sister, says that I was the first person Cyndy called about the cancer. I don't think this is true, though Laura insists. I'm certain Cyndy called my father, the doctor, and that he told her to fly home to Boston. He demanded her return even though the doctors at Penn's health service pooh-poohed her concern. Finally, after a long conversation, I realize why Laura thinks Cyndy called me first and I tell her: "I think you're thinking about the rape."

"Oh, yeah," Laura says. "That's probably right."

When my father called me in Wisconsin to tell me about Cyndy, I said, "Oh, well, I'm sure, she's okay. Lots of women have fibrous breasts."

"No, Debra," my father said, sternly. "That's not what this is about."

"Do you think she'll have to have a biopsy?"

He was quiet.

"A mastectomy?"

"That's the least of my concerns."

I guess I wasn't quite able to hear him right then. I hung up the phone and pulled out my copy of *Our Bodies, Ourselves* to look at that book's photograph of a jubilant naked woman—out in the sun, with one breast gone, the stitches running up her chest like a sideways zipper. I remember wailing, literally wailing, at the image and at the prospect of my sister losing her breast.

I didn't know yet that my father had examined my sister when she came home from college. My father is an endocrinologist, a fertility specialist. He examines women every day in his office, but to feel your adult daughter's breast—breaking *that* taboo, because medical care is shoddy and you *do* love your daughter desperately and *appropriately*—and to know, right away, what it is you are feeling...I have to stop myself from imagining it. And I think my father has to disremember it, too, because even though he knew, right then, she had cancer, he tells this story about himself: When the x-ray of Cyndy's chest was up on the lightboard, my father pulled the x-ray off the board and turned it over to look at the name. "Spark, C." He looked back at the picture. Turned the x-ray over again to check the name. "Spark, C." He did the whole thing again. And again.

Later, two weeks before she did die, I remember seeing her x-ray up on a lightboard. Not something I was supposed to see, I know, but Cyndy's treatment all took place at the same hospital my father has worked for twenty-five years. I knew my way about and I knew how to take silent advantage when I needed to. I looked, but from a distance. I was out in the hall, standing over Cyndy in her gurney, as orderlies were about to move her out of the emergency ward and up to a floor. My view was oblique and once I knew there was nothing happy to see there, I said, Don't look. Though later, all I would do was say, Look, Debra. Look, this is a person dying. Look, this is Cyndy going away.

My mother was always the most pessimistic of all of us, and I used to hate her for it. "She'll be okay," I'd say. And, "We can't read the future." My mother said we were lucky we *couldn't* read the future or we'd never get through it. Which is probably true. That night in Manhattan, things seemed tragic but manageable. In the past was the lumpectomy and the radiation. Now, the mastectomy was completed. The chemo was to come. Cyndy had cut her hair short so the loss of it wouldn't be too upsetting. Back in Boston, she'd gone with my mother to buy a wig. Now, she was trying to wear it over her hair. That was the advice she had been given: to start wearing it so it would be like a new haircut and no one would notice. I thought, Who cares who notices? I was for announcing the illness as just another fact, among many, about Cyndy. To keep it secret was to imply that it was either shameful, like a sin, or special, like a surprise gift, and it was neither.

The wig bothered Cyndy. It was itchy and, though we'd tell her otherwise, it had a dowdy look, a look that owed nothing to the haircuts Cyndy had always had—the funky asymmetrical do she'd sported when she'd gone to London for a year or the long red mane she'd had as a child. One day, while I was still visiting with her in New York, we went out to lunch with some friends of mine who had never met Cyndy. In the middle of lunch, Cyndy, impatient and in the midst of a story (she was a magnificent and voluble talker), pulled off her hair—to my friends' surprise, especially since there was another head of hair under the one she'd pulled off.

After all the preparation for baldness, however, Cyndy's hair didn't fall out. At least, not that year. The first round of chemo was bad, but, again, in the realm of the get-overable. Every three or four weekends, my mother would come into New York and take Cyndy to the hospital and then out to my grandmother's house for a weekend of puking. Cyndy handled it well. The biggest long-term effect was that she wouldn't let anyone say the words "pot roast" when they were around her. And she couldn't stand the smell of toast for years to come.

Some time later, after Cyndy had finished up the chemo, she decided to go to business school, to get a degree in arts administration at UCLA. She loved school. She had never been too happy as an undergraduate, but UCLA was right for her. Her goal had been to make opera, which she adored, accessible to people who ordinarily wouldn't go. She had a special column in the school newspaper called "Kulture, Kulture, Kulture"; she was proud of her ability to drag business students (a surprise! stiff business students!) to the opera. I imagine Cyndy as the life of the party in those days. Cyndy going to the graduate-student beer bashes; Cyndy leading the talk at the business-school study sessions; Cyndy still earning her nickname "Symphony."

I know she slimmed down in those years, too. She had an intermittent problem with her weight, and it was probably the real clue that Cyndy—handle-everything-Cyndy—sometimes had her unhealthy way of handling things. When I visited Cyndy in Chelsea, after her mastectomy, we were toying with the idea of living together. At the time, I was profoundly (read "clinically") depressed. I had left the man I had been living with for four years and had been unenthusiastically debating what I should do next. Cyndy was moving up to Inwood, and we had found a small apartment that would accommodate the two of us should I decide to move with her. I remember that one of her real enthusiasms about the two of us living together had to do with food. She was convinced that I'd have her eating large green salads for dinner, that my own good habits would rub off on her, and she would no longer find herself in the middle of secret, ruinously upsetting food binges.

Cyndy had been a chubby kid, but never really fat, even when she weighed a lot. When she was older, her figure was sensual if robust. Still her weight was an occasional issue: my father telling her, at dinner, not to be a *chazar*, my mother spinning her own anxiety about weight onto Cyndy. At Cyndy's college graduation, Cyndy said "No, thank you" to the dessert tray that a waiter was offering our table. We were all too full. My mother said, "Oh, I'm so proud of you," to Cyndy. Cyndy said, "I'll have that chocolate cake," to the waiter. And the rest of the children—Laura, David, and I—hooted with laughter. It was our turn to be proud. After all, the request for cake was her version of "Oh, stop it, Mom."

Still, toward the end of Cyndy's stay in Chelsea, I got my first glimpse of how painful the problem with food could be. Like many women, I had my own issues, and Cyndy and I would often have long talks about what all this meant. Once, she told me about how she used to have a secret way of slipping cookies silently out of the cookie jar and hiding under a dining-room table to eat. This might have struck me as funny—so often our childhood stories charmed me—but I wanted to sob when she told me. I felt stricken but stricken by our—her, my, everybody's—desires. How easily they became desperate or grotesque or hateful, especially to the person who did all that desiring.

Her desires must have been met in L.A., however, because she looked so good. At the end of her first year there, she organized a student show, a big, campy celebration that everyone dressed for. She brought a videotape of the show back to Boston for the rest of us to see. Now, we fast-forward through the tape so we can see the intermission. Someone has filmed her—happy her—backstage exuberantly organizing things. Then we fast-forward again and there is Cyndy in a gorgeous, retro, off-the-shoulder dress. Her hair is long, just above her shoulders. She needs to flip it out of her eyes. She has long dangling earrings. She is glamorous by anyone's account and quite sexy. By this point, she's had reconstructive surgery. The new breast is lumpy and disappointing—not that anyone says this. It's just clear that when my uncle, the surgeon, said, "Sometimes they do such a good job you can't tell the difference," he wasn't one hundred percent correct. Part of the problem is that Cyndy, like all the women in the family, has large breasts. They couldn't reconstruct her breast so it would be as big as the original one, so she had a smaller breast made, and she wore a partial prosthesis. The doctors had asked her if she wanted the other breast reduced—for balance's sake. But she decided no. After all, she didn't want to run the risk of not having feeling in either breast.

In the videotape, when Cyndy starts to sing, the audience is clearly amazed. And they should be: her voice is stunning. She could have had an operatic career if she had wanted it. Months before her death, a singing instructor made it clear to Cyndy that she not only could, but she had to, have a singing career. Her voice was that beautiful.

Now, when I listen to the tape, I watch Cyndy's mannerisms. Each time, I am surprised by the fact that she seems a little nervous about performing. Cyndy nervous? Cyndy is never nervous, as she herself will admit. (Except about men. That's the one exception.) But she gets comfortable as she proceeds, as the audience's approval is clear. She sings, beautifully, the Carol King song "Way Over Yonder." *Way over yonder, that's where I'm bound.*

Even before she died, I knew the irony would always break my heart, once she was gone.

In the summer after Cyndy's first two semesters in L.A., I was living in Lincoln, Nebraska. I was teaching a summer class, and late at night, I'd get tearful calls from Cyndy. Mostly about men, for I was, in many things, Cyndy's confidante. Sometimes, now, I think that I am wrong about this. I *was* Cyndy's confidante, wasn't I? She *was* the person who I was closest to, wasn't she?

When we were young, I always thought that Cyndy and I belonged together, and David and Laura belonged together. Laura always had a special way with David. Laura and I were close (the twins, after all), and Cyndy and David (the youngest) were playmates. Still, I felt Cyndy and I were a pair. When they met Cyndy, people used to say, "Oh, so she's your twin?" And I'd shake my head no. "Your older sister?" No, I'd say again. Cyndy loved being mistaken for my older sister. "I really am the smartest one in the family," she'd say, even when she was in her twenties. I'd have to disagree; it was a distinction I thought I deserved if by smart you meant (and Cyndy did) commonsensical.

Our closeness was somewhat competitive. We delighted in being competent—more competent than the one in the family who was spacey, the one who was overemotional. We just had things together, and we understood the world. The one fight I remember us having (I'm sure we had many when we were young, but I can't remember them) is about driving the car. She snapped at me for correcting her driving. She hated it when I played older sister.

When Cyndy first started making her tearful phone calls to me, I was proud. I took a secret pleasure in the fact that she confided in me, that she came to me first. I'd even felt a slight pleasure—mixed with my horror—when she called to tell me, and, at first, only me, that she'd been raped. It was during her first year at college. I was in my senior year at Yale. It was a date rape, I suppose, although that term doesn't fit exactly. The man was someone she met in a bar—a sailor, good God—and Cyndy got drunk and later, after some flirting, he didn't understand that no meant no. I honestly don't think he knew he raped her. I think for a while Cyndy was bewildered, too. Her previous sexual encounters had not amounted to much, and, later in college, her experiences remained disappointing.

Given her history, Cyndy's tears on the phone made sense to me. I thought she was finally addressing the issue that had always so frightened her. She spoke, with uncharacteristic frustration, of the way her women friends were always talking about *their* relationships, and she didn't have any relationships, and how upset it made her. With the encouragement of the family, Cyndy started talking to a therapist. I was all for this, I would tell Cyndy, as I sat late at night in my small rental in Nebraska. After all, I had been helped, enormously, by a psychiatrist. My parents agreed with my assessment, I think, although Cyndy spent less of her time on the phone with them talking about men and more time talking about her headaches, her terrible headaches, that stopped her from getting any work done.

So, it's clear where this goes, no? We hope it's not, we hope it's not—as with each test or checkup we have hoped—but it is. Cyndy has cancer in her brain. When they do the initial radiation on her brain, and later when they do an experimental treatment that *does* shrink the tumor, it becomes clear that all that crying had a physiological base. Her tumor shrunk, her headaches go away. She stops crying or talking about men.

But, of course, she does cry, though only once, when she learns about the brain tumor. When I find out, I am standing in my kitchen and kneading bread. I get the call, and then I phone MIT to tell a friend of Laura's not to let her go to lunch. I want to come get her and take her to the hospital. I feel like a rock when I do all this, like a cold rock. I throw the dough in the trash and hear the *thump-swish* of it hitting the plastic bag. Then, I go and get Laura, who screams—as in bad movies, screams—and I drive to the hospital. Laura, instantly feeling everything, spins out of control with grief. She's sharp with nurses who seem to be blocking her way to Cyndy. She won't allow what my father says when he says it. She just tells him, No, no, you're wrong. She turns to me and says, Why aren't you acting like anything? And I think, Because I am so very competent.

In the fall, Cyndy comes and lives with me in my big apartment in North Cambridge. This is so clearly better than staying with my parents in their suburban home. She is immensely disappointed about having to take time off from UCLA. But it is only time off, we reassure her. She will get back there. And she does. After a year with me, she goes back for a semester. But she is too sick and has to come back to live with me for good. She lives with me for two years. This is the part that I'm glad I didn't get to see when I was in my Wisconsin apartment and worrying about the possibility of my sister having a mastectomy. I think now, A mastectomy! A lousy mastectomy! Who cares? I remember once, not long after I'd moved to Cambridge and before Cyndy moved in with me, I was in bed with a temporary lover. He was an old college friend, a doctor, in town to do some work for the year. Cyndy and I had been talking, earlier that day, over the phone, about men. I was encouraging her to approach a young man she was interested in, in L.A. She'd said, "But, it's so complicated. Like at what point do I say, 'Hey, buddy. One of these isn't real.'" I knew she'd be gesturing, even though we were on the phone, to her chest, pointing to first one, then the other. ("I can always tell," she'd said, "when someone knows and they're trying to figure out which one it is.") That night, in bed, I'd said to my friend, "Well, if you loved someone, it wouldn't make a difference...say, before you were involved...if you found out they had a mastectomy, would it?" He looked at me. "Yeah," he said. "I don't mean to be horrible, but of course it would."

"But," I said, as if he'd change his mind because I needed him to, "*I* said it wouldn't. That's what *I* said."

Cyndy and I had fun in the apartment where we lived. My boyfriend, Jim, would come by in the evenings, and they would talk music or we'd go out for dinner. Nights when Jim was working, we'd get George, a musician friend from around the corner, to come over. Cyndy took classes at Boston University. She worked for the Boston Opera Theatre. She got involved with a project involving musicians in Prague. Related to that, Vaclav Havel's press secretary and her son came to live with us for a while. And during all this, cancer would pop up in one place or another—her knees, the back of her tongue. Still, it always honestly seemed to me that we could make her better. Healthy denial, I suppose. Certainly, Cyndy had a lot of it. She was always willing to be cheered up, to imagine her future.

Some things stand out, but I can't (I won't) put them in order. Like: the number of times I would be in bed, making love with Jim, and hear Cyndy hacking away in the next room. That would be the cancer in her lungs.

Or the way she would call out to me each morning that Jim wasn't there: "Derba, Derba, Derba," she'd say, in a high-pitched silly voice. And I'd call back, "Der-ba Bird," because that was what she was, chirping out the family nickname for me. Then, I'd go crawl into her bed and rub her back. There was cancer in the spine by then, and she could never get comfortable. Sometimes, she'd wail at her pillows. She couldn't get them in the right position.

Or the way, one night, when I was making dinner, she said, "Oh, God," and I said, "What is it?" and she snapped, angry as could be, "You *know* what it is!"

There was an odd stretch when I felt her oncologist was trying to convince her that her symptoms were psychosomatic. Like when she couldn't get enough energy to move, and we'd spend days inside, only making an occasional trek to the back porch. Perhaps, he seemed to be suggesting, she was only depressed?

The few times Cyndy did snap at me, I felt like I would dissolve. My mother said, "Well, I guess you're getting a sense, before your time, of what it's like to have an adolescent." In truth, my mother got the brunt of it. When Cyndy was in the most pain, she would leave the apartment for a stay with my parents. When she was well enough, she would come back to stay with me. Wherever she was, though—my house, my parents' house—we were all there, all the time.

And even when she was doing relatively well, there were lots of visits back and forth. One day, in the beginning of her stay with me, Cyndy and I were driving out to our parents' house for dinner. We were talking about death, and Cyndy said, "Oh, well, you know, sometimes I think about death. And I try to force myself to imagine what it would be like but then I'm like... whoa... you know, I just can't do it."

"Yes," I said, for I knew exactly what she meant. "I'm like that, too."

Now I'm even more "like that." For if a parent's job is to protect his or her child, a sister's is to identify with her sibling. Which means, of course, that the whole family gets, in the case of a terminal illness, to fail in what they most want to do for one another. So I push my imagination to death, make myself think "no consciousness." I have, regretfully, no belief in heaven, an afterlife, reincarnation. I believe in nothingness. I try not to let myself pull back, try not to say, "Whoa, that's too much." But my brain—its gift to me—is that it won't let me do what I want.

I think, in this regard, of the time ten-year-old Cyndy came home from school in a snit. She'd learned about black holes in science class. She'd stomped up to her room and flopped on her bed. As she went, she ordered the family never to talk to her about black holes. I thought she was joking. So, I opened the door to her bedroom, stuck my head in—cartoon-fashion, the accordion player poking his head through the stage curtain to get a peek at the crowd—and I said, rapidly, "Black hole, black hole, black hole." Cyndy, already lying on her bed, threw herself against the mattress so that she bounced on it like a just-captured fish hitting land. She started to sob. "I'm sorry," I said. "I was kidding. I thought *you* were kidding." But why should she have been? What's more terrible than everything going out?

Once, during one of her final stays in the hospital, Cyndy said to my mother, "I'm going to be good now," as if that would make her healthy, as if a planet could blame itself for being in the wrong part of the universe.

"Oh, honey," my mother had said. "You *are* good. You are so *good*."

One trip out to my parents that stands in my mind: Cyndy had the shingles, an enormously painful viral infection that runs along the nerve path on one side of the body. Just getting her down the staircase into my car was horrible. Cyndy was sobbing and sobbing, and ordinarily she didn't cry. I put her in the passenger's seat and cursed myself for having the kind of life that made me buy such an inexpensive and uncomfortable car. The requirement of bending was too much, and Cyndy wept and wept. I drove as fast as I could and neither of us talked. I thought, I'll just get her home and it will be all right. My father, the doctor, would know what to do. My mother would be, as she could be, the most comforting person in the world. When we got there, I said, "It's okay, it's going to be okay," as Cyndy walked, with tiny paces, from the car to the front steps. My parents were at the front door and it was night. My mother brought a kitchen chair to the front hall so as soon as Cyndy got up the stairs, she could sit down. I stood behind her, and my parents stood at the top of the six stairs that lead to our front door. My mother (blue turtleneck and jeans); my father (stooped). Both of them had their hands out and were reaching for Cyndy but they couldn't get her up the stairs. She had to do that herself. And I thought, looking at them in the light, and Cyndy still forcing herself up through the night—*Oh, my God. All this love, all this love can't do a thing.*

But that wasn't completely true. The love did do something. It just didn't save her.

Laura, my twin sister, gave Cyndy foot rubs and Cyndy loved them. Laura would give foot rubs, literally, for hours. I gave back rubs but I never liked giving them, would wait for Cyndy to say I could stop. When Cyndy told Laura she could stop if she wanted to, Laura would ask for permission to keep going—as if Cyndy were doing her a favor by putting her feet in the vicinity of Laura's hands. One day, Cyndy was lying on her bed in our apartment and Laura was on a chair at the end of the bed and she was rubbing Cyndy's feet. I was "spooning" Cyndy and occasionally rubbing up and down her spine where the cancer was. We were talking about masturbation. "I can't believe you guys," Laura was saying, telling us again about how amazing it was that, of the three of us, she had discovered masturbation first. We were giggling. This conversation wasn't unfamiliar. We'd had it before, but we could always find something new to tell each other.

"What was that bathtub thing you were talking about," Cyndy said.

Years earlier, I'd instructed both of my sisters about the virtues of masturbating in the bathtub. Something I'd learned from my freshman-year roommate at college. "Got to try it," I said now.

"Exactly how do you do it again?" asked Cyndy.

"Lie in the tub. Scoot your butt under the waterspout and put your legs up on the wall and let the water run into you. Guaranteed orgasm."

"De-bra," Cyndy said, hitting me, as if I'd gone too far in this being-open-with-sisters conversation.

"Sor-ry," I said. "Still, you've got to try it, but wait till this thing gets better." I pointed at her head. There was a new problem these days, something that caused Cyndy to get, on occasions, dizzy. She had some new medicine, so I talked as if the problem would be solved in a matter of weeks. (Aside from the dizziness, Cyndy had occasional aphasia. One night when I was on the phone, Cyndy screamed from her bedroom. I ran in. She'd forgotten a word, couldn't produce it, and felt her head go weirdly blank. The word, she realized, five minutes later, was cancer.)

We decided to leave the topic of sex behind for something else. But not before I insisted, once again, that Cyndy try this bathtub thing. I was rubbing her back and Laura was still rubbing her feet, and I was thinking, as I stroked her skin, Yes, an orgasm. Let this body give her some pleasure.

You *do* get inappropriately intimate with a body when the body is ill. Sometimes there's something nice about it. Cyndy used to sit on the toilet in our bathroom and I'd take a soapy washcloth and wash her bald head. I'd say, "Stamp out dry scalpy skin." This struck us, for some reason, as terribly funny. We'd soak our feet in the bathtub and talk about our favorite Gogol stories. We'd walk arm-in-arm. Say: "This is what we'll be like when we are old ladies."

When Cyndy's symptoms were at their worst, my own body struck me, especially my legs, which stretched—it seemed amazing—from my torso to the ground. The miracle of walking. I still feel it. The air behind my legs is creepily light as I move. Who would have ever suspected that you can feel grief behind your kneecaps?

One very bad night: Cyndy was upset about everything, but especially men, relationships, never having had a boyfriend. According to her, I didn't, *couldn't* understand because I had had a boyfriend. This was a point of connection between Cyndy and a few of her intimates, an absence they could discuss and from which I was excluded. It didn't matter that I felt, for the sadness of my own relationships, included. I had had sex. Many times even—enough to have had a sexually transmitted disease which I (paranoid, irrational) thought I could pass on to Cyndy through ordinary contact. It didn't matter that I was cured of the problem. Her immune system was down. Anything I did might hurt her. My own desires might kill her.

This one night, Cyndy was crying, so I went into her room to put my arm around her, and she said, "Don't. Don't you touch me." Fierce, again. Vicious. I retreated to my bedroom. Cried softly, but still felt I had to do something. I stepped back to her bedroom, and she started to scream, waving me away, but saying, "It's just that I realize that nobody but my family or a doctor has touched me in the past five years."

It'll change, it'll change, it'll change. That was always my mantra for these relationship conversations. But it didn't. She died before it could change.

After that terrible night when Cyndy had the shingles and had to struggle out of our apartment to the car, she spent six weeks at my parents' house. Those were miserable times. She couldn't move from her bed. We'd all climb onto the double bed, a ship in the ocean of her room, and play word games or watch TV or be quiet because a lot of the time she couldn't stand for anything to be going on. As she started to feel a bit better, she worked on the course that she was going to teach in January of 1992. It was going to be called "Opera—What's All the Screaming About?" and it was going to be for high school girls, for kids who, presumably, could care less about opera. We rented opera videos and watched them with her. Then, she decided she was ready to come back to our apartment to work on her course syllabus. I cleaned the kitchen while she worked. At one point, she started to faint, but she grabbed the doorjamb, and I came in and caught her, wrapped my arms around her waist—big now, she was bloated with steroids—and set her down on the ground. She was okay, so she started to work at her computer, and I made us some cocoa. She handed me her syllabus to proofread. She sipped, while I read it, and she said, in a sort of campy voice, "Mmmm...this is love-ly." I laughed, still reading. She made a funny gurgling noise. I thought it was a joke but when I looked up from the syllabus, Cyndy was slipping out of her chair. I ran the few feet to her. She was crumpled on the ground. I rolled her onto her back and saw blood. There was water on the floor—

her urine. "Are you okay? Are you okay?" I screamed. Her wig had rolled off her head and she looked like a gigantic toppled mannequin. She was gasping, breathing oddly. A seizure, I knew. I am, after all, a doctor's daughter. When the convulsive breathing stopped, she said, "What happened? What just happened?" She was as purely frightened as I'd ever seen her.

"Close your eyes," I said. "You just fainted. Close your eyes." I didn't want her to see her own blood. I thought that would scare her. I ran to the bathroom to get a towel and wipe her up. I tried to see where the blood was coming from.

"It's okay, you bit your tongue."

I felt—I have to say this, only because it's so horrible—a slight pleasure. It was the old thing; I would be competent, take care of this trouble. I was good in an emergency. But, there was also part of me—small, I promise myself now, very small—that thought, with some relief, It's over.

The ambulance came. We rode over to the hospital. My parents were there before us. When they rolled Cyndy away, I cried to my mother, "Oh, Mommy. I thought she was dying. I thought she was dying."

Inside, Cyndy was saying the same to my father, "I thought I was dying. I thought I was going to die."

And about two weeks later she did. But not before her body put her through enormous suffering. Not before she had a little more fun with the family. So, last things. The last thing she ever produced was a picture from a coloring book. She had asked for the book and some crayons, and we all earnestly filled in Mickey Mouse's ears and then signed our names and ages. Debra, twenty-nine. Laura, twenty-nine. David, twenty-four. Mommy, fifty-three. Daddy, fifty-five. Cyndy signed hers, "The Queen." (A joke from our two years together. When she was queen, Boston drivers were not going to be allowed to be obnoxious.) Under "age," Cyndy wrote, "None of your damn business." Last meal: gray fish from the kosher kitchen, but she didn't eat it. Last thing she *did* eat: Jell-O. I know, I spooned it into her mouth. Last thing I said to her: I told her that the man she was interested in was in love with her, that I knew because of what he'd said when I called to tell him she was in the hospital. (I was making this up, but who cares?) Last thing Cyndy ever said to me: "Oh, good. Well, tell him we'll get together when I get out of here." Last thing she ever said: I didn't hear this because I wasn't in the room, but she woke up, delusional and panicked and worried because she was going on a long trip and she hadn't packed her suitcase.

As my fiction-writer friends always say, You can't make this stuff up. No one would believe you if you tried.

And I have to agree: real life is just too heavy-handed.

Very last thing: her body still desiring life, she takes every third breath, though her fingers are dusky, though her kidneys have already shut down. We give the funeral director the pretty purple dress she bought for special occasions. We put her in the ground.

*Our desires,* I sometimes think now, as I'm walking down the street.

Today, outside a bakery, I stop myself and say, "Yes, Debra? What about them?" And I realize I don't know. "What? What?" I stand for a while feeling disgusted with the world—those horrible leering men in the greengrocer's; that stupid sailor in the bar; foolish me, making love with my sister dying in the next room. *Our desires, our desires, our desires.* I know what the refrain is; I just don't know what to do about it. It's a reproach for me, an always unfulfilled wish for my family, and a sad song—it's a dirge—for Cyndy. Still, since I am here, stuck among the living, I have to remind myself that the song owes nothing to the beautiful ones that Cyndy sang. So I go into the bakery and get a short-bread cookie, dipped in chocolate. It is so delicious I start to cry.

# JOSEPH FEATHERSTONE

## *My Good War*

The other day I was wondering how to make onion soup, and my mind served up the bowl I had in Seattle just before we shipped out to Yokohama—my first onion soup, with a slice of toasted french bread and some melted Guyere cheese. This was the end of 1946. I was six and a half, and the restaurant in Seattle was dark and warm, as well as fancy. We were heading for Japan in the morning, where my father had a job as a civilian lawyer with the U.S. Occupation. The good soup took my mind off the strangeness of having a father I did not recognize—he had been in the Pacific during the war—and the misery of leaving Wilkes-Barre, Pennsylvania, and the grandfather and aunt I loved.

The group moving across the country into chosen exile included my mother and my older brother, and a brand-new baby sister. Crossing the Pacific in winter was bad. There was a typhoon, and we were seasick. Worse for me was the fact that the Pacific had just been a war zone. Our gray navy ship was still equipped with guns. I dreaded confronting the Japanese, who I had thought about and dreamed of every day in a sheltered and lucky childhood rocked by rumors of war.

When the men went off to fight, many families regrouped, like us, into a kind of commune. Ours was a commune of women and children, except for an occasional male cousin home from the merchant marines—and my grandfather. Papa combined a railroad man's cap with an elegant cigarette holder, like FDR's. He was lovely to pets and children, assuring us that pine trees heal, and telling us to always speak well to our cat, Colors. A skeptic about many things, he was a believer in the rights of ordinary working people. The world, he always said, constantly screws up the one workable idea—that everyone should help each other, and be kind.

I noticed that he found kindness toward other grownups a difficult spiritual discipline. He could be a hard man to those who worked under him at the railroad yards, and to those at home at 481 South Franklin St. He was not a tyrant in the family commune—all the patriarchs were off, in uniform—more of a dissident, really, a rebel from established ways. I helped him in his long campaign to permit the cat to have her kittens in the linen closet—the first of many good losing causes for me, though another routine defeat for him. When my mother in exasperation gave our heroic cat away—Colors could leap to the garage roof in one jump, and had all the neighborhood dogs cowed—Papa roamed the city and found her, bringing her home on his back in triumph. The cat and my mother glared at each other, enemies.

It was tough for my mother to do business with the likes of Papa and the family commune all the time. The setup gave my brother and me odd-angled, but roomy, tribal space in which to grow with our dogs and adventures. I went off to kindergarten and came home the first afternoon insisting that I had been fired. My aunt Mary let me stay home for the rest of the year, the sort of ruling you were not likely to get from a parent. We were part of a safe and cozy neighborhood on the Susquehanna River that knew Bing Crosby was a Catholic, too. Everyone understood that the country lost something big when FDR died.

The war was an invisible version of the terrible Susquehanna floods, soaking our lives. It formed a vast pressure system in our heads. There were the missing men, of course, constant presences, though in fact all of our family's hostages came home safe—they had what people called a good war. Each day my grandfather showed me the progress of the various fronts in the maps in the four newspapers he pored through. Even before I could read I always checked the newsstand on the square to see if the headlines were in big Bodoni type, which meant war news, maybe casualties, perhaps with the names of neighbors on the list.

Every Saturday morning, my brother and I walked uptown to see movie matinees, which always included newsreels of combat along with the serials like Terry and the Pirates. I don't know if you have ever looked at World War II–era comic books—people collect and sell them now—but the dark, overpainted, claustrophobic colors can still take me back. The Japanese soldiers were inked bright yellow in fierce dark panels, and they had fangs for

teeth and they wore glasses with lenses thicker than the bottoms
of Coke bottles, magnifying their terrible insect eyes, and they
killed babies and tortured women and said stuff like "Aieee, ten
thousand purple demons!" when the brave American soldiers
overran their jungle foxholes. My father had been near them in
New Guinea, where he caught malaria, and I supposed they had
been trying to kill him—he once wrote of someone finding a
Japanese sniper and wiping him out of a cave with a flame throw-
er. Now here I was going away to live with beings little better than
murderous bugs.

There was something else, which I never told a soul at the time.
My thoughts were on making my first communion, and learning
to confess my sins. The one sin I could not bear to tell anyone,
even Aunt Mary, was a sin inadequately dealt with in the questions and answers in our blue Baltimore Catechism, which
seemed to dwell on puzzling offenses involving sex, or else dis-
obedience toward rightful authority. In a time and place awash in
the Catholic homily, no nun or priest or text ever gave us a single
piece of advice about how to stay intact in the face of war. "Offer
it up," they said of suffering. What did this mean? My big problem was that I sometimes had to be or pretend to be—I wasn't
clear on the difference—a Jap or a German. I wondered if my per-
plexity stemmed from the weakness and confusion that some
people located as one source of sin. It was surely a product of a
small but systematic injustice. My friend Alan and I were the
youngest on the block. All through the years of playing war under
the two big cherry trees in our backyard, the bargain was clear:
little kids often had to agree to be the German or the Jap, or the
big kids might not let you play. I may have had a choice, but I
didn't feel I had one. So I played, risking my soul.

Christ himself, I was sure, had never faced anything so complex, although for him becoming human might, I supposed, have
created a similar feeling of shame and betrayal. "Jap" was our
word for the Japanese. It conveyed more horror than "German."
It's curious that, although my mother's family was political, on
the left, and profoundly anti-fascist, we kids seldom called the
Germans Nazis. In the game, you were the German, not the Nazi.
I think we hated Japs more than Germans because the Germans

were like us—my brother's best friend was named Fritzi, after all—whereas we saw the Japanese as less than human. And there was a summary playground verdict: the Japs had started the war. We took our ideas from the war's weather system, storming along inside our heads on some principle of unfolding chaos. The times made it hard to be good.

So I spent the war in combat for the enemy—always losing, sometimes crying, wounded and dying from gunshot and bayonet damage and bombs and grenades and flame throwers, haunted by the pictures of Jap insects in the comics, and a kid's version of Japanese and Nazi horrors pressed in the mind by the steady pressure of real and imagined violence. We kids were enacting the war, making a replica we could experiment with, and maybe understand, but the war was a planet on fire, and even the replica burned.

On VE day, my aunt and I were uptown when we heard the news. We stepped inside the nearest church, which had a large German congregation. The choir was singing thanks for peace in German, and I breathed a sigh of relief. The war was not over for those of us assigned to the Imperial Japanese Army, however. We had to soldier on, every day bringing more young lives lost under the cherry trees. On a lucky day we had a furlough. We could join Robin Hood's men, and escape the nightmare of current history.

I got more and more scared as our ship approached Japan. We docked in Yokohama at night. Everybody was sleeping. I got up first and went out on deck in the early light. The fog was lifting. You could start to make out the new piers and those bombed by the Americans in the great raids my grandfather read to me about in the papers, the vast incalculable tonnage of bombs and fire bombs we had exulted in, the flaming rivers in which, in the backyard, I had sometimes died along with my fellow insects. Later my brother and I explored in fear the bombed-out buildings, and Yokohama neighborhoods where all the cats and dogs had been eaten in the hungry time. A mind trained in war by my grandfather could begin to guess even from the state of the docks that the city had been twisted by strange hot storms.

I could smell land, a few pine trees, scents of a port city, foreign garbage. In the fog on the pier there was one man stooping over.

He was collecting cigarette butts in a large khaki shoulder bag. He had only one leg, and a crutch for the missing leg. He was wearing the ruins of a Japanese army uniform. He was the first Japanese I saw outside of a comic or a newsreel. I went below where everyone else was still asleep and fished quietly in my parents' dresser for cigarettes, and took a full unopened carton up to the deck and threw it down on the pier. At first the Japanese soldier didn't notice the Lucky Strikes. Then he did, staring down, astonished. He looked up at me, caught my eye, grinned, paused a second, and gave a formal military salute of thanks. I felt the first shock of a short life rich in what to that moment I believed were certainties: with his wire-rimmed glasses and his frayed cap and his cigarette holder and his hungry old face he looked exactly like my grandfather.

It felt as though I was starting to push back against some great coercive pressure, fighting to stay intact. I think I began to sense from that moment that, whatever the intricate balance of sin and virtue surrounding the incomprehensible, monstrous fact of the war, something had messed with my mind, and filled it full of lies and hatred and fear.

I was a winner, looking down on the face of defeat. I hated myself for being the side that took the man's leg, for the bombings, for being a German and a Jap, for letting myself be made a Jap, for the hatefulness of faces staring at other humans and calling them bugs. I feared and hated the Germans and the bug people, too, the Japs most of all. I hated them for losing, and would have hated them even more for winning. Even my bones felt confused. I don't know to this day how I didn't explode, or how I found the beginning of a way out, except that what I did made things start to feel better.

I look at myself looking at the old Japanese man (who may in years have been as old as I am now), my mind awash with the firestorms that ripped apart the world. The war was a civil war, taking place inside all of us, whether we realized it or not. I was trying to mend its tears, and to fit my sense of dislocation and fear and exile to a startling new reality: my hunger for a human web.

The war was history's loudspeaker blaring at us, flooding our thoughts, ordering me and my store of experience to get lost. It was

an enemy, too. In fighting back against its flood of words and images, it helped, strangely, sadly, that I was a migrant now, that I had
left my own sweet valley—that I was one of all the others who had
to make a new, provisional home out where nothing was solid,
where everything floated, like my gray ship. Every migrant in the
new floating world would have a name and a different story.

My picture of my grandfather and my aunt was next to my
migrant's heart; nobody was going to take it away. I was forever a
product of America and Wilkes-Barre, but even as one of the new
conquerors of Japan, it would be impossible for me from that
moment on to believe that truth has only one face.

I wanted, finally—it seems so simple—to meet the world without hatred or coercion. Even a small boy could see that it was
time to shed some hard, ancient skin in 1946. How much more so
in 1994. Not to see this is to be far more blind than the blind children my brother and I were soon playing with at the famous big
school in the bluffs over Yokohama. These Japanese were our
neighbors now. They gave us our puppy, Dusty, whose mother
was one of the school's Seeing Eye dogs. Some of the children
were blind from birth, others from the U.S. firebombings. We
started games of hide and seek at night out where the blind knew
the terrain—hiding in tall bamboo thickets, our faces lit moony-
green by the cool explosions of fireflies. We were young boys,
playing together like crickets in the same cage.

I count myself doubly lucky—I grew up easy, and I once found,
by an accident of grace, or the fortunes of war, an imaginative
moment in which I floated up out of the dark mirror that most of
us in this terrible century have been forced to look into. No wonder I feel tender toward myself on the deck of my ship, still afloat,
and reaching out. I like to see the sources of my childish bravery
in my own small sufferings. I savor the roots of dissent in the love
and curious example and teachings of my harsh old grandfather.
Lapsed Catholic that I am, I have enjoyed making my confession
to you: I was a thief, like my hero, Robin Hood, on behalf of
humanity.

I relish the Japanese soldier, too. He and my rebel grandfather
are surely two of a kind. His military salute has more than a hint
of mockery, at the same time that it manages respect and even

affection for the small stranger in the temporary role of the colonial big shot. Man to man, I want to look him in the eye today and laugh. We fought together on the same side in the world's stinking war.

CHARLES BAXTER

# Dysfunctional Narratives
## Or "Mistakes Were Made"

Here are some sentences of distinctive American prose from our era.

> From a combination of hypersensitivity and a desire not to know the truth in case it turned out to be unpleasant, I had spent the last ten months putting off a confrontation with John Mitchell.... I listened to more tapes.... I heard Haldeman tell me that Dean and Mitchell had come up with a plan to handle the problem of the investigation's going into areas we didn't want it to go. The plan was to call in Helms and Walters of the CIA and have them restrain the FBI.... Haldeman and I discussed [on the "smoking gun" tape] having the CIA limit the FBI investigation for political rather than the national security reasons I had given in my public statements.... On June 13, while I was in Egypt, Fred Buzhardt had suffered a heart attack. Once I was assured that he was going to pull through, I tried to assess the impact his illness would have on our legal situation.

These sentences are *almost* enough to make one nostalgic for an adversary with a claim upon our attention. There he is, the late lawyer-President setting forth the brief for the defense, practicing the dogged art of the disclaimer in *RN: The Memoirs of Richard Nixon.* (I've done some cut-and-pasting, but the sentences I've quoted are the sentences he wrote.) And what sentences! Leaden and dulling, juridical-minded to the last, impersonal but not without savor—the hapless Buzhardt and his heart attack factored into the "legal situation," and that wonderful "hypersensitivity" combined with a desire "not to know the truth" that makes one think of Henry James's Lambert Strether or an epicene character in Huysmans—they present the reader with camouflage masked as objective thought.

In his memoir, Richard Nixon does not admit that he lied, exactly, or that he betrayed his oath of office. In his "public statements," he did a bit of false accounting, that was all. One should expect this, he suggests, from heads of state.

Indeed, the only surprise this reader had, trudging gamely through *RN*, looking for clues to a badly defined mystery, was the author's report of a sentence uttered by Jacqueline Kennedy. Touring the White House after *RN*'s election, she said, "I always live in a dream world." Funny that she would say so; funny that he would notice.

Lately I've been possessed of a singularly unhappy idea: the greatest influence on American fiction for the last twenty years may have been the author of *RN*, not in his writing but in his public character. He is the inventor, for our purposes and for our time, of the concept of *deniability*. Deniability is the almost complete disavowal of intention in relation to bad consequences. This is a made-up word, and it reeks of the landfill-scented landscape of lawyers and litigation and high school. Following Richard Nixon in influence on recent fiction would be two runners-up, Ronald Reagan and George Bush. Their administrations put the passive voice, politically, on the rhetorical map. In their efforts to acquire deniability on the arms-for-hostages deal with Iran, their administrations managed to achieve considerable notoriety for self-righteousness, public befuddlement about facts, forgetfulness under oath, and constant disavowals of political error and criminality, culminating in the quasi-confessional, passive voice–mode sentence, "Mistakes were made."

Contrast this with Robert E. Lee's statement after the battle of Gettysburg, the third day and the calamity of Pickett's Charge: "All this has been my fault," Lee said. "I asked more of men than should have been asked of them."

These sentences have a slightly antique ring. People just don't say such things anymore.

What difference does it make to writers of stories if public figures are denying their responsibility for their own actions? So what if they are, in effect, refusing to tell their own stories accurately? So what if the President of the United States is making himself out to be, of all things, a *victim*? Well, to make an obvious point, they create a climate in which social narratives are designed to be deliberately incoherent and misleading. Such narratives humiliate the act of storytelling. You can argue that only a coherent narrative can manage to explain public events, and you can reconstruct a story if someone says, "I made a mistake," or "We did that," but you can't reconstruct a story—you can't even know what the story *is*—if everyone is saying, "Mistakes were made." Who made them? Well, everybody made them and no one did, and it's history anyway, so we should forget about it. Every story is a history, however, and when there is no comprehensible story, there is, in some sense, no history; the past, under those circumstances, becomes an unreadable mess. When we hear words like "deniability," we are in the presence of narrative dysfunction, a phrase employed by the poet C. K. Williams to describe the process by which we lose track of the story of ourselves, the story that tells us who we are supposed to be and how we are supposed to act.

One spiritual godfather of the contemporary disavowal movement, the author of *RN*, set the tenor for the times and reflected the times as well in his lifelong denial of responsibility for the Watergate break-in and coverup. He claimed that misjudgments were made, though not necessarily by him; mistakes were made, though they were by no means his own, and the crimes that were committed were only crimes if you define "crime" in a certain way, in the way, for example, that his enemies liked to define the word, in a manner that would be unfavorable to him, that would give him, to use a word derived from the Latin, some culpability. It wasn't the law, he claimed; it was all just politics.

A curious parallel: the Kennedy assassination may be *the* narratively dysfunctional event of our era: no one really knows who's responsible for it. One of the signs of a dysfunctional narrative is that we cannot leave it behind, and we cannot put it to rest, because it does not, finally, give us the explanation we need to enclose it. We don't know who the agent of the action is. We don't even know why it was done. Instead of achieving closure, the story spreads over the landscape like a stain as we struggle to find a source of responsibility. In our time, responsibility within narratives has been consistently displaced by its enigmatic counterpart, conspiracy. Conspiracy works in tandem with narrative repression, the repression of who-has-done-what. We go back over the Kennedy assassination second by second, frame by frame, but there is a truth to it that we cannot get at because we can't be sure who really did it or what the motivations were. Everyone who claims to have closed the case simply establishes that the case will stay open. The result of dysfunctional narrative, as the poet Lawrence Joseph has suggested to me, is sorrow; I would argue that it is sorrow mixed with depression, the condition of the abject, but in any case we are talking about the psychic landscape of trauma and paralysis, the landscape of, for example, two outwardly different writers, Don DeLillo (in most of *Libra*) and Jane Smiley (in the last one hundred pages of *A Thousand Acres*).

A parenthesis: Jane Smiley's novel has been compared to *King Lear*, and its plot invites the comparison, but its real ancestors in fiction are the novels of Emile Zola. *A Thousand Acres* is Zola on the plains. Like Zola, Jane Smiley assembles precisely and carefully a collection of facts, a Naturalistic pile-up of details about—in this case—farming and land use. As for characters, the reader encounters articulate women (including the narrator, Rose) and mostly frustrated inarticulate men driven by blank desires, like Larry, the Lear figure. Lear, however, is articulate. Larry is not. He is like one of Zola's male characters, driven by urges he does not understand or even acknowledge.

Somewhat in the manner of other Naturalistic narratives, *A Thousand Acres* causes its characters to behave like mechanisms, under obscure orders. Wry but humorless, shorn of poetry or any lyric outburst, and brilliantly observant and relentless, the novel at first seems to be about 1980's greed and the destruction of resources that we now associate with Reaganism, a literally exploitative husbandry. Such a story would reveal clear if deplorable motives in its various characters. Instead, with the revelation of Larry's sexual abuse of his daughters, including the narrator, it shifts direction toward an account of conspiracy and repressed memory, sorrow and depression, in which several of the major characters are acting out rather than acting.

The characters' emotions are thus preordained, and the narrator herself gathers around herself a cloak of unreliability as the novel goes on. It is a moody novel, but the mood itself often seems impenetrable because the characters, even the men, are not acting upon events in present narrative time but are reacting obscurely to harms done to them in the psychic past, from unthinkable impulses that will go forever unexplained. Enacting greed at least involves making some decisions, but in this novel, the urge to enact incest upon one's daughter is beyond thought, and, in turn, creates consequences that are beyond thought. Rose herself lives in the shadow of thought (throughout much of the book she is unaccountable, even to herself) by virtue of her having been molested by her father. This is dysfunctional narrative as literary art, a novel that is also very much an artifact of *this* American era.

Watergate itself would have remained narratively dysfunctional if the tapes hadn't turned up, and, with them, the "smoking gun"—notice, by the way, the metaphors that we employ to designate narrative responsibility, the naming and placing of the phallically inopportune protagonist at the center. The arms-for-hostages deal is still a muddled narrative because various political functionaries are taking the fall for what the commander-in-chief is supposed to have decided himself. However, the commander-in-chief was not told; or he forgot; or he was out of the loop. The buck stops here? In recent history, the buck doesn't stop anywhere. The buck keeps moving, endlessly; perhaps we are in the era of the endlessly traveling buck, the buck seeking a place to stop, like a story that cannot find its own ending.

We have been living, it seems, in a political culture of disavowals. Disavowals follow from crimes for which no one is capable of claiming responsibility. Mistakes and crimes tend to create narratives, however, and they have done so from the time of the Greek tragedies. How can the contemporary disavowal movement not affect those of us who tell stories? We begin to move away from fiction of protagonists and antagonists into another mode, another model. It is hard to describe this model but I think it might be called the fiction of finger-pointing, the fiction of the quest for blame.

In such fiction, people and events are often accused of turning the protagonist into the kind of person the protagonist is, usually an unhappy person. That's the whole story. When blame has been assigned, the story is over. (In writing workshops, this kind of story is often the rule rather than the exception.) Probably this model of storytelling has arisen because, for many reasons, large population groups in our time feel confused and powerless, as they often do in mass societies when the mechanisms of power are carefully masked. For people with bad jobs and mounting debts and faithless partners and abusive parents, the most interesting feature of life is its unhappiness, its dull constant weight. But in a commodity culture, people are *supposed* to be happy; this is the one tireless myth of advertising. In such a consumerist climate, the perplexed and unhappy don't know what their lives are telling them, and they don't feel as if they are in charge of their own existence. No action they have ever taken is half as interesting to them as the consistency of their unhappiness.

Natural disasters, by contrast—earthquakes and floods—have a quality of narrative relief: we know what caused the misery, and we usually know what we can do to repair the damage, no matter how long it takes.

But corporate and social power, any power carefully masked, puts its victims into a state of frenzy, the frenzy of the *Oprah* show, of *Geraldo,* and Montel Williams. Somebody must be responsible for my pain. Someone *will* be found; someone, usually close to home, *will* be blamed. TV loves dysfunctional families. Dysfunctional S&L's and banks and corporate structures are not loved quite so much. In this sense we have moved away from the Naturalism of Zola or Frank Norris or Dreiser. Like them, we believe that people are often helpless, but we don't blame the corporations so much anymore; we blame the family.

Afternoon talk shows have only apparent antagonists. Their sparring partners are not real antagonists because the bad guys usually confess and then immediately disavow. The trouble with narratives like this without antagonists or a counterpoint to the central character—stories in which no one ever seems to be deciding anything or acting upon any motive except the search for a source of discontent—is that they tend formally to mirror the protagonists' unhappiness and confusion. Stories about being put-upon almost literally do not know what to look at; the visual details are muddled or indifferently described or excessively specific in nonpertinent situations. In any particular scene, everything is significant, and nothing is. The story is trying to find a source of meaning, but in the story, everyone is disclaiming responsibility. Things have just happened.

When I hear the adjective "dysfunctional" now, I cringe. But I have to use it here to describe a structural unit (like the banking system, or the family, or narrative) whose outward appearance is intact but whose structural integrity may have collapsed, so that no one is answerable within it—every event, every calamity, is unanswered, from the S&L collapse to the Exxon Valdez oil spill.

So we have created for ourselves a paradise of lawyers: we have an orgy of blame-finding on the one hand and disavowals of responsibility on the other.

All the recent debates and quarrels about taking responsibility as opposed to being a victim reflect some bewilderment about whether in real life protagonists still exist or whether we are all, in some sense, minor characters, the objects of terrible forces. Of course, we are often both. But look at *Oprah*. (I have, I do, I can't help it.) For all the variety of the situations, the unwritten scripts are often similar: someone is testifying because s/he's been hurt by someone else. The pain-inflicter is invariably present and accounted for onstage, and sometimes this person admits, abashedly, to inflicting the ruin: cheating, leaving, abusing, or murdering. Usually, however, there's no remorse, because some other factor caused it: bad genes, alcoholism, drugs, or—the cause of last resort—Satan. For intellectuals it may be the patriarchy: some devil or other—but an *abstract* devil. In any case, the malefactor may be secretly pleased: s/he's on television and will be famous for fifteen minutes.

The audience's role in all this is to comment on what the story means and to make a judgment about the players. Usually the audience members disagree and get into fights. The audience's judgment is required because the dramatis personae are incapable of judging themselves. They generally will not say that they did what they did because they wanted to, or because they had *decided* to do it. The story is shocking. You hear gasps. But the participants are as baffled and bewildered as everyone else. So we have the spectacle of utterly perplexed villains deprived of their villainy. Villainy, properly understood, gives someone a largeness, a sense of scale. It seems to me that that sense of scale has probably abandoned us.

What we have instead is not exactly drama and not exactly therapy. It exists in that twilight world between the two, very much of our time, where deniability reigns. Call it therapeutic narration. No verdict ever comes in. No one is in a position to judge. It makes the mind itch as if from an ideological rash. It is the spectacle, hour after hour, week after week, of dysfunctional narratives, interrupted by commercials (in Detroit, for lawyers).

Here is a koan for the 1990's: what is the relation between the dysfunctional narratives and the commercials that interrupt them?

But wait: isn't there something deeply interesting and moving and sometimes even beautiful when a character *acknowledges* an error? And isn't this narrative mode becoming something of a rarity?

Most young writers have this experience: they create characters who are an imaginative projection of themselves, minus the flaws. They put this character into a fictional world, wanting that character to be successful and—to use that word from high school—"popular." They don't want these imaginative projections of themselves to make any mistakes, wittingly or, even better, unwittingly, or to demonstrate what Aristotle thought was the core of stories, flaws of character that produce intelligent misjudgments for which someone must take the responsibility.

What's an unwitting action? It's what we do when we have to act so quickly, or under so much pressure, that we can't stop to take thought. It's not the same as an urge, which may well have a brooding and inscrutable quality. For some reason, such moments of unwitting action in life and in fiction feel enormously charged with energy and meaning.

It's difficult for fictional characters to acknowledge their mistakes, because then they become definitive: they *are* that person who did *that* thing. The only people who like to see characters performing such actions are readers. They love to see characters getting themselves into interesting trouble and defining themselves.

. . .

Lately, thinking about the nature of drama and our resistance to certain forms of it, I have been reading Aristotle's *Poetics* again and mulling over his definition of what makes a poet. A poet, Aristotle says, is first and foremost a maker, not of verses, but of plots. The poet creates an imitation, and what he imitates is an action.

It might be useful to make a distinction here between what I might call "me" protagonists and "I" protagonists. "Me" protagonists are largely objects—objects of impersonal forces or the actions of other people. They are central characters to whom things happen. They do not initiate action so much as receive it. For this reason, they are largely reactionary, in the old sense of that term, and passive. They are figures of fate and destiny, and they tend to appear during periods of accelerated social change, such as the American 1880's and 1890's, and again in the 1980's.

The "I" protagonist, by contrast, makes certain decisions and takes some responsibility for them and for the actions that follow from them. This does not make the "I" protagonist admirable by any means. It's this kind of protagonist that Aristotle is talking about. Such a person, Aristotle says, is not outstanding for virtue or justice, and she or he arrives at ill fortune not because of any wickedness or vice, but because of some mistake that s/he makes. There's that word again, "mistake."

Sometimes—if we are writers—we have to talk to our characters. We have to try to persuade them to do what they've only imagined doing. We have to nudge but not force them toward situations where they will get into interesting trouble, where they will make interesting mistakes that they may take responsibility for. When we allow our characters to make mistakes, we release them from the grip of our own authorial narcissism. That's wonderful for them, it's wonderful for us, but it's best of all for the story.

A few instances: I once had a friend in graduate school who gave long, loud, and unpleasantly exciting parties in the middle of winter; he and his girlfriend usually considered these parties unsuccessful unless someone did something shocking or embarrassing or both—*something you could talk about later.* He lived on the third floor of an old house in Buffalo, New York, and his acquaintances regularly fell down the front and back stairs.

I thought of him recently when I was reading about Mary Butts, an English writer of short fiction who lived from 1890 to 1937. Her stories have now been reissued in a collection called *From Altar to Chimneypiece*. Virgil Thomson, who was gay, once proposed marriage to her. That tells us something about the power of her personality. This is what Thomson says about her in his autobiography:

> I used to call her the "storm goddess," because she was at her best surrounded by cataclysm. She could stir up others with drink and drugs and magic incantations, and then when the cyclone was at its most intense, sit down at calm center and glow. All of her stories are of moments when the persons observed are caught up by something, inner or outer, so irresistible that their highest powers and all their lowest conditionings are exposed. The resulting action therefore is definitive, an ultimate clarification arrived at through ecstasy.

As it happens, I do not think that this is an accurate representation of Mary Butts's stories, which tend to be about crossing thresholds and stumbling into very strange spiritual dimensions. But I am interested in Thomson's thought concerning definitive action, because I think the whole concept of definitive action is meeting up with a considerable cultural resistance these days.

Thomson, describing his storm goddess, shows us a temptress, a joyful, worldly woman, quite possibly brilliant and bad to the bone. In real life people like this can be insufferable. Marriage to such a person would be a relentless adventure. They're constantly pushing their friends and acquaintances to lower their defenses and drop their masks and do something for which they will probably be sorry later. They like it when anyone blurts out a sudden admission, or acts on an impulse and messes up conventional arrangements. They like to see people squirm. They're *gleeful*. They prefer Bizet to Wagner; they're more Carmen than Sieglinde. They like it when people lunge at a desired object, and cacophony and wreckage are the result.

The morning after, you can say, "Mistakes were made," but at least with the people I've spent time with, a phrase like "Mistakes were made" won't even buy you a cup of coffee. There is such a thing as the poetry of a mistake, and when you say, "Mistakes were made," you deprive an action of its poetry, and you sound like a weasel. When you say, "I fucked up," the action retains its meaning, its sordid origin, its obscenity, and its poetry.

Chekhov says about this, in two of his letters, "...shun all descriptions of the characters' spiritual state. You must try to have that state emerge from their actions.... The artist must be only an impartial witness of his characters and what they said, not their judge." In Chekhov's view, a writer must try to release the story's characters from the aura of judgment that they've acquired simply because they're fictional. It's as if fiction has a great deal of trouble shedding its moral/pedagogical origins in fable and allegory.

In an atmosphere of constant moral judgment, characters are not often permitted to make interesting and intelligent mistakes and then to acknowledge them. It's as if the whole idea of the "intelligent mistake," the importance of the mistake made on an impulse, had gone out the window. Or, if fictional characters do make such mistakes, they're judged immediately and without appeal. One thinks of the attitudes of the aging Tolstoy here, and of his hatred of Shakespeare's and Chekhov's plays, and of his obsessive moralizing. He especially hated *King Lear*. He called it stupid, verbose, and incredible, and thought the craze for Shakespeare was like the tulip craze, a matter of mass hypnosis and "epidemic suggestion."

In the absence of any clear moral vision, we get moralizing. There's quite a lot of it around, and I think it has been inhibiting writers and making them nervous and irritable. Here is Mary Gaitskill, commenting on one of her own short stories, "The Girl on the Plane," in a recent *Best American Short Stories*. It's a story about a gang rape, and it apparently upset quite a few readers.

> In my opinion, most of us have not been taught how to be responsible for our thoughts and feelings. I see this strongly in the widespread tendency to read books and stories as if they exist to confirm how we are supposed to be, think, and feel. I'm not talking wacky political correctness, I'm talking mainstream.... Ladies and gentlemen, please. Stop asking "What am I supposed to feel?" Why would an adult look to me or to any other writer to tell him or her what to feel? You're not *supposed* to feel anything. You feel what you feel.

Behind the writer's loss of patience one can just manage to make out a literary culture begging for an authority figure, the same sort of figure that Chekhov refused for himself. Mary Gaitskill's interest in bad behavior is that of the observer, not the judge. Unhappy readers want her to be both, as if stories should come prepackaged with discursive authorial opinions about her own characters. Her exasperation is a reflection of C. K. Williams's observation that in a period of dysfunctional narratives, the illogic of feeling erodes the logic of stories. When people can't make any narrative sense out of their own feelings, readers start to ask writers what they are supposed to feel. Reading begins to be understood as a form of therapy. In such an atmosphere, already-moralized stories are more comforting than stories in which characters are making intelligent or unwitting mistakes.

Marilynne Robinson, in her essay "Hearing Silence: Western Myth Reconsidered," calls the already-moralized story, the therapeutic narrative, part of a "mean little myth" of our time. She notes, however, that "we have ceased to encode our myths in narrative as that word is traditionally understood. Now they shield themselves from our skepticism by taking on the appearance of scientific or political or economic discourse...." And what is this "mean little myth"?

> One is born and in passage through childhood suffers some grave harm. Subsequent good fortune is meaningless because of this injury, while subsequent misfortune is highly significant as the consequence of this injury. The work of one's life is to discover and name the harm one has suffered.

As long as this myth is operational, one cannot act, in stories or anywhere else, in a meaningful way. The injury takes for itself all the meaning. The injury *is* the meaning, though it is, itself, opaque. All achievements, and all mistakes, are finessed. There is no free will. There is only acting out, the acting out of one's destiny. But acting out is not the same as acting. Acting out is behavior that proceeds according to a predetermined, invisible pattern created by the injury. The injury becomes the unmoved mover, the replacement for the mind's capacity to judge and to decide. One thinks of Nixon here: the obscure wounds, the vindictiveness, the obsession with enemies, the acting out.

It has a feeling of Calvinism to it, of predetermination, this myth of injury and predestination. In its kingdom, sorrow and depression rule. Marilynne Robinson calls this mode of thought "bungled Freudianism." It's both that and something else: an effort to make pain acquire some comprehensibility so that those who feel helpless can at least be illuminated. But unlike Freudianism it asserts that the source of the pain can *never be expunged.* There is no working-through of this injury. It has no tragic joy because within it, all personal decisions have been made meaningless, deniable. It is a life-fate, like a character disorder. Its politics cannot get much further than gender-injury; it cannot take on the corporate state.

Confronted with this mode, I feel like an Old Leftist. I want to say: the Bosses are happy when you feel helpless. They're pleased when you think the source of your trouble is your family. They're delighted when you give up the idea that you should band together for political action. They love helplessness (in you). They even like addicts, as long as they're mostly out of sight: after all, *addiction is just the last stage of consumerism.*

And I suppose I am nostalgic—as a writer, of course—for stories with mindful villainy, villainy with clear motives that any adult would understand, bad behavior with a sense of *scale,* that would give back to us our imaginative grip on the despicable and the admirable and our capacity to have some opinions about the two. Most of us are interested in characters who willingly give up their innocence and decide to act badly. I myself am fascinated when they not only do that but admit that they did it, that they had good reasons for doing so. At such moments wrongdoing becomes intelligible. It also becomes legibly political. If this is the liberal fallacy, this sense of choice, then so be it. (I know that people *do* get caught inside systems of harm and cannot maneuver themselves out—I have written about such situations myself— but that story is hardly the only one worth telling.)

It does seem curious that in contemporary America—a place of considerable good fortune and privilege—one of the most favored narrative modes, from high to low, has to do with disavowals, passivity, and the disarmed protagonist. Possibly we have never gotten over our American romance with innocence. We would rather be innocent than worldly and unshockable. Innocence is continually shocked and disarmed. But there is something wrong with this. No one can go through life perpetually shocked. It's disingenuous. Writing in his journals, Thornton Wilder notes, "I think that it can be assumed that no adults are ever really 'shocked'—that being shocked is always a pose." If so, there is some failure of adulthood in contemporary American life. Our interest in victims and victimization has finally to do with our constant ambivalence about power, about being powerful, about wanting to be powerful but not having to acknowledge the buck stopping on our desk.

What I am arguing against is *not* political or social action against abusers of power, corporate or familial. I am registering my uneasiness with the Romance of Victimization, especially in this culture, and the constant disavowal of responsibility by the abuser. Romantic victims and disavowing perpetrators land us in a peculiar territory, a sort of neo-Puritanism without the backbone of theology and philosophy. After all, *The Scarlet Letter* is about disavowals, specifically Dimmesdale's, and the supposed "shock" of a minister of God being guilty of adultery. Dimmesdale's inability to admit publicly what he's done has something to do with the community—i.e., a culture of "shock"—and something to so with his own pusillanimous character.

The dialectics of innocence and worldliness have a different emotional coloration in British literature, or perhaps I simply am unable to get Elizabeth Bowen's *The Death of the Heart* (1938) out of my mind in this context. Portia, the perpetual innocent and stepchild, sixteen years old, in love with Eddie, twenty-three, has been writing a diary, and her guardian, Anna, has been reading it. Anna tells St. Quentin, her novelist friend, that she has been reading it. St. Quentin tells Portia what Anna has done. As it happens, Portia has been writing poisonously accurate observations about Anna and her husband, Thomas, in the diary. Anna is a bit pained to find herself so neatly skewered.

Bowen's portrait of Portia is beautifully managed, but it's her portrayal of Anna that fascinates me. Anna cannot be shocked. Everything she has done, she admits. In the sixth chapter of the novel's final section, she really blossoms: worldly, witty, rather mean, and absolutely clear about her own faults, she recognizes the situation and her own complicity in it. She may be sorry, but she doesn't promise to do better. Portia is the one who is innocent, who commands the superior virtues, not she herself. Speaking of reading private diaries, she says, "It's the sort of thing I do do. Her diary's very good—you see, she has got us taped. . . . I don't say it has changed the course of my life, but it's given me a rather more disagreeable feeling about being alive—or, at least, about being me."

That "disagreeable feeling" seems to arise not only from the diary but also from Anna's wish to read it, to violate it. Anna may feel disagreeable about being the person she is, but she does not say that she could be otherwise. She is the person who does what she admits to. As a result, there is a clarity, a functionality to Bowen's narrative, that becomes apparent because everybody admits everything in it and then gives their reasons for doing what they've done. It's as if their actions have found a frame, a size, a scale. As bad as Anna may be, she is honest.

Anna defines herself, not in the American way of reciting inward virtues, but in a rather prideful litany of mistakes. In her view, we define ourselves at least as much by our mistakes as by our achievements. The grace and honor of fiction is that in stories, mistakes are every bit as interesting as achievements are; they have an equal claim upon truth. Perhaps they have a greater one, because they are harder to show, harder to hear, harder to say. For that reason, they are rarer and more precious.

Speaking of a library book that is eighteen years overdue, but which she has just returned, the narrator of Grace Paley's story "Wants" says, "I didn't deny anything." She pays the thirty-two-dollar fine, and that's it. One of the pleasures of Paley's stories is that the stories, as narrated, are remarkably free of denial and subterfuge. Their characters explain themselves but don't bother to excuse themselves. City dwellers, they don't particularly like innocence, and they don't expect to be shocked. When there's blame, they take it. When they fall, there's a good reason. They don't rise; they just get back on their feet, and when they think about reform, it's typically political rather than personal. For one of her characters, this is the "powerful last-half-of-the-century way." Well, it's nice to think so. Free of the therapeutic impulse, and of the recovery movement, and of Protestantism generally, her characters nevertheless *like* to imagine various social improvements in the lives of the members of their community.

Dysfunctional narratives tend to begin in solitude and they tend to resist their own forms of communication. They don't have communities so much as audiences of fellow victims. There is no polite way for their narratives to end. Richard Nixon, disgraced, resigned, still flashing the V-for-victory from the helicopter on the White House lawn, cognitively dissonant to the end, went off to his enforced retirement, where, tirelessly, year after year, in solitude, he wrote his accounts, every one of them meant to justify and to excuse. His last book, as of this writing not yet published, is entitled *Beyond Peace.*

# The Encroaching Forest:
## Southeast Asian Memories

### Plants & Houses (Northern Thailand)

Several months after I come to live in the house, I begin to realize that nothing in the compound exists without effort or purpose. The lush, tangled gardens surrounding us serve as constant reminder that until only recently the neighborhood belonged to the encroaching forest. The house, a perfect cube with glass walls and a frame and floors of solid, polished teak, is just big enough for Khun Ma and Khun Pa, my host parents, their daughter, Nuan-wan, and me. Gleaming and new, the house sits unobtrusively in the space it has claimed for itself. With all the glass louvers open, it is as if there are no walls at all and we are living in the midst of tropical wilderness.

It takes a while before I notice things—that the family never buys medicine, that the lemony-smelling bushes hedging the house repel mosquitoes. I attribute it to sheer luck that the trees droop heavily with red finger bananas, fat pomegranates, and softening, sugary guavas whenever I'm hungry, that randomly grabbed twigs are always flavorful, that a rambutan, with its rubbery red and green antennae resembling sea life, slipped inside someone's sheets, never fails to elicit a terrified shriek. I do not question the things I notice, any more than I question the fact that every morning I awake to the fragrance of mango, orange, and fig trees ripening in the sun outside my glass walls.

Once she sees my interest, however, Khun Ma spends hours trying to teach me about the surroundings she has created. I trail her through the gardens, a basket looped over my arm, as she pinches annatto seeds and sniffs galangal root. "I planned *every* plant you see in this compound," she tells me, handing me a stalk of lemon grass to test. Its clean, hot bite sears my mouth, and she nods briskly. "As a developing nation we need to know our environment," she explains, "in order to liberate ourselves."

At the dinner table she is continually fishing one plant or another out of the soup. Brandishing it aloft, she announces: "This prevents sore throat!" or perhaps, "This one is clearing your sinuses!"

I nod dutifully at the dripping leaf, which—no matter how hard I stare—looks to me like a weed, indistinguishable from any other.

The house has three different cooking/eating areas, each with a different name and function, each of which translates into English as, simply, *kitchen*. The first, a sleek room with Western appliances, is where we take our meals. Here, thanks to the maid, Phi (Older Sister) Niew, a steady supply of hot drinks and chilled fruits appears almost magically to replenish itself all day long. The second kitchen, located behind the house in the same small cement building that contains Phi Niew's quarters and the laundry, is used to store bulk foods and a baking oven—quite rare in the tropics. The last cooking area, my favorite, is simply an open clearing in the garden where a slab of cement has been poured on the ground. The wok and gas burner stand on one side, the chopping board and mortar and pestle on the other. This is the real kitchen.

There are two sounds I associate with this last kitchen: the metallic staccato of Phi Niew's heavy Chinese knife against the worn chopping board—a solid cross-section of tamarind tree—and the steady, hollow *thwap* of the wooden pestle against the side of the mortar as she pounds chili peppers, the seeds spraying into the air and tears streaming down her face.

I sit for hours on the warm cement at her feet, half-asleep from the soothing rhythm of her chopping and pounding. Giant flies hover just out of reach, driven wild by the stench of warm meat. I close my eyes and pretend that the noises are those of trees being cleared in the nearby jungle.

One evening early in my stay, a sudden wave of heat sweeps through the house during dinner, followed by an unprecedented chill. Immediately the kitchen is flooded with the overpowering perfume of night-blooming jasmine. There follows a deafening crack, as if all the glass panels in the house have shattered simultaneously, and it begins to rain.

"First rain!" someone cries, and the entire family leaps up from the table, shouting directions to each other in *pasat nua*, the local dialect I don't speak. They seem excited but not upset, so I try to stay out of the way. Each person grabs a basket and rushes outside. No one thinks to direct me, and I am too surprised and too new to the household to demand an explanation.

Once they all leave, I run to the glass louvers and peer out. I can hear the family laughing and calling to each other in the rain, but the wind blows their words away. Blind outside the glass perimeter of light, I chart their progress from inside the house, following the sounds from room to room. They move along the outside corners of the house, keeping low to the ground. After twenty minutes, family members begin to straggle in, flushed and triumphant. Nuan-wan extends a basket crawling with plump black beetles for my inspection.

"Good thing we remembered!" Khun Ma says, rejoicing. "The first rain last season we forgot all about them!" She turns to me and promises, "I'll roast them for your breakfast tomorrow!"

I grin weakly.

The next morning I find a basket of small bugs awaiting me. The almost weightless creatures are still intact, their tiny legs permanently curled in the air above them. As I stir them with my finger, wondering how to begin, the dry bodies make a faint rustling sound.

On one of her trips from one kitchen to another, Phi Niew shows me how to peel off the head casing and dip the body in chili sauce. The crisp insect pops on my tongue, a rich, oily taste like nuts or fried meat flooding my mouth. Relieved, I smile, and just then Khun Ma comes in. Surveying the scene, she beams. "And *twice* the protein of meat!" she crows.

Another morning I accompany Khun Ma to a Buddhist temple. At the front entrance we pass two nuns dressed in white, their heads and eyebrows shaved. They stand outside the door to the sanctum, clutching meager posies in the folds of their robes, their faces shining as brightly as their polished heads. I linger to smile at them, while Khun Ma looks on, a strange expression on her face.

When we're out of earshot she leans close to me. "See how they sell flowers to support themselves?" she whispers. "They can't even take the vow not to touch money!" She explains that, though circumstance forces nuns to support themselves, using money relegates them to a lower spiritual plane. While monks receive food, clothing, and shelter from both the church and devout laypeople, nuns are no one's concern.

Inside the sanctum, we prostrate ourselves before the altar three times and light three sticks of incense. Like Christianity, Thai Buddhism is based on a Trinity: the Buddha, his teachings, and the community of monks. The importance of the number three runs strong throughout Thai society, even secular life. Everything must be constructed, articulated, allocated in threes, Khun Ma explains.

When we leave the temple compound, the nuns look up to say goodbye. Once again I linger, trying to imagine what makes these hungry women smile so. We walk slowly to the parking lot, and at the car door I turn to find one of them hurrying after us. As she nears, I see that she is holding out one of her flowers. Reaching me, she tucks the golden blossom into my palm in a single, smooth movement.

"For you," she says, her face aglow. Then, with a final smile, she is gone, her bare feet crunching over the gravel of the parking lot as she returns to her vigil at the temple entrance.

Stunned, I stare at the gift in my hand, and even Khun Ma looks surprised. The flower is so delicate, its veined, buttery-colored petals so thin, that it looks made of paper. I turn it over and over in my hand to convince myself that it is real.

Inside the car, I put the flower on the dashboard and immediately, a full, heady perfume fills the sunny car. If I close my eyes, the fragrance reminds me of summers as a child, when I would ease my way through a cloud of bees to reach the trumpets on the honeysuckle vine, break off an orange blossom, and suck the nectar from the warm neck.

When I feel the car pulling into the compound, I open my eyes to find that the flower has disappeared. The papery petals have burned up in the sun, leaving nothing but a scattering of pale, scented ashes across the dashboard like the residue of incense.

The best time of day in the compound is early evening. This is when I like to emerge into the quiet cool and ride my moped around the neighborhood. I pedal down narrow roads overhung with giant wild banana and coconut palms, leaving a cloud of red dirt behind me. Dwarfed, I feel on the verge of discovery.

I pass young housemaids with smooth, shy faces who look up from their laundry to smile at the first black woman they have ever seen, children sprawled asleep on porches, their mouths open, still wearing their school uniforms. The faint rasp of their snores is like the distant buzz of drowsy bees. Occasionally a new cluster of houses surprises me, almost hidden in the underbrush: modern glass-and-stucco bungalows, all pastel whimsy and odd geometry; traditional wooden houses on stilts, simple except for handmade lace curtains behind scrolled window grilles.

One evening as the sun is fading, I turn a corner and come upon a middle-aged woman in a clearing. Dressed in a white bra and faded print sarong, she rakes weeds into a roaring bonfire. She works furiously, never once looking up. Just as the sky turns to night, the thick black smoke of the fire billows up around her, and she disappears before my eyes—first her bare feet, then the sarong, the gleaming bra, the brown of her shoulders, and finally her head. I am left alone in the dark clearing.

Turning the moped around, I start pedaling for home as fast as I can. I think about the first time I took out my contact lenses. My entire host family stopped talking and watched me, their eyes round. After a few weeks, we devised a system where each morning before breakfast I wash and rinse my contacts then place them on the counter near the back door. Phi Niew boils the lens case for ten minutes along with Khun Pa's eggs and brings it to me in a little cut-glass bowl, still steaming. She walks slowly, the dish clutched in her hand, her eyes trained on the sterilized case rolling around inside.

This particular evening when I approach the compound gate, I notice for the first time the tall cement walls surrounding the house, the tops glittering with barbed wire and crushed glass.

. . .

Besides the glass house, there are two other houses in the compound. The old house stands cool and dim in the back, everything about it worn smooth with years. It is quiet with sleeping children and women. Khun Ma's mother lives there with her teenage daughter-in-law, the daughter-in-law's two children, and the maid, Nong. Hidden in the garden between the two homes is the family shrine, a miniature house with the traditional three-tiered roof of a Thai temple. Every morning Phi Niew and Nong pass between the houses, delivering the food they have prepared. With each trip they pause at the shrine to leave offerings for the ancestors—balls of sweet rice, waxy jasmine blossoms, tiny cups of green tea.

One morning at breakfast Phi Niew looks distracted. She watches Nong carefully, worrying a cold sore at the corner of her own mouth. I help clear the table, and she tells me that years ago Khun Ma took in a foster child—a teenage boy who had been orphaned when two car accidents within one year claimed first his mother and siblings, and then his father and the father's mistress. When the boy himself was twenty years old, a truck struck the motorcycle he was driving, and he was killed.

Because it was a violent death, Khun Ma engaged a spirit medium to hold a special ceremony that would recall the soul from its exile on the side of the road and grant it peace. According to Phi Niew, the medium went into a trance, selected the boy's favorite clothes from a large pile in front of her, and put them on. Speaking in a young male voice, she demanded foods that had been the boy's favorites. After eating and then answering a number of questions to establish the authenticity of the spirit, the medium said that the boy wanted to confess to murdering his father's mistress. The second car crash had not been accidental, the voice said. Everyone in the room was stunned.

The medium then bowed before Khun Ma and begged forgiveness for destroying her motorcycle and leaving this world. At the end of the session, the boy's spirit moved to a tree above the shrine between the houses and refused to be born again.

A year or so later the maid, Nong, who passed the tree regularly on her way to and from the two houses, fell ill. She came down with a high fever, and large blisters covered her face and her body. Khun Ma took her to doctor after doctor, but no one could cure her or explain her illness. Finally they went to another spirit medium who claimed that the spirit of the orphan boy was lonely. He had looked down and seen Nong passing through the bushes below. He was trying to kill her, the medium explained, so that her spirit could join him in the tree. Khun Ma and the medium made offerings at the shrine beneath the tree, and Nong recovered that night.

Phi Niew ends the story with a shy smile. "It is nothing," she assures me, touching the sore at the side of her mouth. "Perhaps a reminder."

Nong says nothing. Hoisting a load of dishes, she disappears into the vegetation between the two homes. It is difficult to see her—though the walls of the house are glass—but I can smell the plants she brushes against. Long after she is gone, a fading trail of lemon grass and ripening persimmon marks her path.

Later, as I wheel my moped out from behind the house, I think about the boy whose spirit who has climbed a tree and refuses to come down, about how even death could not destroy his ravenous loneliness. I wonder how offerings of things like orange sections and sticks of incense are supposed to help him. So far, no food, no scent, has helped fill that hungry space in me. Only movement.

I leave the compound and ride towards town. This time along the road I recognize meaning in things I previously could not even see. Nearly every few miles there is a cluster of white flags and string with chalk lines etched in the dirt. The highway is crowded with them. They are not, as I had always assumed, traffic markings, but sites where spirit mediums have lain the souls of countless transit victims to rest.

I now understand why the third home is crucial to the compound. It serves to remind us that death drives along the side of the road with us, eating the same food we do. The thin white string and chalk lines not only bind the spirit's essence to earth, but show how slender is the boundary between the two worlds.

I see why Khun Ma works so hard to make ancestral offerings

and engage spirit mediums: It is, after all, a full-time job helping those who have suffered violence, those who are lonely, those of us in trees who refuse to be born again. Sometimes the work is not so much saving those who have left their souls at the side of the road, as it is keeping the survivors alive.

## Love Tourists (Southern Thailand)

It is a neon night in the sex resort, the balmy air weightless against our tanned faces. Thatched-roof bars strung with bright paper lanterns and girlie calendars line both sides of the town's only road. This is not what we expected.

Things have changed since we were here last. Then it was a cheap student vacation. We slept on the beach and bought fresh crab and coconuts from the native islanders. No one paid attention to us, two friends from school. This row of bamboo bars, looking like something from the set of a South Pacific movie, did not exist.

Now the entire city dedicates itself continually to sex. Packs of men on "love tours" swagger the Strip, undressing all brown women with their eyes. Arab men, American men, Australian men, German men, Japanese men. We learn to walk with Scott's proprietary white hand on my brown arm.

Local teenagers crowd the free discos. Flamboyant, heavily made-up mixtures of fashion and race, they do the latest dances from London and New York, next to tourists who could be their unknown fathers. Their younger siblings haunt the streets and bars, draped in chains of jasmine, selling packs of Lucky Strikes. The police maintain paradise by rounding up beggars, revolutionaries, the deformed, anyone who ruins the ambiance.

As foreigners fluent in the native tongue, we attract attention. Countless child vendors approach just to hear us speak. We paw through basket after basket in hopes of discovering some halfway-useful trinket to buy. At last I come across a find. "Look, Scott," I cry, holding up a flat yellow box.

He looks up from his basket to smile. "No way!" he shouts. "*Chiclets!* I can't believe it!" We buy the gum and keep moving.

Grinning pimps swarm everywhere, pressing business cards

against us that advertise the skills of their sisters and daughters. Scott pushes away their advances, shaking his head *no,* holding up his hands to ward them off.

There is a flurry, two men shouting, a brief scuffle, then somebody flees and a fan of cards falls to the street. The squares of paper lay face-up in the mud, boasting *Live live American-style show! See pussy eating banana! See pussy to blow out candle!*

We ignore the offending cards like road kill, stepping over them to enter the safety of a quiet, open-air bar. There, firmly ensconced on rattan stools, we order drinks and giant saffron prawns. The drinks—local rot-gut whiskey distilled from rice—are dressed up with pastel paper umbrellas. As I take a sip of the harsh fermented rice, I feel a softness at my knees and look down to find a child gripping my leg. It is a young boy. He beams up at me, one tiny hand steadying himself, the other clutching a wire loop strung with plastic bags of pink shrimp crackers. His huge eyes meet mine easily. His unself-conscious touch in this place of pimps almost makes me cry.

As if pulled by strings, Scott and I both bend forward on our stools to reach him. The boy stands bravely between us, beautiful and so very, very small. He wears a scruffy yellow sweater over a powder-blue safari suit. I reach out and cup the point of his chin loosely in my hand, half-afraid of leaving a stain on his translucent skin. He flushes and ducks his head deeper into my palm. Scott asks his name at the same time I ask his age.

"Thum," he replies, too young to be surprised that we speak *pasat thai.* "I am five." He is the size of a three-year-old American child. He braces himself sturdily against our barrage of questions and answers each with great seriousness. Yes, he has already eaten. No, he doesn't go to school yet. Six, he has six brothers and sisters. At the mention of his siblings, his face blooms into smile.

We ask him what time he goes home, but he is either unable to understand or unwilling to answer. Already it is after ten o'clock.

I ask the price of the shrimp crackers, and Scott bolts upright, smacking his forehead with the ball of his hand. "Oh no!" he groans. "I *hate* those things!"

Thum hoists up the wire loop to show that someone has carefully drawn the number three in red marker on each bag. Three baht. About ten cents. I hold up one finger. One bag. Thum gnaws his lower lip as his tiny fingers wrestle to pull a bag off the wire loop. After great effort, he hands me the crackers in exchange for three coins.

Instinctively, I reach for the box of Chiclets and Scott begins to laugh. He shakes his head. "God, you're a pushover!" he says.

I hold out the gum to Thum, who immediately sets down his wares and pads his palms together, tiny fingers splayed. He bows to me, bringing his hands up to his forehead in a *wai,* a sign of respect and thanks. He is a child, so instead of returning the gesture as I would with an adult, I hold out my hand to receive it. As he brings his hands down into mine, I can feel the faintest brush of his fingers across my palm. Only then does he accept the box. In perhaps just another year he will learn to put away such gifts to sell to the next tourist, but tonight he is still a child.

Again he chews his bottom lip until he succeeds in extracting a piece of gum and puts it in his mouth. Again his face flowers into a smile. He then labors to find his shirt pocket under his sweater, managing after several tries to slip in the box.

"I can't believe you're giving him all our Chiclets," Scott moans in mock distress. "*All* our Chiclets!"

At that exact instant someone takes Thum by his left arm. We look up to protest. A teenage girl stands in the street behind him. She starts to pull Thum away, the resolve in her expression silencing us. A split second later a policeman takes his right arm. The policeman's grasp is gentle but determined. The girl looks at the policeman. She does not let go of the boy. The policeman returns her look. He gives his head a single, firm shake, and then Thum is gone, our empty hands around the space where he used to be, our silent mouths still open.

A few moments later a dark Nissan police truck creeps by, clearly on a sweep. Half a dozen child vendors lounge in the open pickup bed, their eyes at half-mast. The studied boredom on their faces resembles that of their sisters, the painted bar girls who throng the street, looking on with only the vaguest of interest.

The policeman tosses the boy's shaking body into the back of the truck, and Thum crouches where he lands. A second later, his face crumples and he begins to scream, his three-year-old's body shuddering with the force of his cries. I barely recognize him, the intensity of his unhappiness almost unreconcilable with the soft child of five minutes before.

The girl flutters, distressed, near the back of the truck, the flesh of her palm still warm from holding him. She says nothing. None of the other children move. Thum is by far the smallest and the youngest among them. The truck moves on. Minutes later, though the truck is gone, Thum's shrieks hang on the warm night air.

Long after life in the street has resumed, long after we have finished two plates of prawns in silence and several drinks each, we still do not look at each other. Though we don't know it, we are already checking out, we are already getting ready to leave. A few days later, in the final incident that prompts our departure, one of the posh international hotels burns to the ground, and the remains of at least five native women are found chained to beds. But tonight we dream of children.

"No," Scott finally says, shaking his head curtly and once again holding up his hands. *No.*

He may be saying *no* to what happened, *no* to what will happen, *no* to this place of pimps. Perhaps he is saying *no* to action, or to responsibility. But this time innocence is not so easy. It is not as simple as walking away from the obscenity of business cards. We are here, and though perhaps we can never save five women or even one five-year-old boy, we are somehow responsible. Even if we never speak of this again, we have already by our presence said *yes.*

### Coffee Break (Java)

I come upon the Jakarta Pizza Hut feeling a bit extravagant and giddy. I have spent days trudging around fetid, steaming Jakarta, my least favorite Asian city, black tears of pollution streaming down my sticky cheeks, getting the bureaucratic run-around. I am tired of being in transit, tired of worrying about potential thieves and fakers, tired of trying to squeeze myself into native life. At last my stolen traveler's checks have been replaced, and in two hours I have a flight out of this labyrinth of rubbish heaps and open sewers.

I stand outside the Jakarta Pizza Hut, bastion of Western culture, feeling at once compelled and repelled. It looks like any Pizza Hut anywhere in the U.S.A., and I haven't eaten for thirty hours. Still I hesitate. I pride myself on being a true traveler, able to withstand hardship, scornful of Western luxury. As I ponder, it begins to rain—big black drops that sizzle ominously as they hit the street.

The inside of the Jakarta Pizza Hut is nearly empty. A young waiter ushers me to a table with all the pomp and ceremony due a dignitary attending a state funeral. A second waiter presents a menu with great flourish. Two others, apparently joined at the shoulders, take my order.

Already drunk at the mere thought of my first cheese in a year—and soon to discover that I have picked up lactose intolerance along with other native customs—I develop a craving for wine. A fifth waiter passes by, and I call out in *bahasa indonesia*. Caught off-guard, he nearly topples over in his eagerness to stop. He leaps to my table, responding immediately in English. Then, apparently taken as much aback as am I, he stands speechless, blinking at me.

The fifth waiter at the Jakarta Pizza Hut is distressingly perfect. Indonesians tend to be lovely, but his beauty is universal, completely lacking ethnic stamp. He is tall and well-built, with luxuriant, blue-black hair and sculpted features. His dazzling smile relaxes into a generous mouth; his dark eyes gleam with what I choose to interpret as sincerity. As conservative in dress as a Connecticut college boy, he is well yet not overly groomed—reassuringly unlike the pretty island boys in clicking-heeled shoes who prey on and are preyed upon by foreigners.

Though such smooth beauty does little for me, I am suitably impressed. I explain that I want to order a glass of wine and ask him please to send my waiter.

"Yes," he answers promptly. "A glass of wine. Certainly!" He leaves, glancing back over his shoulder at me. Almost immediately he reappears and places an entire carafe of wine on the table. I am surprised, but a year on the road has taught me not to question any perks along the way. As I thank him, I notice my gestures becoming expansive and more gluttonous.

After a year, the simple act of having wine with a meal is thrilling. The cheap juice enters my system like a fun childhood friend who doesn't really care what's best for me. Once I glance up just as the fifth waiter happens to be passing by. He feels the movement and falters in his path, watching me out of the corner of his eye. Confused, I look away.

A bit later I raise my head to find him facing me, standing perfectly motionless with his arms folded behind his back like every uniformed native in every tropical travel poster. At my gaze he promptly glides forward, asking, "Yes?"

"Oh no, nothing!" I protest, wondering if I had indeed summoned him.

He asks in faltering English what I am reading, and it pleases me that his first question is not where am I from and why am I alone. His name tag reads Sudirman.

"About Bali," I answer, touching my guidebook. "It's where I'm going next."

He steps to my right and picks up the book, his movements respectful yet confident. I wonder if he comes from money. We chat, and as it turns out, he is a student at the National Institute for Hotels & Tourism. This job is his field experience rather than his livelihood. I am somewhat intrigued. Though I attend the occasional gala expatriate event, most of my friends are hungry priests, artists, activists. Sudirman is not the kind of Indonesian I usually meet.

He offers politely to take me sightseeing. I thank him and decline. I have plane reservations to Bali tonight.

"Tonight?" he asks, his eyes widening. "Then please, when you return, to come here—or to my home." He takes out his pen and opens my book. "May I?" he asks, before writing his address on the inside cover.

I am explaining that I do not plan to return, that I hate Jakarta, when the twin waiters appear and stand behind him, clearly impressed by his self-assurance. We are all impressed. They peek over his shoulder and when I laugh, they blush, nodding to me.

Sudirman looks up, smiles, and touches first one and then the other lightly on the cheek. "My friends," he says tenderly, and something in my chest shifts.

He turns back to me, still incredulous at my news. "You don't come *back* from Bali?" he asks, and I nod. He considers this and then makes a gentle suggestion: "I think you had better cancel?" Eyes wide, he nods encouragement. "Yes, *please* to cancel your flight to Bali."

Bali. The place everyone in Indonesia seems to be dreaming about, travelers and natives alike. I am only passing through Jakarta on my way from one such dream place to another, my loose itinerary based on adding excursions to not-so-well-kept secrets gleaned from the travelers' circuit. What keeps me moving is the belief that the best in travel are the unexpected treasures that appear (and disappear) along the way—that which can't be planned or held. I tell myself that I don't need Sudirman. I don't need any of his possibilities. I've never before stopped moving for anything or anyone.

I consider the fifth waiter's proposition, anyway, twirling my empty wineglass. I wonder what would happen if I stopped just once. *I wonder.* With all this wine and cheese in my stomach, I feel as warm and relaxed as if Bali were inside me. *Should I cancel?*

Sudirman nods, smiles, waits; and I realize that I spoke out loud.

I have been avoiding local pick-ups, though recently I have been regretting this decision. I was in Central Java during the month of Ramadhan, and the entire city sat up every night, gathering at tiny candlelit stalls to watch flickering shadow-puppet plays and wait for the four a.m. meal. On every dark street corner Muslims grouped together, murmuring and laughing quietly. Crouched among the *wayang* musicians, sleeping children and their dogs in my lap, I could have fallen easily in love and stayed on, settling into the rhythm of the sleepless city.

I think about rushing back to the guest house tonight before my flight to say goodbye to my Jakarta family: Edina from Berlin and Bud from Portland whom I keep running into throughout Southeast Asia and who have been feeding me since the robbery. Mary, the beautiful Malaysian anthropologist who brings us treats from Embassy fêtes. Rudy, the Sumatran owner, who has been letting me stay at the guest house for free. Later he will take me to the airport, kiss me on both cheeks and the forehead, and say, "You shouldn't trust anyone, even me. You're always welcome. Send a telegram if you run into trouble." I think about arriving to yet another unknown city at night with my bag that never unpacks completely.

I hadn't noticed Sudirman leave, yet suddenly he appears with garlic bread and another carafe of wine. "You have decided?" he asks, putting the food I haven't ordered on the table before me. "You cancel?" We laugh, openly appraising each other, and he nods slowly until I am nodding, too. "Tomorrow and tomorrow," he says with a smile. "Keep canceling."

"Okay," I say. If I didn't stay for something in Central Java, I decide, I can stay for something, here, now. "I cancel."

He pours the wine. "It is okay," he asks, watching me. "I visit after working tonight?" We both know his question is a formality.

A young well-dressed couple enters the restaurant, and after excusing himself, Sudirman runs over to shake hands with the man. Immediately another waiter takes the opportunity to refill my glass and ask where I am from, why I am alone. I pay the bill, which consists only of the order taken by the Siamese twins. As I expected, there is no garlic bread, no two carafes of wine.

Sudirman returns and walks me out. "I finish at twelve o'clock," he says quietly, and his words caress the space between us. I feel them like the back of his hand against my cheek. "Don't fall asleep."

Startled at this sudden intimacy, I take a step back. "But I'm exhausted!" I warn him. He smiles, says nothing. "Well," I concede. "You better really show up, then!"

"I will," he promises. "Don't sleep."

At eleven-thirty we are all lounging at the guest-house kitchen table, debating the best cities in Asia to receive mail *poste restante*, when Sudirman strides in, immaculate in pressed royal blue corduroys, polished loafers, and a long-sleeved, blue and white tuxedo-style shirt. Gleaming in the light of the dingy kitchen, he is even more than I remember. I realize that I hadn't really expected him to come.

"Uh, hi," I say, at a loss.

Placing two large pizzas on the table, he bows to the circle of stunned foreigners and sits down next to me. I feel as if a gentleman caller has wandered into my grandmother's parlor. After a moment he holds out his hand and asks me, "Will you walk?" As we stand up, the group of travelers comes to life, ripping into the pizza boxes with cries of delight.

Edina turns to me, stuffing cheese into her mouth and shaking her head. "There you go again, Faith!" she mumbles between bites. "Just this morning you were broke, hungry, and hating this Jakarta. Now we are all indulging in expensive imported food! How *do* you do it?"

Later, when Sudirman and I return from our walk, I find the kitchen dark, the pizza boxes empty. All that's left on the table is a matchbox with the words *Pizza Hut: Jakarta • Singapore • Bangkok* emblazoned on the cover—my itinerary in reverse. I smile and turn the matchbox over to find a drawing of a prickly durian fruit on the underside.

Though durian flesh is reportedly rich and intoxicating, its stench is so overpowering that no Westerner I know has ever tasted it. There are countless stories of travelers fainting in durian fields or abandoning cars they thought were about to explode because of ripe durian in the trunks. Transport is virtually illegal, as durian are banned from ships and airplanes. It is the quintessential Asian fruit, relegated to the shores of its homeland.

Days later, when I awake, rested, the wine and lactose purged from my system, and move on, this will be my only souvenir.

### The Splendor of Fruit (Burma)

It is dusk in Rangoon. I sit smoking in my room at the famed Strand Hotel. I am alone and feel as though I am the hotel's sole occupant. Since my arrival I have seen no evidence of any other guests. Because of delays in Bangkok, I missed the friends I was supposed to meet. I am pleased at the way things have turned out, pleased to have been left behind. Closed to the West since the forties, Burma is a country that has been left behind. Solitude seems somehow fitting in this place.

After the harsh, modern reality of Jakarta and Bangkok, Rangoon feels like an abandoned movie set. I can picture the dramas that took place: mysterious foreigners with strange appetites lounging downstairs in the smoky lobby; opium smugglers vanishing into the murky lighting of the black market; colonial wives escaping the capital to summer in the cool hills of Maymo. Dressed in tennis whites, they sit fanning themselves on the verandah. Below, native servants crouch in the garden, transplanting imported strawberries by hand.

The postwar flight of the British must have been similar to the departure of a film crew—the fantasy cut short, the elaborate, impractical structures beginning to crumble into disuse. Today rotting colonial mansions house small cities of the homeless. Families squat in the echoing halls of deserted ministries. Outside, the sons of military officials rumble through the streets in the country's few cars—antique fin-tailed Cadillacs, their radios smuggled over the border from Thailand.

Listless, I do nothing. At seven in the evening, the city is no cooler than at noon. A book of stories by Somerset Maugham lies abandoned on the dresser next to a half-empty bottle of beer. The warm, root smell of malt clings to the open mouth. Mandalay beer is notorious among travelers on the Asia circuit. Perhaps its foul taste is due to a missing ingredient that can't be imported from the West. Perhaps it is simply a matter of local preference. Either way, the result is a dark, yeasty concoction, served warm in a country without ice. It is still fermenting as it touches the tongue.

The hand-drawn label on the bottle depicts a famous pagoda not in Mandalay at all but in Pagan, miles to the north. Pagan, where my friends are. Burma's ancient capital. *Village of one hundred temples.* Favorite among the four cities to which each closely guarded phalanx of tourists is rushed. I think I understand the marketing strategy: Mandalay is the country's most famous city, Pagan's temples its most recognizable image.

The Strand Hotel used to be the center of colonial society, and being here is like stepping into someone's faded memory. I close my eyes to fix the scene: the bed covered with soft chenille nubs, the fragile, yellowing lampshade that coughs like an old drum at my touch. Draped over the rattan whatnot, my freshly washed underwear drips slightly like someone perspiring. The carpet is indistinct; years ago it may have been red or violet but can no longer remember.

I open my eyes, and Maugham stares out. As reflected in the dresser mirror, the room makes an old photograph, stained and curling at the edges. Something about the reflection is wrong: me, a black woman holding a cigarette. When did I take up smoking? It is difficult to isolate my own memory. Originally I must have been dreaming of menthol and thought that cigarettes would keep me cool, but Burmese cigarettes are made of cloves. Their warm, cloying scent hangs over the entire country. There is no escaping the fragrance.

Suddenly it is an hour later—eight o'clock. The ceiling fan whines, languidly revolving its arms. Even on high speed it is virtually useless. It swirls cloves and malt into the thick atmosphere, unbreathed in years. Sporadically the air shifts like a musty animal, placing a damp, scented hand on my shoulder, the back of my neck.

In search of anything cool, I leave my suite. The hallway is as wide as the street outside. My bare feet slap against the cool marble, and I am tempted to lie down on the unswept floor. I pass through anterooms and parlors and sitting rooms crowded with dark furniture: settees and writing desks; dusty ebony and teak. There is no sign, no sound of anyone else. At the end of the dimly lit corridor, the communal bathroom gleams white.

I enter and sit on the edge of the claw-footed bathtub. The room is easily five degrees cooler. Everything in the long, narrow space is white. Glittering white tile walls and floor. Oversized white ceramic fixtures. Stubbly white towels. The only spot of color is the pale orange toilet tissue that feels made of corrugated cardboard. Envisaging a long, cool bath, I twist the bathtub knob, and a ribbon of rust sputters out. I remember that there is also a soap shortage.

I climb into the tub and mop up the rusty water with toilet paper. The tissue is the exact same color as the water. Once the tub is dry, I take off my shirt and lie on my stomach. Pressing my face and chest against the cool, hard porcelain, I dream. Of ice cream. Cold beer. Lemonade.

It is nine-thirty when I awake, blue light streaming across my body. The light comes from the open window above. If I stand up and climb onto the edge of the bathtub, I can just squeeze my head through the narrow opening. The window faces a shanty-town behind the hotel, leaning on the verge of collapse: wormy planks patched together with scraps of cloth and cardboard, the eerie glow of battery-run blue lights after curfew. Noise and light spill out of every crack of the structure. Michael Jackson on black-market cassette. Voices raised in laughter and anger. The cries of children and bark of dogs. In contrast, the dark street is utterly barren, as hushed as the hotel corridor. I am protected and yet trapped.

In my best Gloria Swanson imitation, I sweep down the grand staircase to the hotel lobby. Two white-gloved attendants in frayed uniforms spring up, leaving their conversations behind. They usher me through a stately set of glass doors off to the left. I enter another series of empty formal rooms, pale blue walls stretching to twenty-foot ceilings. I wander, already having for-gotten why I came. Finally, something feels out of place: an Eng-lish-language newspaper strewn on the floor, an abandoned slab of papaya growing soft on a plate. Only a hotel guest would be allowed to do this—someone else has recently been here. I hurry ahead.

The dining room, an elegant Old World affair with ornately carved ceilings, is nevertheless empty. Everything stands ready: tables swathed in snowy linen, set with china, crystal, and silver; wicker screens curving inwards to isolate private conversations. A young waiter, his face dramatically scarred by pockmarks, rushes forward from his post.

Leading me to a chair, he suggests that "Madame is wanting a nice bottle of Mandalay beer?"

"No," I respond, staring hungrily at his hands. His manicured nails are the color of raspberry sherbet. "I want fruit," I declare. "Lots of fruit. Any fruit. All the fruit you have." Anything to relieve this thirst.

In what seems like only seconds, the waiter returns with a large silver tray. He begins to pile dishes and dishes of fruit atop the

table until every inch of cloth is covered. He works quickly, silently. I gape at the staggering still life, at the splendor of fruit. The
musky perfume of mango and pineapple. The whimsy of rambutan with its red and green tentacles. Plum-colored mangosteen, so
quick to stain. Huge juiceless pomelos, tinted rust. With a flourish the waiter places before me a cut-glass bowl, set inside a larger
dish of chipped ice. "Chilled strawberries," he announces proudly
at my startled look. "Just brought down from Maymo Hills!"

As I pick up a heavy silver spoon, I begin to understand the
colonial aesthetic—the addiction to privilege—the seduction of
creating a role and starring in one's own fantasy. This, then, must
be progress: that for the right price, now anyone—even a black
woman—can play.

SUSAN JANE GILMAN

# Meeting Mick Jagger

When my mother was a teenager, she kept scrapbooks on Marlon Brando and Ingrid Bergman. She pressed their photographs, magazine clips, and movie stills behind cellophane like dried flowers, and wrote them fan letters which they never answered. Recently, a boy I once baby-sat had "Guns 'n' Roses Lives" tattooed on his right shoulder blade. It was a heart pierced by a dagger, colored red, black, and blue. His younger sister wants one now, too, and their mother is not pleased. Each year, my friend Ed and his old high school buddies pile into a van to follow the Grateful Dead around for three weeks. We are a nation that prostrates itself before celebrities. Everyone knows this: Books have been written.

In 1979, when I was fifteen years old, I had my first experience with fanaticism. I fell in love with a rock star. For anyone who has been an adolescent, this is hardly news. But unlike most teenagers, I met my idol. I had dinner with Mick Jagger one night, purely by coincidence, and this became the seminal event of my adolescence. For quite a while afterwards, I was a celebrity at my high school, the envy of my girlfriends, and a giddier, somehow more confident person.

I am now twenty-nine; the experience, half a lifetime ago, is not something I dwell upon. Yet once in a while, I'll hear a song from that period in my life that dilates my memory like perfume. I'll remember what it felt like to be fifteen and starstruck, and then what it had been like to meet *the* Rolling Stone. And it will occur to me that my experience has resonated throughout my life in substantial ways. I have grown up understanding the absurd negotiations the heart can make despite politics and reason. I know how a single human being can be construed as the ticket to salvation. I know addiction; I know recklessness. And, having been entranced by one of rock's preeminent sexists, I am a more forgiving feminist. Meeting Mick Jagger was my coming of age.

My obsession began when I was working as a mother's helper in Southampton, New York. I still needed a mother myself; I had thumbtack-sized breasts and was longing to be kissed. I was employed by a family named the Maysels. The father, David, was a film producer who had made *Gimme Shelter,* a documentary about the Rolling Stones that recorded the murder at Altamont.

One evening, *Gimme Shelter* was on television. I was friends with a girl next door, Gwynne; the Maysels gave me the evening off so I could watch the movie with her. The two of us sat around in damp Speedo bathing suits watching *Gimme Shelter* on an old, portable RCA television that had a wire hanger for an antenna. About ten minutes into the film, my skin started to tingle. Gwynne, who usually talked through anything, stared at the screen in silence. We were watching Mick Jagger. Neither of us had seen him before. He was swaggering, almost tongue-kissing the microphone, and his eyes were half-closed. "Oh my God," I whispered. Gwynne looked at me. I looked at her. We didn't say anything and stared back at Mick, whirling about the stage. Then we both moaned.

From that day on, no one could hold a rational conversation with us. All we talked about were the Rolling Stones. The adults made it clear to us we were being unbearably adolescent, and this, somehow, increased our fervor. When fall came, Gwynne went away to boarding school and I went home to Manhattan, where I proceeded to build a shrine in my bedroom.

I bought Rolling Stones records, Rolling Stones posters, Rolling Stones buttons, Rolling Stones books. When I trooped home carrying a Rolling Stones mural—an overblown album cover, six feet long and three feet high—my parents stopped coming into my bedroom. I read every magazine I could get hold of, including *People* (which, as an aspiring "serious writer," I considered sacrilegious), in hopes of finding so much as a paragraph about Mick, or even his ex-wife, Bianca.

Eventually, my infatuation became so consuming I called up my best friend, Rebekah, who lived in the apartment below me. Alcoholics hate to drink alone, and I stayed up all night playing her Rolling Stones music and showing her photographs. By the end of the session, she, too, was hooked.

After that, Rebekah and I went about constructing our own little meta-reality, in which the Rolling Stones replaced the sun at the center of the solar system. We fantasized about them, talked about them as if they were our intimate friends, even worried about them.

"Do you think Mick is lonely?" I remember asking her one night. "His last hit was 'Miss You.' What if underneath all his fame, he's really pining away for intimacy, and that song is like his plea for help? Oh God, wouldn't that be terrible? Could you imagine him, lonely? God, I hope Mick isn't lonely. Please don't make Mick lonely..."

Before then, our puberty had been calm and insecure. We had spent a lot of time copying makeovers out of *Seventeen* magazine, doing our homework, making earrings, and going on Alba '77 milkshake diets. Neither of us had boyfriends; we'd been kissed maybe once each. If we went out at all, it was to the movies or an occasional high school party.

Once we became groupies, however, we started smoking clove cigarettes and pot, and took No-Doz to simulate amphetamines. We avoided having anything to do with our parents, and stopped talking to most of our "square" friends at school. We spent every day in Rebekah's bedroom or mine, listening to the Rolling Stones and embroidering their "lapping tongue" logo on Rebekah's overalls. We were so frustrated and sexual, we didn't know what to do with ourselves.

It was October 1979, and Jimmy Carter was still clinging to the presidency. AIDS had not yet emerged. In New York City, drugs were still considered glamorous; cocaine, in particular, was pricey and chic. Discotheques were in full swing: It was customary to start an evening at midnight and stay out until dawn. People thought nothing about getting high and having sex with strangers.

Both Rebekah and I felt terribly left out. We had no conception of a world beyond Manhattan's underground culture. We were convinced there was a wonderful party going on somewhere in a fancy hotel full of photographers, artists, musicians, and movie stars dressed in gold lamé. They did cocaine, had sex, and were admired and beloved by the world. Our own lives, in comparison, were marginalized and full of longing. We decided that if we could emulate the Rolling Stones—the ministers of decadence—and then meet them, we would somehow be transformed into sophisticates.

Not surprisingly, losing our virginity counted heavily in this transformation. We wanted *lovers*, not boyfriends. After all, Warhol girls and courtesans always had *lovers*; high school virgins had makeout sessions with their *boyfriends*. We regarded virginity as the sexual equivalent of training wheels and braces: the quicker disposed of, the better. And through some twisted, fifteen-year-old logic, we equated losing our virginity with losing our virginity to Mick Jagger.

We were overdosing on estrogen and progesterone, and spent a lot of time speculating who in school had "lost it" thus far. I, in particular, had a deep-seated, vaguely recognized fear that my virginity was the hallmark of failure. I had only that year, at the late age of fifteen, begun to develop a figure, and I did not consider myself graceful or pretty. My virginity seemed like testimony to the fact that I was undesirable. Anytime I found out that somebody else I knew had "lost it," I got stomach pangs. I believed that the number of non-virgins was directly proportional to the extent of my inadequacy.

To help substantiate our fantasies, Rebekah and I began dressing like underground movie stars—all sparkles and funk. I had a pair of Lucite cocktail pumps (you could see the nails in the heels) with rhinestone ankle straps, which I wore with gold socks, an oversized fake-fur coat, and a gray fedora. Rebekah wore layers upon layers of antique clothing.

We bought most of our outfits at a clothing dump on East 10th Street called Bogie's, which has since closed. It was run by two old Rumanian immigrants, and the merchandise consisted of one enormous heap of clothing. Everything was all mixed in together: trench coats, old negligees, baseball jerseys, lace bed jackets, sheets. The women would hand us a bag and we'd climb to the top of the pile—it was the size of a haystack—and sort through the clothes until we found things we liked. Almost everything was faded, stained, or frayed, but the price was right. The women would weigh the bags and charge us a dollar for every ten pounds of clothing. We ended up with all these fancy old clothes for two or three bucks. We wore silk camisoles as shirts, petticoats as skirts—and traipsed through the city in other people's underwear. We also bought loads of earrings. Rebekah wore one, I the other: lavender feathers, loopy gold fleur-de-lis, fake tourmalines. We'd also cover ourselves with bracelets and Rolling Stones buttons. We must have been quite a sight, even by New York standards: once we walked into Tavern on the Green looking for a friend, and the headwaiter asked us to leave.

We took immense pleasure in lying and sneaking around. We'd tell our parents we were going out for ice cream and instead take the bus up to Columbia University to smoke pot by the statues with some fraternity boys. Or we'd go to Lincoln Center to look for celebrities. One night, a thirty-five-year-old man picked us up, took to us to French restaurant, and got us drunk on hard cider. We excused ourselves to go to the bathroom and left him there with the check. Our mothers thought we were baby-sitting.

Often, we talked in British accents and told people we were the Rolling Stones' illegitimate daughters. We convinced some women on the crosstown bus that we were the Rolling Stones' mistresses. We told boys from Yorktown Prep that we were Rolling Stones groupies who had hitchhiked from San Francisco. We felt enormous power, fooling them.

It is not at all ironic that in our broader lives, we felt anything but in control—though at the time, we were too naive to recognize this. Rebekah's parents were on their way to a divorce, fighting so terribly that upstairs in my apartment, I could hear them screaming and slamming furniture. While my family was eating dinner, we'd hear several thuds beneath the table; a few minutes later, our doorbell would ring. Rebekah would be standing there, crying in the hallway.

"Oh, Susie, oh, God..."

Similarly, I'd come home from school every day to find my mother moody and seething. She was often enraged at my father (they, too, were headed for a divorce), but since I was the only one around, she took it out on me. Sometimes, something as simple as a fork left in the sink would set her off; other times, my attempts to make her proud of me backfired. I remember once showing her a poem I had written, which won a prize at school.

She read it, looked at me icily, and threw it on the floor.

"So?"

"Well, my English teacher liked it."

"So go live with your English teacher."

Then she told me to make my own dinner and slammed her bedroom door in my face. My father came home just then.

"What happened?" he asked.

"I don't know. I just showed her a poem I wrote. Do you want to see it?"

He shook his head. "I think you owe your mother an apology," he said. "You shouldn't upset her."

He walked into their bedroom and closed the door sharply behind him. I stood there for a minute. Through the door I could hear my mother yelling. Then I walked slowly down to Rebekah's. She answered the door and I could hear her mother in the background, shouting, "Paul! Listen to me for a minute, goddamn it!"

Rebekah looked at me. We didn't say anything. She just went and got her cigarettes and we went and sat out in the concrete stairwell. I unfolded my poem and handed it to her, and she read it as she smoked. When she was done, she hugged me.

"That's wonderful! That's really, really wonderful."

I eyed her. "You really think so?"

"Of course! Susie, you're a poet!"

"Oh. Rebekah."

We hugged, and then we both started to cry.

After a little while, when we felt better, we went back to our continuing saga with Mick. Although we'd repeatedly told each other our fantasies, we never tired of hearing them, embellishing details, or making up new ones. Rebekah's main fantasy was that she would meet Mick Jagger at a nightclub and he'd take her around to the apartments of all the other band members so she could meet them. Then she'd hit it off with the guitarist Keith Richards and travel with the band for a while.

My favorite fantasy was that one evening I would meet Mick Jagger at a dinner party. We would talk about music and literature; he would find me intelligent and attractive. Then we would get romantically involved and he would pick me up from school in his limousine so that all the boys who never looked at me would see that I was pretty.

In November of 1979, Rebekah came running upstairs with a newspaper article.

"They're here," she shrieked.

According to the *Daily News,* the Rolling Stones were in New York, putting the finishing touches on their album *Emotional Rescue* at the Electric Lady Studios. We looked it up in the Yellow Pages and found out Electric Lady was on Eighth Street in Greenwich Village. I told my mother I was going to Rebekah's house to bake cookies; she told her mother she was going to mine. Then we both took the Eighth Avenue subway downtown. It was ten p.m. The studio was probably the most nondescript doorway in Greenwich Village. Located next to a movie theater, it was a small, windowless, brick storefront with a door set in far from the street. Only a small brass plaque saying "electric lady" in lowercase letters distinguished it. You could walk by it a thousand times and never notice.

For the next two hours, Rebekah and I stood in front of this doorway, stopping people on the street who looked like they might know something, asking them if they'd seen the Rolling Stones.

After that, we spent every weekend camped out in front of Electric Lady. (Luckily, it was a mild winter.) We'd get downtown at about ten a.m., position ourselves on a car right near the entrance, and wait. Rebekah would smoke cigarettes and I, ever the conscientious student, would bring along books and do my homework. We flirted with strangers a bit, if we thought they were *somebody,* and took beer from guys on the street. Sometimes Rebekah would ring the bell at the entrance and say she was sent over from *The Village Voice* with a package for Keith Richards, but they never let her in.

We fell in with some other hippie-groupie types from Rebekah's school who often threw "the parents are away" parties out in Flushing. Since the parties lasted all night, we rarely slept at them; at three a.m., a bunch of us would try to set up beds on the floor using sofa cushions and towels, but when the sun rose, we'd all be up listening to "Freebird" and cooking frozen pizza in the kitchen.

Most of the time, none of us knew where we were, or who we were with. People were taking speed, smoking grass, dropping acid, making out with whoever was around: it was a druggie, psychedelic mess. There would be beer and cigarette butts all over the basement floor, cans and paper, little pools of wax where candles had melted down on the coffee tables. By the morning, I always felt battered from alcohol. All I ever wanted to do was take a hot shower and slide between the cool, fresh sheets of my own bed. But instead, Rebekah and I would take the train to Greenwich Village and spend a few hours replacing whatever it was we had lost at the party: lipstick, change purses, socks.

We were walking across Eighth Street one of these afternoons when we saw a limousine pull up in front of the recording studio.

"Rebekah!" I grabbed her and we tore down the block. Then we leaned against an Oldsmobile parked in front of the cinema next door and waited to see who was coming out; we wanted to appear very nonchalant about it.

Two minutes later, the door to Electric Lady swung open and the Rolling Stones' guitarist, Keith Richards, sauntered out with his little blond son in tow. He looked, if this was possible, scraggly and regal. I remember his black hair was all tousled and he was wearing a pair of gold mirrored sunglasses. I sized him up as fast as possible: tight black-velvet pants pulled over boots, black jacket, a red-green-yellow scarf slashed around his neck. When he walked into the sunlight, he recoiled a little. Then he spotted me and Rebekah, and for a second acknowledged us with a nod before staggering towards his limousine.

Rebekah whispered, "Let's go with him, Susie. Let's jump into the limousine..."

I had completely jelled. He was walking down the street, I remember, and all I could look at was his ass. I was watching his proud legs and his ass, packed in black velvet, pull and move, pull and move, with a bit of a jiggle, as he moved towards his car. Keith Richards's ass, I remember thinking. I'm watching Keith Richards's ass as he goes to his limousine.

Rebekah grabbed my wrist and pulled me to the curb. "Let's do it, Susie," she said. "We're really going to do it."

The chauffeur opened the door and Keith's son scuttled in, followed by Keith, who paused for a moment before dipping down into the back seat. He seemed to take one last look at the studio, the street, and the people, and as he did, the sunlight glared off his glasses in flashes of gold. Rebekah and I froze. The door slammed, the motor growled, and the limousine leered away from the curb, leaving us standing at the edge of the gutter, shivering, tears running down our faces.

"Keith," we shouted as the car drove away, "Keith, we love you!"

When it was absolutely out of sight, we started laughing, crying, and shouting all at once: "We saw Keith! We saw Keith Richards!"

Then Rebekah said to me, "I'll bet you anything Mick is still in the studio. We're going to meet him. We'll wait out all night if we have to."

When she said this, I remember, I started to panic. Up until then, my fantasy life with Mick Jagger had allowed me to be, in my own heart, beautiful, sexual, and confident. In reality, I was not popular at school; boys did not like me. At home, my mother had, on occasion, thrown me out of the house. But in my fantasies about Mick Jagger, I was always adored and taken in. They were small wishes for my own redemption.

I think I must have realized that standing there on Eighth Street, because suddenly the prospect of actually meeting Mick Jagger sickened me. The last thing I wanted to do was wait outside for him all night and approach him like a beggar with an autograph book. To be cast that way in his eyes—and in mine—would leave me with nothing.

At the time, however, I could not articulate any of this. I simply told Rebekah I couldn't do it: I had to baby-sit.

"Susie," she cried. "This is our dream come true."

So then I explained that even though we'd been waiting in front of Electric Lady for a month, I suddenly realized I didn't want to meet Mick Jagger this way. In my dreams, I always met him at a dinner party. "And someone introduces us," I said. "I don't come up to him."

Understandably, Rebekah looked at me as if I'd gone insane. "Susie, that's fantasy. This is reality. Mick Jagger is in this recording studio, and you and I have the opportunity to meet him."

It was one of those moments that could have disintegrated a friendship; the fact that it didn't is testimony to how close we were. After an argument on the street, I went home that night and Rebekah stayed. The next morning I got a phone call: at five o'clock in the morning, Mick Jagger had come out of the studio.

"Oh Susie, oh Susie," Rebekah sobbed, as I screamed with delight. "He was so beautiful. I waited outside with three other groupies until the sun was starting to rise. When he walked out of the studio, we almost missed him because he's grown a beard and none of us recognized him. But then we realized who he was, and we started following him down the street. Susie, I must have been only three feet away from him. Then, all of a sudden, he turned right around and starting yelling at me, 'Fucking ridiculous.'

"Susie, I couldn't believe it. I thought I was going to die. I thought he was angry at me for following him. But then, he smiled right at me and said, 'This is so fucking ridiculous. I can't get a fucking cab in fucking New York City at fucking five o'clock in the morning!' It was so unbelievable. Just like that, Mick Jagger starts talking to us! I just froze. I couldn't even speak. Mick Jagger, standing right next to me, talking to me about taxicabs and New York City! Oh, Susie. I wish you had been there."

At that moment, I wished so, too.

At the end of January, I got a telephone call from Gwynne, my friend from Southampton. She was home from boarding school, staying at her mother's house five blocks away. She wanted to know if I would come over: her mother was having "a really boring dinner party" for "some snooty people from France." Gwynne was allowed to have one guest to help make it bearable.

Gwynne's mother lived in a sprawling, high-ceilinged apartment on Central Park West with views of the park. Gwynne's father and godmother were well-known artists; paintings and sculpture filled the house. No sooner did I arrive when Gwynne got a phone call from her boarding school boyfriend, and I was left alone in the middle of a crowded living room, wondering what to do with myself. Everyone else was French and at least twice my age; all I could see were the backs of people huddled in groups for conversation. Since I spoke some French, I could tell they were speaking about antiques and a baron's estate. I sat by myself and studied the bottom of my drink.

Then the doorbell rang, and Gwynne appeared from her bedroom to answer it. I started to follow her, but stopped at the entrance to the living room. Although the party was still in full throttle, everything suddenly got very quiet around me. My blood raced like quicksilver. I had to clutch the back of the sofa to keep from trembling. There, five feet in front of me in the vestibule, stood Mick Jagger. He said hello to Gwynne's mother and unknotted his scarf.

The surge of adrenaline I felt at that moment was so powerful that fourteen years later, my heart still quickens as I write about it. For a moment, I thought I would faint. My breathing was staccato, nearly asthmatic. I gripped the upholstery and tried to calm myself down.

Taking the cue from my daydreams, in which I was always blasé at the moment of encounter, I decided it would be best if I was not standing there gaping as Mick unsnapped his parka. But, I found, I couldn't move my legs. So I stood there and tried to avert my eyes, pretending to look for Gwynne. Then Mick looked up and saw me. Most likely, he saw a small fifteen-year-old girl with eyes as big as chestnuts and a mouth as round as an apple, making a deliberate effort not to look at him. He seemed amused. Smiling, he called out, "Hello."

It took me a moment to realize he was addressing me. After I said hello back, Gwynne appeared in the doorway and asked me if I wouldn't like to talk to her for a minute. We both tried to sound as casual as possible. We walked down the hall to her bedroom very calmly, then shut the door and proceeded to shriek and jump on the bed. "Oh my God! Can you believe it? Mick Jagger! Right here, in this house!"

Frantically, we brushed our hair, put on lipstick, doused ourselves in perfume, and tried to look as grown-up as possible. Then we zoomed out of her room and, acting as if we had all the cool in the world, arrived at her mother's elbow just as she was making introductions. She introduced Mick to Gwynne, then turned to me. Her words to me were like the opening bars of a symphony: "Mick, this is Susie. Susie, this is Mick."

He reached out and took my hand.

From then on, the evening was all candles and glitter, clouds of white wine, and a room the color of amethysts. I was absolutely delirious with adrenaline.

Mick, it turned out, spent most of the evening talking to me and Gwynne. I'm not sure whether he was simply bored by the Parisians, or if he felt most comfortable playing to a teenage audience. Perhaps, tickled by our adoration, he enjoyed giving us the thrill of our lives. In any event, soon after we were introduced, he beckoned me over to him, took my hand, and proceeded to ask me about myself. I told him about school and that I planned to be a writer. Later, we talked about religion and movies. I do not remember anything specific that was said, only that it was a conversation with Mick Jagger, and that he was holding my hand.

What I do remember about him, however, was that he could not sit still. He was constantly moving: drumming his fingers, winking at us, making funny faces, rolling his eyes. He had a small diamond set in one of his front teeth; when he spoke, first his eyes (blue) would sparkle, then his diamond, then his whole smile. He seemed to glitter blue-silver-white, blue-silver-white, like Christmas lights. I also remember he was dressed very casually—a sweater and slacks—not at all like a rock star.

As the evening wore on, my pulse slowed and I began to feel more comfortable. After dinner, Gwynne and I sat with Mick and Gwynne's godfather, Earl (who, it turns out, was the one who knew Mick and had invited him to the dinner), drinking champagne out of Dixie cups. By that point, Mick seemed like any other family friend—biting, funny, and uneventfully human. It never once occurred to me to flirt with him. He was thirty-six years old, and looked much too adult.

Yet he remained, in my eyes, heroic. At one point after dinner, Mick, Gwynne, Earl, and I were all in the kitchen, telling jokes. Earl began one, "There's this Jew, you see..."

Mick and I had talked about religion, and he knew that I was Jewish. As Earl launched into the joke, Mick looked at me, rolled his eyes, and said, "Hey, Earl, I don't want to hear that one right now. Save it for later, huh?" then looked back at me and smiled.

A few minutes later, as he was leaving the kitchen with Gwynne's mother, he asked her, "The girl in the kitchen, the one who's not your daughter?"

"Oh yes," she said. "That's Susie."

"Oh," he said. "She's *charming*."

In retrospect, I am sure he deliberately said this within earshot, knowing the impact it would have on me. At the time, however, overhearing his praise made me reel: my fantasy had come true to the finest detail.

Yet towards the end of the evening, something else happened, too. I wandered into one of the rooms looking for Gwynne, and found her, Mick, and a handful of other guests watching *Saturday Night Live* on television. Mick told me to join them; I stood before the television with my hands in my pockets. After a few minutes, he looked up at me and said: "You know, you've got the biggest titties out of all the girls here."

"Excuse me?" I said. Some of the other guests giggled.

"Do you know you've got the biggest titties out of all the girls here?" he repeated. Then he smiled at me, and winked.

Today if I were to write this as a short story, his comment would be the moment of epiphany: A young girl, whose sexuality is just being awakened, fantasizes about a rock 'n' roll star. She dreams that one day they will meet, and that he will find her desirable. Then, miraculously, she has dinner with him. But instead of being the charming man she dreamed he would be, he humiliates her, making lewd comments about her body in front of the other guests. When he says these things, she suddenly realizes that the man she has idolized for so long is in fact vulgar and arrogant. The event marks the beginning of her disillusionment, and thus, her coming of age.

Yet while this chain of events seems the most narratively and morally logical, it is not what actually happened. When Mick Jagger said to me, "You've got the biggest titties," I simply stood there. For one moment, my insecurity and self-loathing, my bickering parents, and my loneliness all melted away. I looked at Mick and beamed. I said shyly, "Thank you."

# Degenerates

Not long ago I accompanied a Trappist abbot as he unlocked a door to the cloister and led me down a long corridor into a stone-walled room, the chapter house of his monastery, where some twenty monks were waiting for me to give a reading. Poetry does lead a person into some strange places. This wonderfully silent, hiddenaway place was not as alien to me as it might have been, however, as I've been living on the grounds of a Benedictine monastery for most of the last three years, and have steeped myself in the community's daily rhythm of prayer, work, and play.

Trappists are more silent than the Benedictines, far less likely to have work that draws them into the world outside the monastery. But the cumulative effect of the liturgy of the hours—at a bare minimum, morning, noon, and evening prayer, as well as the Eucharist—on one's psyche, the sense it gives a person of being immersed in the language of scripture, is much the same in any monastery. What has surprised me, in my time among monastic people, is how much their liturgy feeds my poetry; and also how much correspondence I've found between monastic practice and the discipline of writing.

Before I read a few poems of mine that had been inspired by the psalms (the mainstay of all monastic liturgy), I discussed some of those connections. I told the Trappists that I had come to see both writing and monasticism as vocations that require periods of apprenticeship and formation. Prodigies are common in mathematics, but extremely rare in literature, and, I added, "as far as I know, there are no prodigies in monastic life." This drew a laugh, as I thought it might.

Related to this, I said, was recognizing the dynamic nature of both disciplines; they are not so much subjects to be mastered as ways of life that require continual conversion. For example, no matter how much I've written or published, I always return to the blank page; and even more importantly, from a monastic point of view, I return to the blankness within, the fears, laziness, and cowardice that, without fail, will mess up whatever I'm currently writing and, in turn, require me to revise it. The spiritual dimension of this process is humility, not a quality often associated with writers, but lurking there, in our nagging sense of the need to revise. As I put it to the monks, when you realize that anything good you write comes *despite* your weaknesses, writing becomes a profoundly humbling activity. At this point one of the monks spoke up. "I find that there's a redemptive quality," he said, "just in sitting in front of that blank piece of paper."

This comment reflects an important aspect of monastic life, which has been described as "attentive waiting." I think it's also a fair description of the writing process. Once, when I was asked, "What is the main thing a poet does?" I was inspired to answer, "We wait." A spark is struck; an event inscribed with a message—*This is important, pay attention*—and a poet scatters a few words like seeds in a notebook. Months or even years later, those words bear fruit. The process requires both discipline and commitment, and its gifts come from both preparedness and grace, or what writers have traditionally called inspiration. As Bill Stafford wrote, with his usual simplicity, in a poem entitled "For People with Problems About How to Believe": "a quality of attention has been given to you: / when you turn your head the whole world / leans forward. It waits there thirsting / after its names, and you speak it all out / as it comes to you..."

"Listen" is the first word of St. Benedict's *Rule* for monasteries, and listening for the eruptions of grace into one's life—often from unlikely sources—is a "quality of attention" that both monastic living and the practice of writing tends to cultivate. I'm trained to listen when words and images begin to constellate. When I'm awakened at three a.m. by my inner voice telling me to look into an old notebook, or to get to work on a poem I'd abandoned years before, I do not turn over and go back to sleep. I obey, which is an active form of listening (the two words are related, etymologically).

Anyone who listens to the world, anyone who seeks the sacred in the ordinary events of life, has "problems about how to believe." Paradoxically, it helps that both prayer and poetry begin deep within a person, beyond the reach of language. The fourth-century desert monk, St. Anthony, said that perfect prayer was one you don't understand. Poets are used to discovering, years after a poem is written, what it's really about. And it's in the respect for the mystery and power of words that I find the most profound connections between the practice of writing and monastic life.

The *lectio divina* (loosely and inadequately translated as "prayerful reading") practiced by followers of Benedict, including Cistercians and Trappists as well as Benedictines, strikes me as similar to the practice of writing poetry, in that it is not an intellectual procedure so much as an existential one. Grounded in a meditative reading of scriptures, it soon becomes much more: a way of reading the world and one's place in it. To quote a fourth-century monk, it is a way of reading that "works the earth of the heart."

I should try telling friends who have a hard time comprehending why I like to spend so much time going to church with monks that I do so for the same reasons that I write: in order to let words work the earth of my heart. To sing, to read poetry aloud, and to have the poetry and the wild stories of scripture read to me. To respond with others, in blessed silence. That is a far more accurate description of morning or evening prayer in a monastery than what most people conjure up when they hear the word "church."

Monks have always recognized reading as a bodily experience, primarily oral. The ancients spoke of masticating the words of scripture in order to fully digest them. Monastic "church" reflects a whole-body religion, still in touch with its orality, its music. Both poetry and religion originate in the oral, and I suspect that they stray from those roots at their peril, becoming rigid, precious, academic, irrelevant. In the midst of today's revolution in "instant communication," I find it a blessing that monks still respect the slow way that words work on the human psyche. They take the time to sing, chant, and read the psalms aloud, often with a full minute of silence between them, in order to let the words sink in. The community I'm most familiar with keeps two minutes of silence after brief readings from scripture—in the time I've been with them, we've heard much of Isaiah, Job, Jeremiah,

Acts, Romans, and Revelations read this way, as well as the entire books of Jonah, Ruth, and the Song of Songs—and it is astonishing how words will resonate in the vast space that our silence creates. It's not easy listening, or the hard-sell jargon of television evangelists; it's more like imbibing language—often powerfully poetic language—at full strength.

This style of reading and listening also allows fully for response, for one's own unruly thoughts to rise up out of the unconscious, sometimes in comical fashion. Once, at morning prayer during Easter season, when I heard that an angel in the book of Revelation said to John of Patmos, "Write what you see," my gut response was, "Easy for *you* to say." But when we ended a vespers reading with a passage from Job, "My lyre is turned to mourning, and my pipe to the voice of those who weep," I was awestruck, not only with the beauty of the words, but also with the way those words gave a new dimension to watching the nightly news later that evening, leading me to reflect on the communal role of the poet.

Poets and monks do have a communal role in American culture, although it alternately ignores; romanticizes, and despises them. In our relentlessly utilitarian society, structuring a life around writing is as crazy as structuring a life around prayer, yet that is what writers and monks *do*. Deep down, people seem glad to know that monks are praying, that poets are writing poems. This is what others want and expect of us, because if we do our job right, we will express things that others may feel, or know, but can't or won't say. At least this is what writers are told over and over again by their readers, and I suspect it's behind the boom in visits to monastic retreat houses. Maybe it is the useless silence of contemplation, that certain "quality of attention" that distinguishes both the poem and the prayer.

I regard monks and poets as the best degenerates in America. Both have a finely developed sense of the sacred potential in all things. (Think of Mary Oliver, or Galway Kinnell. Of Philip Levine or Denise Levertov. Joy Harjo, Lucille Clifton, Linda Hogan, Li-Young Lee, Gary Snyder.) In a world in which "meaningless" and "ritual" are taken to be synonymous, many desperately seek meaningful symbols in the empty rituals of drug use, pornography, shopping, sports. But the absurd practices of monks and poets are healthier. They value image and symbol over utilitarian purpose or the bottom line; they recognize the transformative power hiding in the simplest things. In a culture that excels at artifice, at creating controlled environments that serve a clear commercial purpose (shopping malls, amusement parks, chain motels), what poets do, what monks do, is useless. Worse than that, it's scary; it remains beyond consumerism's manipulation and control.

Not long ago I viewed an exhibition at the New York Public Library entitled "Degenerate Art" that consisted of artworks approved by Hitler's regime, along with art the Nazis had denounced. As I walked the galleries it struck me that the real issue was one of control. The meaning of the approved art was superficial, in that its images (usually rigidly representational) served a clear commercial and/or political purpose. The "degenerate" artworks, many crucifixes among them, were more often abstract, with multiple meanings, or even no meaning at all, in the conventional sense. This art—like the best poetry, and also good liturgy—allowed for a wide freedom of experience and interpretation on the part of the viewer.

Pat Robertson once declared that modern art was a plot to strip America of its vital resources. Using an abstract sculpture by Henry Moore as an example, he said that the material used could more properly been used for a statue of George Washington. What do poets mean? Who needs them? Of what possible use are monastic people in the modern world? Are their lives degenerate in the same sense that modern art is—having no easily perceptible meaning, yet of ultimate value, concerned with ultimate meanings? Maybe monks and poets know, as Jesus did when a friend, in an extravagant, loving gesture, poured nard on his feet and washed them with her hair, that the symbolic act *matters;* that those who know the exact price of things, as Judas did, often don't know the true cost or value of anything.

## A Spare Umbrella

Cold. Wet. Sloppy. Traffic on the bridge is heavy even though I waited for morning rush hour to end. Perhaps there *is* no end to rush hour. Fax. E-mail. Supersonic jets. We're all racing at greater and greater speeds, going around and around, stuck behind each other on the bridge. Except Mom, who in her characteristically subtle wisdom has maintained her own pace at the nursing home, moving slowly in reverse, faded to her adolescence now, recognizing me occasionally as daughter, sister, mother.

Mom used to love this ride from my place in Oakland to her apartment in San Francisco, particularly once we got past Treasure Island. She would point at Alcatraz and Coit Tower, as if I had never seen them, as if I were twelve years old, as if she were behind the wheel. The truth was she never learned to drive. Rather, she became an expert rider of buses.

How can you let your mother visit you on the *bus* from San Francisco? friends would ask. How can you let her live in the Tenderloin? I never *let* my mother do anything. Some people need food; my mother sustained herself on will. Born in a city, she was going to die in a city. And she almost did.

I have taken a day off work to clear out Mom's studio apartment. The back seat is cluttered with a dolly, boxes and twine and large, green plastic sacks, body bags for memories. I reach her neighborhood and immediately prepare the vulture swoop for a parking space. You have to be quick in San Francisco. People swerve in front of you from nowhere, from the next block, from the sky. All that City of Light nonsense evaporates in the parking duel. Ten minutes. Fifteen minutes, circling, a buzzard on wheels. Suddenly, stunningly, there is a space right in front of her apartment building. The meter eats seventy-five cents an hour, but I have come laden with quarters. Rain pours heavier now, soaking me before I duck under the front awning.

Damn keys don't work. It's a dangerous building and they

change the lock every few months. How can I let my mother live in the Tenderloin? Drenched, cold, I summon her common sense and ring the manager's bell.

Nell, a stocky woman in her mid-sixties, waves to me as she approaches with a ring of keys. Sister Matthew used to wear the large brass ring of school keys on her wrist and tell us it was a charm bracelet; wearing it, she could charm her way through any door. Charm has never been one of my talents. Nell nods at my discouraged, shivering body. She is followed by two of the ugliest dogs I have ever seen. Short, squat Winston Churchills. Somebody's sons, Mom used to joke. I miss my mother's ironic laughter.

"How is Mary? We talk about her all the time. Please give her my best." She says all this in rapid succession as if she forgets Mom's Alzheimer's. Maybe Nell is developing dementia; lately I have begun to wonder seriously about my own memory. Nell has been kind to Mom. Took her to the movies. Phoned immediately when she broke her arm. Let us keep the apartment for months after Mom moved, just in case. Just in case there was a miracle. A Presbyterian, my mother never had a taste for miracles.

The building has been only modestly maintained over the last fifteen years and the red flowered carpet suffers into a painful pink. Lately, here, they have started to take more monthly and weekly tenants. The downstairs lobby is lined with menacing plastic trees; two large chairs are chained to the floor; thick iron grillwork grips the window and door. I check the mailbox, saddened that unlike the others, it bears no name, just an apartment number. Briefly I am indignant for Mom; after all, her rent is still being paid. The box is empty.

Waiting for the familiar elevator, I think about my mother being held up here between the second and third floors. "Well," she had shrugged after a couple of margaritas, "it happens. I don't carry much cash." On the third floor, I safely disembark from the elevator and walk down to the end of the corridor where she used to stand with the door open, welcoming me with a cup of afternoon tea or a drink before I took her out to dinner. Never did she cook a meal for me in that place. Didn't cook for herself, either, preferring to eat between her work shifts at the café, saving money, evading loneliness. The fridge was always stocked with Coke and cheddar cheese. Today she is not waiting for me. Stupid, clichéd to feel abandoned, yet I do. Lost about how to begin this task, this life, ahead without her. The door to apartment No. 310 is closed.

We walked along the shore at Long Beach, a balmy evening, the final night of the last family holiday. That evening Dad took my brother to a baseball game. Mom and I had a blast shopping, seeing an Elvis Presley film (*Blue Hawaii*, I think, but the King is dead and they all mush together now), ambling barefoot along the beach. It seemed a perfect time to confess I wanted to go to college. A quiet, peaceful, private moment. Both of us feeling optimistic. And although her cautious response was entirely predictable, I had hoped for more. Okay, if college was what I wanted, she said. "Remember to take typing. It's something to fall back on." That was the difference between us—I was conscious of climbing; Mom of falling. As we strolled, I swung the bag with the "drastically reduced" sale blouse, a secret audition for my Ivy League wardrobe. Oh, yes, I insisted, talking hectically to cover my panic, I *had* to go to college if I was going to become a teacher. She smiled and turned toward the ocean, her eyes even with the horizon.

Now, in the grim corridor light, I notice that the beige and brown art nouveau design on her door is peeling. Tentatively I approach the locks. But the keys work and soon I am inside the studio apartment, smelling a familiar stuffy sweetness: the room is redolent with the aromas of her sweat, Ivory soap, and whatever shampoo has been on sale at Walgreen's. She never wore deodorant or perfume. I am enveloped by her, as if she were really here and whole and not fragmented into ten thousand detached synapses in a room across San Francisco Bay.

We cannot say goodbye in person. She slipped away before either of us understood what was happening. I can say goodbye to her here. With this understanding, I am immobilized, recalling times we sat in this living room—the Murphy bed invisible behind the wall—gossiping and recollecting and laughing. I think about our dinners at cafés like Nathan's and Mama's and, for special occasions, some of the fancy downtown hotels. I remember our excursions to Macy's. Shopping was in her blood; she could sniff out a sale weeks ahead of time, hide her item in the size sixteens, and then snap it up on the right day. This frugality—this poverty—drove me nuts, and I promised myself that once I got a full-time job, I would buy something straight off the new arrival rack. When I showed this fashionable suit to my mother, she looked vaguely betrayed. In fact, I wound up giving away the outfit. I came to understand that in our family, shopping was more than bargain-hunting, it was a social event, an outing, an entertainment. While my college friends told me about childhood excursions to museums and galleries, I thought about those shopping trips, but was too embarrassed to mention them.

As I move through the apartment for the last time, I remember flying home from my new job and surprising her at this door. Her face revealed utter disbelief. Then doubt. Then pleasure. Nothing has ever been more gratifying to me than the look of pleasure in my mother's eyes.

First I will pack the clothes. Three small closets. One behind the Murphy bed, next to the bathroom. The dresses are hung neatly, ready to wear to work. The shoes, carefully selected compromises between style and comfort for her corn-encrusted feet, are evenly lined on the floor. I don't have my mother's talent for tidiness but whenever I do manage to straighten a shelf or drawer, I feel an enormous sense of accomplishment, approval, pleasure.

The noise of the traffic outside is deafening. In futile response, I keep turning on more and more lights. It's only eleven a.m., but I am fading. The rainy gray weather seems to have oozed right into this room. During the first few years after I moved back to California, I would often spend the night here with her, sleeping together in the lumpy double Murphy bed or, when her snoring grew serious, lying on the couch. I never slept through the night because of the street noise. Drunks shouting at the Creator. Horns honking. Buses wheezing. Sirens whizzing down the street. And so it became more common for her to spend the night in Oakland, where she complained about the morning racket of jays and doves, but always managed to fall back into a sound, long slumber. I wonder now about her capacity to shut out this inner-city cacophony; perhaps it explains her ability to dismiss my father's static for so long. Perhaps she found the noises reassuring and that says something else about their marriage.

Next I approach the dishes, chipped Noritake that Dad proudly brought home from Japan. Smudged jam jars and dusty cocktail glasses. My heart catches at the orderly line of dirty glassware and I consider how her eyesight has gone in recent years. As well as her sense of smell. How many late nights did I stay awake worrying if she had left one of the unlit burners on? Perhaps it would have been better if she had died that way, her pride would have preferred asphyxiation to Alzheimer's. And I admit this; there have been times in the last year of forgetfulness and high anxiety that I have prayed for her death.

In the cutlery drawer, behind the mismatched stainless, is the Norwegian cheese slicer I bought her. Still in the box. I should have remembered she liked to use that wobbly serrated knife with the wooden handle to cut her cheese. I thought I had ceased trying to improve her when I was in college. Apparently not.

Everywhere in the flat—around her desk, by her bed, on the bathmat—lies evidence of how bad her psoriasis had gotten. Once meticulous about cleaning her apartment, eventually she gave up trying. On the floor around her desk and on the rug beneath her bed are beaches of white flakes which had once been skin covering her muscles and bones.

We did become friends in the last ten years—a break between her mothering me and me mothering her—we did go to movies, had passionate arguments, took road trips. Sometimes we attended Saturday matinees when her friend, the prop man at the Geary Theatre, could get free tickets. Sometimes concerts—she liked modern dance, hated atonal music—when she was feeling daring. But what she liked best was to take the bus to Oakland for the weekend, go out to dinner with me, and then watch TV, laughing and interrupting the show with her barbed comments. I've never understood people who thought my mother was a saint. She was a bawdy, critical, tough old bird. We had roaring fights, fuming silences, hilarious reconciliations. She was a hero, perhaps, but no saint.

All over the apartment now, I find what she would have called, in her better days, J-U-N-K. Boxes within boxes. Assiduously folded paper and plastic bags. Used casings from her casts. Crutches. A three-year-old Christmas card from her boss. Some of the clutter makes sense. Hairpins and pennies lie everywhere. Gelusil. Matchbooks from the restaurants where I took her to dinner. Bureau drawers are littered with scraps of paper to combat dimming memory. "Annie, 7 p.m., Saturday." "Mary will call Friday." But she would forget where she had put these notes and phone repeatedly to check on a date or a plan.

I also find a number of things belonging to my brother, who has disappeared since Mom developed Alzheimer's. He is closer now to Dad, and in this family you have to make choices. Here are his jogging shorts, a knee bandage, underwear, a jacket. I should leave them for Goodwill, but stupidly, perhaps, I take the stuff with me. Currency for some future détente.

The morning Mom entered the nursing home was a turmoil of relief, guilt, and terrible sadness. Nothing compared to my sheer panic hours later when I learned she had disappeared. Disappeared? How can you lose a slow old woman? I found her, back in the apartment, of course, a specter at the end of her couch. "Don't scold me," was the first thing she said. Both of us weeping, I held her tightly as she pleaded, instructed, "I just need one more night here. One more night alone."

The bathroom is the sparest part of the flat. Just aspirin and Merthiolate in the cabinet. Do they still sell Merthiolate or should I donate the vial to a museum? Even the half-full aspirin bottle looks ancient. She never believed in mind-altering drugs, with the exception of that margarita now and then. When Dr. Hanson gave her Valium, Mom asked me what it did and then flushed the whole bottle down the toilet. The peppermint bubble bath I brought her every three months has turned color, from green to purple. So much for Berkeley natural products.

At her desk, I lift the disintegrating drapes, peering out the window at the boarded-up hotel and the coffee shop where she worked for many years. How depressing it must have been for her at times, with such a view, in this shadowy, loud apartment. The furniture is sunken, sooty. The plastic ficus tree thrives in the corner. Turning back to the desk, I pack the *Learn to Type* book. Goodwill can use the typewriter. Her adding machine—she was always proud of her ability to balance her checkbook, another talent I didn't develop—is missing its cord. The calculator remains on the desk as a kind of testimonial.

Almost finished, I look around. My eyes fill again, with anger, grief. I don't mind picking up the pieces; I wish there were more to pick up. Just *this* after eighty years? It could have been worse, is my mother's reply. Whenever I would ask if she regretted immigrating she shook her head vehemently and said here she found work, for a time the love of a man, and she would always have her children. It is hard not to feel guilty in my spacious place across the Bay where I have lots of light, and an answering machine to screen calls from a mother who rings ten times each morning to ask the same question. Yet pointless guilt was never something she courted (she only used shame occasionally, to win an argument) and I feel myself encompassed by a genetically linked trait of practical cheer. Get on with it, I tell myself, she tells me. You've run out of quarters for the damn parking meter.

Left for last are the nightgowns and underwear. Perhaps I'm still terrified of the adolescent taboo hovering over my mother's "confidential drawers." Sorting through the slips, I am struck by how tiny she is. It's hard to think of your mother as small. I have her slightness and if I had a daughter, she would be a short woman, too. I have also inherited a penchant for saving things. I pack the three umbrellas from the bottom drawer—even the one with the broken handle—you never know when you might need a spare umbrella.

Shifting the remaining boxes onto the dolly, I lock Mom's door for the final time. She wouldn't want me to cry out here in the corridor, in public. I compose myself, breathing deeply, thinking there is plenty of time for weeping and raging. There are months, perhaps years, ahead of visiting and listening to and nodding at a person who sometimes reminds me of my mother. Although this feels sentimental and faintly sacrilegious, I am seized by a desire to go shopping at the winter sales. As I press the elevator button, I imagine the two of us together again.

# ALBERT GOLDBARTH

## *My Week Aboard a UFO!!!*

A bitter Wichita, Kansas, winter day. The air is hard, and everything tempted to appear in an afternoon hour or two of tepid sunlight moves with recognition of that hardness, circles overhead as if turning an adamant mill wheel (crows), or raises a lavish tail the shape—and I would swear the brittleness—of the ice-fronds on a window (a squirrel).

Only the cardinal feasting at my neighbor's backyard feeder seems to maintain its usual flickering movement. All of the other birds about it seem to peck and squabble and drably rustle their bodies with what looks like, in comparison, arthritis. The cardinal, though—that *scorch*—is too quick for my eye. I miss so much, its motion seems to be all disconnected jerkiness, as if I'm only given every second frame of a reel of film. In fact, the cardinal *is* the lesson of moving pictures: the human eye is fallible, and can't keep up, and invents. But the movies are paced to match that invention, while the cardinal supersedes it.

The cardinal says: what the universe is, is mainly hillocks of sumptuous curlicued film on the cutting-room floor we'll *never* see. Dark matter. Infrared. The dreams in the skull a finger-width away from yours on the pillow. Flying saucer abductions—so often repressed. Satanic abuse—repressed. The puff of a moment in which we opened our eyes and their first light filled the residual gum of the womb the way light travels through a pane of stained glass, saying its stories of glory in an untranslatable language...

All, on the cutting-room floor.

The Missing Link. *Cut.* Amelia Earhart. *Cut.* The taste of our own tongues. *Cut.* The carefully hidden love life of the cuckold's wife, in a series of gaudily, honkytonkily decorated motel rooms usually highlighted (faucets, phone rim) in a *trés faux* mother-of-pearl, so that her fancy calls back each of those rooms in its place along a lovely nacred curve like that of the local museum's chambered nautilus. *Cut, cut, cut.* Dropped out of the line of ongoing-ness we live along.

The cardinal's motion is snippets. And I know if we could see its movement as fluidly as it happens, as it *really* happens—if we could see with the time geology keeps, or the stars—then there would be no secrets from us, no puzzles, not the subatomic rhumba lessons by which the physical universe is kept in its ver-sion of order, not the fierce pinwheeling outward of the galaxies, not the intimate greed- and lust-noise of the fourplex human heart, no, not the secrets of the hummingbird's tongue or the whale's vagina or any of the antimatter thereof would be opaque to us, and we would know what the gods know, which would be an example of contents overmuch for their container; we would explode, from the burden of wholeness.

2.

*Dropped out of the line of ongoingness . . .*

· · ·

Was the night especially eldritch? Did its moon bob in a wisp of skyey fish-milt, and did shadows splay across the land? We don't know. What we know is that it *was* night, in the Vale of Heath, South Wales, and "a certain Mr. Rhys," who with his fellow work-er Llewellyn was driving a string of horses back to the farm, re-marked that he heard fiddles nearby and thought he'd seek them out to "have a dance." Llewellyn returned alone. Rhys never re-turned. A thorough daylight search of the area failed to turn up Rhys or any clue, and soon Llewellyn was suspected of his murder.

A week had already passed when a local farmer wise in the ways of the mysteries convinced a group—Llewellyn was included—to revisit the scene of the disappearance under his sage direction. "There Llewellyn heard the music. His foot was on the edge of a fairy ring." Anyone touching Llewellyn could also hear the music, "and saw a crowd of figures dancing in the ring, with Rhys among them." Still with one foot in the world of humankind, and with the rest of the party anchoring him in that world, Llewellyn snatched at Rhys, and over the dancer's squealing protests dragged him out of the ring.

Rhys somberly blinked the haze from his eyes. "It seemed to

him he had been dancing only five minutes or so," goes the story.
Lost time.

One hundred and fifty years later it happens again, although in the language of one hundred and fifty years later. At night, on her way home from a class she teaches in urban planning, Elizabeth Ultman's car stops dead. "I don't mean it sputtered and slowed down. First it's going fifty miles an hour, then *bingo* it's stopped." This happens between one small Wisconsin town and another. There's no one around. There's *nothing* around. "And then there's a light, and I'm out of the car, and fizzing up through the light as if I'm an Alka-Seltzer."

Aboard the saucer, she's prodded and rayed and electroded— not ungently—by a team (a pod? a pirate gang? a technical crew?) of the ancient-seeming, yet fetally featured, beings one reads so much about in the literature of contactees. "Then everything misted over, and I woke up back on Earth"—she's found, a little disheveled, a lot disoriented, walking directionlessly on a back-woods road in downstate Illinois. It's seven days since her parents reported her missing.

"I thought I was in their ship for two or three hours, it couldn't have been more than that."

Or Multiple Personality Disorder—two or more coterminous, separate personalities "alive" in the same fraught mind. Each has its detailed history, networks of friends, and distinctive speech. There might be a four-year-old child and then, in immediate segue, a slinky bar girl—both of them whole and convincing. Usually, they "have no recollection of their intervening 'sleep,' picking up in mid-speech or action at the exact point at which they were interrupted, the hiatus ranging from minutes to several years." Lost time. Lost people.

The power the state takes on in Orwell's *1984* is precisely that of the cutting room: an office makes a decision, say, at the Ministry of Truth, and somebody "unexists"; it's not that someone vanish-es, but *never was; is* scissored out of the fabric and out of the his-tory of the fabric. Someone never traced the fluted neck and cool paunch of that sea-green crystal bud vase in the kitchen window, someone never ran his hand across you, trembling, *here* and even *here.* The air reorganizes: someone never ambled through it.

Stains and stinks reorganize. The molecules undo their winding conga lines, and then redo them anew. Australopithecus never existed: the grasses reshuffle. That photograph doesn't exist: the wedding-ring line on your finger tans over.

I'm thinking about the painful weekly witnessing of the marriage of my friends Celeste and Eddie as it further shattered. The atmosphere of an easy social evening in their company would crawl across your scalp. And then "Oh you can kiss my ass," and worse; the make-you-cringe appearance of invective like the living toads we hear about sometimes, freed from the heart of a rock. Those scenes were finally no surprise any longer; so neither was, when they first got around to trying it out in public, like a name for the only child they'd ever have together, the word "divorce."

For that bad while, the people I knew as "Celeste" and "Eddie" were gone, replaced by eerily look-alike changeling friends, who might sport her hoop earrings, his alpaca coat, might even be robotically repeating the conversational tropes I knew to be an "Eddiehood" or a "Celesteism"—yes, but uttered with the necessarily shaken-empty grimness we work up to face adversity; or with the manic overkill of an amateur clown; until nothing was left of the actual "them" except jewelry and a wardrobe. "When I'm with him," she said, "I try to be only a hanger for my clothes."

And as they disappeared in front of me—in space—they made each other disappear in time as well. She *wasn't* there, he swore, the day he such-and-so-forth'ed. Yeah?—she sure the goddamn hell *was*, buddy: *he's* the one who never thus-and-furthermore'd. The fundament of Memory collapsing. Each of them, meditatively studying a face in the bathroom mirror: who *is* that? Brandishing the shears by which we recognize a petty functionary at the Ministry of Truth. "A new future," Bernard Lewis says in his *History: Remembered, Recovered, Invented*, "requires a different past." The mountains of certainty? . . . Snowmelt. Static.

"It *happened*," Elizabeth Ultman says as the final line of her narrative—says it quietly, half to herself, so says it all the more persuasively for lack of histrionics. Do I believe in these other-planetary bipeds with their slightly-more-than-Terran rockets and medical probes, and their oh-so-very-human curiosity? Do I think they ride the skies in swooping paisley-shape space vehicles, and intervene, with people-catcher tongs and great hypnotic eyes, in the muddled affairs of Mineral Wells, Wisconsin? I think not.

But *something's* happening out there, swarming auditoriums at conventions of the UFO-abducted—more each year, and more emphatic. Something's feeding the surface ire of my lawyer-counseled, loggerhead friends. Whatever it is, however deep it surges from, we've all been evicted from Eden, I mean the womb—the original cutting-room slice—and, even before that, been the bird- and lizard-us which wouldn't stay unchanging, which impelled us up the protein/protean process of evolving that's also a process of always jettisoning a former self, until the nurse's casual slap at the just-delivered bloodslicked tush announced our welcome into a world of "God" and "love" and the first tick lost from our personal clock of mortality.

The police call. Midnight, one a.m. Mrs. Ultman? We've found your daughter. Yes, ma'am. She seems all right, but also she seems to have come through some trying ordeal.

3.

"The brain's chief function is selective forgetting."
(Otherwise presumably we'd go mad from detail overload.)
That's the seductive promise of Big Brother: give control unto me, and I'll do the work of your brain for you. Signing up as a lifer in the military, entering the convent: handing over the sticky bother of decision-making.

By this criterion, Erving Goffman classifies together institutions seemingly so diverse as TB sanitaria and POW camps. And in his book *Asylums* he presents a study of the means (the insistence on uniforms; the partial or total replacement of personal doodads from one's former life; renaming—or maybe numbering; etc.) by which identity is erased—"assaults upon the self," as Goffman says. Lost people. Business as usual—*cut*—at the Ministry of Truth.

Of course the first thing clipped from the record is inevitably a competing Truth; the successors to Akhnaton knocked his face from statues and his name from cartouches and other inscriptions *tens of thousands* of times, a monumental (or, more literally, de-monumental) total tonnage of undone stone.

And often, chance alone conducts some nullifying labor for the

Ministry of Truth, on its behalf: it's chance, bad chance of a particularly irksome sort, that Peter Bruegel's last gift to the world,
*The Triumph of Truth*, is lost to us. We only have Karl Van Mander's after-the-fact account of 1640, in his anecdotal book of "the
lives of the most illustrious painters of the Lowlands," and here
Van Mander says, as his ending lines of the Bruegel entry, "he did
one more painting, entitled *The Triumph of Truth*. It was, he said,
his best work." And then he died—in 1569, about fifty.

What was it like? It was large, no doubt. (The earlier *The Triumph of Death* is almost four feet tall and over five feet long.) And
it was...well, I imagine it existing to him as *The Tempest* did to
Shakespeare—as a grace note, a diminuendo ever-rippling into a
kind of patterned awareness that makes cohesive sense of the gala
fury that's long preceded it; as a swan song, as the music flowering
poignantly out of that lifted slender throat the way the rose is an
explosion at the mouth of its stem.

I imagine this is exactly the cosmology Big Brother and his offi-
cialdom most fervently need to obliterate: a triumph of retrieval,
of the wayward, and the condemned, and the abandoned, of the
ostracized and the taboo, of every castoff clipping, glued back by
the force of Bruegel's vision into the read text of the world: a
Truth that *is* the Truth because—so simple, really—it's Totality. (I
see the smoke plumes of a million bonfired books respooling
back into their volumes, char made whole, the very oxidation
halted and healed, and those pages once again awaiting an
absently licked finger.)

I imagine him, he's forty-nine, he's standing in the attic workshop light, it's dawn, as if the world itself has just opened its eyes,
and he's considering this painting, this still-unresolved and all-
things-possible half-completed painting, as a universe he'd like to
enter (soon, I suppose, he will), and touch the artfully positioned
russets and dove-grays of his grand design as if they truly were
the kitchen ladles and skinned-clean market hares and worn-but-
durable saddle pommels and catches of herring and lace trim and
alembics and buttons and harvesting scythes of what we call, for
lack of anything clearer and finer, "the real world."

Here, in this canvas's forming landscape, all of his earlier paintings, that were isolated units of his life, return—and recombine in

harmony. Here, the disappointed hunters silently print their way home through the snow; and the Tower of Babel impossibly rises skyward, looking like a honeycomb half-swiped to a convoluted stump by a bear; and the chopped-apart bodies of infants (this would be *The Slaughter of the Innocents*) are tossed to the snow like food for the scavenging dogs (there are scavenging dogs); and, in their milky sea-chop, Icarus's scissoring legs are a failing call for attention below the vast untenanted sky.

They're here, they're all here, not one is forgotten.

And isn't it a fact that nothing *does* disappear from the submost annals? Every-breath-we-take-contains-some-atoms-breathed-by-Julius-Caesar, etc. Eidetic memory. Aren't we elements out of star and stone, in newer combination? All of those tabloid-belovéd dogs returning to master (the champion, Bobbie, lost in Wolcott, Indiana, and trekking over three thousand miles home to Silverton, Oregon). Doesn't the force behind What Is—despite all of its fog and casual invention—hold on tenaciously?

Timothy Leary on senility: "It improves long-term memory—in walking to the kitchen I remember fighting another kid when we were four, and all of my grade school teachers, and my first date."

The ancient Jewish fortress Masada "is not mentioned in the rich Rabbinic literature. Jewish tradition knows nothing of Masada...[and] even the Hebrew spelling of the name is conjectural." But 1,900 years later, archeology "remembered" the site. "Today, Israeli armored corps recruits are sworn in on Masada. It is not uncommon to see one saying his sunrise prayers in the world's oldest extant synagogue."

Isn't DNA a "living fossil"? Speaking of which...the Dallas Area Rapid Transit Authority halted work on a subway tunnel "because its tunnel-boring machines released pockets of methane gas that had been trapped in the rock when ancient giant sea worms decayed." A cockroach is the planet remembering perfectly, down to the spiracle, its earlier self. It's remembered itself for 250 million years this way—without alteration.

Bad pennies show up again, mnemonics recall the primary colors, and Wordsworth's daffodils won't remain in psychological banishment, no, they "flash" and "dance" etherically but viably from the paved-over levels of mind.

"Think, sweet."

"I can't, I *told* you, I can't!"

A hand on her head. A mother's hand. "The doctor says."

Elizabeth Ultman squirms on her parents' living-room couch. So many days.

"I don't *care* what the doctor..." Stops. / The doctor. / Doctors. / A medical table. / Exam. / "No."

"Honey...? What, dear? Easy."

"No!"

"Elizabeth? Henry, come in here! Hold her! *Elizabeth!*"

"NO! NO! NO!"

.   .   .

Shakespeare's last play is *The Tempest*. By a surface coincidence, Bruegel's last completed painting (that we still have) is *The Storm at Sea*.

A ship is in distress, in darkly frightening heaves of ocean as tall as its sails. A whale, its mouth agape—its open mouth the entrance to a monstrous, meat-red sleeve—is drawing near. The sailors have vainly thrown a barrel its way, to divert it; and have vainly (this was the lore of the day) poured oil of castoreum over the clashing waters, to frighten it. But it isn't frightened. It isn't diverted. It charges on, powered by primal red.

Next, they'll make an offering of Jonah. He gets flung to the waves, and swallowed into those alien coils, and taken on the mysterious journey.

The whale—the mother ship—diving deep into the only outer space of the time.

4.

It also happened to me.

In the days of my own divorce, when, out of the breach of mild disaffection, the bully-boys Chaos and Enmity stepped forth to declare their reign, I felt myself change, in becoming their loyal subject. Not forever changed, I think; but changed so long as they held sway. And some "essential Albert" slipped with frequency out of my grip like a sliver of soap in the dirty bath water she and I had made of things.

I'd look at Morgan—who *was* this? She'd moved out, and on

the days when we convened to sign a paper or haggle spiritedly over some grain of our mutual possessions, I might slide a side-long glance her way as she'd be counting dogeared paperback books or tarnished silver, and wonder who this prim, itinerary-taking stranger could be, as if I were a child who'd been led without preparation to the cult-house of an angry god. Who *was* this angry priestess of his? I was too small; I couldn't imagine.

There must be an army of strangers waiting in each of us. Replacement selves.

What happened on that wickedly chilly December night in 1926 when Agatha Christie—thirty-six then, and with seven respectable mystery novels behind her—disappeared from the world for eleven days? We know that her recentmost novel had met unfavorable reviews, that her mother had died, that her husband, Colonel Archibald Christie, had lately fallen in love with a younger woman and wanted a divorce; that she was sleeping poorly, eating erratically, moving herself and her furniture dazedly around their splendiferous country house at Sunningdale in Berkshire; and that, on the morning after her vanishing, her Morris two-seater was found slid halfway down a bank of iced grass, with its bonnet stuck in a clump of bushes.

And then...? We don't know. Whatever happens, happens in the land of Bermuda Triangleish speculation, it flies to whatever place Hemingway's legendary early manuscripts went to, in the suitcase that was stolen off the train that day.... The chronicles of unexplainable loss. Sometimes, the chronicles of equally mysterious return. Elaine Caplan, surgeon at New York's Animal Medical Center: "I once pulled a whole blanket out of a Doberman."

Evening. Dinner. The clinking of crystal. Eleven days after her disappearance, December 14, Agatha Christie is recognized by the headwaiter of the Hydropathic Hotel in North Yorkshire. She'd been there for the week and a half, a "visitor from South Africa" (she had registered under the name of her husband's mistress), who "seemed normal and happy, sang, danced, chatted with fellow guests, played billiards," and followed the florid newspaper coverage of the search for her (to the public's cost of £3,000) with the same detached interest the other guests gave it. Wearing a plain gray cardigan and green knit skirt the night of her disappearance, and with a few pounds in her purse, she was found dressed stylishly now and with three hundred pounds upon her.

Amnesia? Nervous breakdown? Publicity ploy (in fact her next book doubled the best of her earlier sales figures)? A spiteful and highly ornate attempt to bring her husband's philandering into the open? Even—part one of a fumbled plan to murder (or sully the name of) the other woman? We don't know. She never 'fessed up. All we can do is picture Agatha Christie–prime and Agatha Christie–parallel: one steps into her Morris, and drives herself into the night like a sentence back into its ink; the other steps out.

"Albert—?"

Where was I? Who was this? My mother.

My father had died, and this was my mother, and we were sitting out the ritual *shiva* mourning at her house.

"I'm okay…"

My father had died, the same month the divorce was final. A week before, he'd loaned me the money to carry me through the basic bucks that kind of breakage costs, and now in the other room my sister was explaining to my niece about "up to heaven" and "with *his* mommy now" and the rest of it. And as for *my* mother…the truth is, it was easier being strong for her (or that's the way I needed to see it: that I was "strong," "for her") than it was to be strong for myself in my alternately broken- and hardhearted shambles.

But such strength is expensive, and he wasn't here any longer to offer me loans. This is the only way I can say it: I must have put my prime-self up for hock for a while, pawned myself, in some required metaphysical way, and left the Albert-parallel dealing with grief maturely. Reciting the mourner's *kaddish* unfalteringly.

And what was this image that everybody recognized on the TV screen? This scraggled smoky Y.

"…I'm just going out for a walk for a minute. I'll be right back."

The trail the spaceship *Challenger* made, exploding.

Maybe some of its import did sink in. Outside, I had the crazy feeling the sky was coming apart above me, coming apart then massing back closed. A symbol, I suppose, that I read into the outside cosmos—of my own, interior phasing-in and -out. Is this the tumult that the saucer-spotters tell themselves they see?

Or it was the *Challenger's* psychic disturbance of the national air. Or my sister was right, and heaven had opened up and was closing.

Those are the kinds of things you think at such moments. My breath was frantic, then calmed. January. Anything I said wore a mask: my own breath.

Yes, or maybe it was just that a cardinal flickered above me in passage, and I filed away its ungraspable movement.

Anyway—*some* confusion of wings, that blurred the still clear morning.

## *This Is No Language*

Because I immigrated to the States from Croatia at the age of twenty, people often ask me why I write in English rather than in Croatian. I give a silly answer that it's owing to my Achilles' heel that I do. The less silly—but not tragic—answer takes longer, even though it might start just as well with my injured foot.

When I was sixteen I sprained my left ankle, tearing its ligaments, and stayed in bed with a cast for a month. My brother, Ivo, to become a rock star and sing in English, bought a dozen of Langenscheidt's books in simplified English, with vocabularies of 450, 750, and 1,200 words. I grabbed the one with 450 words, *Greek Myths.* I used to read fairy tales—and to my mind myths were nothing but tales. Under the guise of learning English I read the book in a couple of days, amazed that the meanings of the words came across, through a shroud of letters, from a long distance of memory and guessing; the chaotic letters ordering themselves through my leaps of faith spoke tales of men and women changing into animals, gods into lusty men. After that, that I should understand a language seemed modest and natural, no hubris. Then I read *Dr. Jekyll and Mr. Hyde.* Jovially I wondered whether the new language would change me into a half-man, a half-goat, or a donkey, or, equally astounding, a foreigner. When I returned to school a week later and the teacher asked me to translate a text the class had studied in my absence, I did it quickly. Till then I'd had a D in English—we had two hours a week of English (mostly in Croato-Serb) since the age of twelve—so my metamorphosis into an Anglophile amazed both the teacher and me.

After that, at night I listened to the Voice of America, the BBC, and Christian broadcasts on shortwave. In the dark, ominously sonorous Texan voices announced the Hour of Decision. I'd wake up early in the morning, when the stations went off the air, to a buzz sliding up and down the frequencies. One morning I wrote to the radio station because the announcer had promised a free New Testament. (That was the second letter I had ever written in English. The first I had written when I was twelve with a dip-in steel pen, in calligraphy, to Roger Moore, who'd sent me his autograph, which I kept with autographs of my dead father.) Along with the New Testament came the station's monthly magazine with my letter printed and highlighted—evidence that broadcasting the Good News into the communist bloc worked. Seeing that my words, not Croatian but English, were printed in Canada, indeed gave me a great confirmation in the faith—not in Christ, but in the word: the English word had become flesh, or at least lead on cellulose.

The library in our town, Daruvar, got a present of one hundred books in English from the U.S. Consulate in Zagreb. I read *The Old Man and the Sea* without a dictionary. Then I read the dictionary, marked the words I lusted after, wrote them down on lists, and walked in the park, memorizing fifty a day. During history lectures, I took notes in English. I remember where I learned some words: *obtuse, obtrude,* and *obese* I learned with my feet dangling in the town swimming pool, in water green from algae and brown from the spring rains. *Mob,* I learned at a cool water fountain in the park, as I let the water pour over my forearms to cool my blood. *Bog,* I learned while bathing in a large oval marble turkish bathtub in our hot springs—the letter sequence meant *God* in Croatian. (Now, years later, those tubs are no longer in service because a Yugoslav federal army jet rocketed the building, but vapors still have to do with both bog and god.)

I became so obsessed with English that I wanted to study in England or the States. I wrote to a hundred colleges, and after a year, Vassar, which did not charge any application fee, offered me admission and full financial aid.

The evening before my departure, I found my childhood friends sitting on a terrace in the park. I said, "Tomorrow I am going to the United States." They made no reply, but continued to slurp coffee and blow out cigarette smoke for a long time, not looking at me; then they raised their eyebrows and went on with their conversation about soccer. Offended and supercilious, I walked away: they did not believe me.

At Vassar, after reading "The Death of Ivan Ilych," I wrote a death story, in Croatian. I mailed it off to a Serb friend of mine, editor of a literary journal in Zagreb. His reply astonished me. "What language are you writing in? This is no Croatian: too many Serb words, too much strange syntax, and not consistently enough to be mistaken for experimentation. First learn the language, then write." It turned out that my friend was half Croat, half Serb, and that he was openly and bravely critical of the Yugoslav police state because Serb police had tortured his father on the Naked Island (our version of Siberia) for pro-Soviet sympathies. So he did not see any reason why Croatian should be filled with Yugoslavisms.

Croatian had been Serbanized for decades to fit the Yugoslav model, ever since the thirties and the dictatorship of King Alexander Karadjordjevic. I could understand why one would wish to distance oneself from Serb imperialism even in language. But whatever vocabulary I had grown up on was a living language, so why not use it and savor its nuances, all the more multiple because of a mix of cultures—and politics, too, is a form of culture. People in Daruvar did speak the way I wrote. The project to ethnically cleanse my native language depressed me since I did not want to deal with any kind of nationalism. Tito had made Yugoslavs terrified of the very word. But had I forgotten my love for English? I read in English, studied in English, wrote papers in English, talked in English for many hours in the dining halls. When it came to talk, students lived in an old-world rhythm. So I had a real friend to turn to, the English language.

I translated my story into English, brimming with conceit once again. Then my new American friends began to point out my awkward syntax—too many winding sentences and misplaced adverbs and wrong prepositions—and lapses in diction: too much mixture of the high and the low style, and too many British words. This sounded familiar. In American culture a strong drive to purify the language by eliminating excessive Anglicanisms still lingered. I fell from the frying pen into the melting pot, in which not many ingredients were allowed to melt. In college, while I was invited to admire Joyce's word permutations, I was discouraged from experimenting, from deviating in any way from an imaginary standard English. I was invited to admire Faulkner's lengthy acrobatics but held fast to the rules of basic word order and exhorted to copy Hemingway's short sentences—which was all fine, but the accountability to write in the least common denominator of the language seemed to me deconstructive, inhibitory, humiliating. Soon, though, I realized that I needed the advice; in Croatia, under Austro-Hungarian and German influence, people strained the language, writing monstrously convoluted sentences. Under bureaucratic communism, where obfuscation was desirable, newspapers became unreadable. A comparative study of national newspapers showed that the Yugoslav press used more acronyms than any other press. I had not deviated from the Croatian style: the longer and the more confusing my sentences were, the prouder I was. My American teachers now taught me to make "precise" and "vivid" descriptions, to select *"le mot juste."*

These days after spending dozens of minutes making word choices, I am disconcerted when friendly writers tell me: "You know what? Your being a foreigner is an advantage. You accidentally pair up words in a strikingly fresh way. You probably don't even notice it. We native speakers have to work at it."

And when I don't get a shade of a word because I haven't grown up listening to American lullabies, my friends patronizingly smile; when I don't do dialects because I haven't grown up with them, my friends treat me as a comic alien, an aquamarine creature. Tell me about the advantage, then! My writer friends show me how superficial my project of writing in English must be. Where in me are those soulful contacts with words that can be made only with mother's nipple between your naked gums? Sometimes, for example in the movie *Crossing Delancy,* you find a stereotype of a foreigner who writes in English, and who for that reason is *superficial.*

But thousands of immigrants write in English as a second language—sometimes superficially, but more often deeply, because their immigrant experience does free them as well as hurt them. I can think of only one expatriated American adopting a foreign language and writing in it, Julien Green. How come? Isn't adventure the spirit of America? Or is the mythical adventure only the sort that comes *to* America, rather than adventuring *from* America? I marvel at American linguistic unexileability.

Yes, it's often troublesome writing in ESL. English, which at first came so quickly and easily, melodiously, in the long run proves highly evasive in its shadings. This is what David Godine, for example, said about a novel of mine several years ago: "Although I found your novel interesting, I cannot make an offer because it sounds like a bad translation of a good book."

And maybe I did sound like an English translation—maybe still do—because I read a lot of literature in translation, afraid to be "limited" to American outlooks. Still, do I have to put up with people constantly knocking down the language in which I write? Why don't I go home? Go back to Croatian?

All right, this is why. I don't know the new Croatian, nor the old Croatian. I remember how when I received a visitor from Hungary in my hometown, Daruvar, she conversed in Hungarian with the local Baptist minister at a dinner party, and she laughed at his Hungarian. He had grown up in a Hungarian family in Croatia, in isolation from Hungary. Hungarian had changed in several decades, but his belonged to the last century. My Croatian is an anachronism, or anatropism: it does not belong to another century but to another country—the Socialist Republic of Croatia in the Socialist Federative Republic of Yugoslavia, the country which has in the meanwhile vanished. The use for my language is gone. In the last three years, Croatian bureaucracy, to prove it is independent, has undertaken a revision of the language. Words I had never heard appear in daily newspapers. For example, *u pogledu toga* (in regard to this) has become *glede.* The linguo-ethnic purge affects not only Serb words and communist jargon but many words of foreign origin. *Avion* has become *zrakoplov* (air-floater, literally). Some Turkish words remain, such as *bubreg* (kidney); perhaps Croat bureaucrats like them because many Serbs hate these words as a reminder of the four-century long Turkish invasion of Serbia. Not only couldn't I keep up with all the changes, but I don't like most of them. Languages mix, inter-link, and there's no such thing as a pure language. Language is used for mixing, not for refusing to communicate, though of course in many cases, yes, we do use language as a shield, a wall, psychologically, and obviously, politically. I prefer the mixing and the shades that come from various regions, like coffee aromas.

Another irksome thing about Croatian. Recently I bought a directory of Croatian writers, published in 1991 by *Most* (*Bridge*) magazine. (Ironically, it's Croats and Serbs who have demolished the bridge in Mostar.) Almost all the Croat writers come from and live in the major cities—Zagreb, Rijeka, Split, Osijek. I met some. They all sounded like the radio, stiffly correct, whatever that happened to be at the time. That, too, I would not want to adjust to. I would use the Daruvar—and Western Slavonian (different from Slovenian)—regional, provincial expressions. But that would not go over well in Zagreb, where I'd be immediately branded as a provincial unless I changed my speech into either standard Croatian (as though there were such a thing) or a Zagreb dialect.

If I meet a Croat, linguistically I'm walking barefoot on nails. Any word might be construed politically to show me to be a Yugoslav nostalgic, which I am not, but my not having purged my tongue of Serb words could create that impression. (For a year I studied in Serbia and that increased my spontaneous Serb vocabulary.) Some words peculiar to my region (many of them Czech, German, and Hungarian) could create a complex relation of Zagreb versus the provinces. I am not interested in proving that I am not a provincial. And if I become interested in that, I prefer to prove that I am not a Zagreber but an American, that is, a cosmopolitan—a different kind of provincial.

And this linguistic insecurity with Croatian is not unique to me. I exchanged several notes in English with a new writer from Croatia—Sanja Brizic-Ilic, now residing in Venice, California—when I edited an anthology of stories in English as a second language, *Stepmother Tongue*. Recently when I talked on the phone with her, we spoke in English. She told me she did that because she was not sure what Croatian was anymore—just in case I was.

This politically induced linguistic confusion particularly affects small and weak countries such as Croatia, but though I sympathize with the confusion, I am not going to throw myself headlong into the muddy waters and write in Croatian again. I never liked jumping into the water headfirst. Stones may be too close to the surface. So I decide to stick with my English, such as it is. Here at least I have an excuse. No matter what awkwardness I commit, I can still say, What do you expect? I'm just a foreigner.

Do you miss Croatian? people ask me. No, I say, though I may, on some hearthy level. In Croatian I could do old dialects—I have a good ear for them—and I could play with old voices, with untranslatable shades of words, their histories and even their politics. But I'm not going to lament. I don't need to pull a Nabokov—the way he tried to show what he'd lost in translation by writing down the original Russian word and explaining its shadings as he did in *The Gift* and *Ada*. I don't mind losing some good stuff in translation because I have lost much more bad stuff.

The politics of Serbo-Croatian and Croato-Serbian and *Croatian or Serbian* (as for a while the language was called)—this was the only language in the world with a hyphen, and then later, even more absurdly and confusingly, with an *or*—these politics troubled me beyond words even when I lived in Croatia. I must admit I did not enjoy being forced to write compositions in the Cyrillic alphabet once a week at school. (In Croatia we wrote in the Latin alphabet.) Nor did I like getting conscription notices from the Yugoslav federal army in the Serbian variant of the language (*ekavski* rather than *ijekavski*). The army used only blatantly Serbian syntax, vocabulary, and it was a mostly Serb institution. Serb officers had ridiculed and abused several friends of mine in the army for their speaking the Croato-Serb rather than Serbo-Croat. Nor did I like Serb nationalists in our town artificially using Serbian vocabulary to make a statement. But I equally disliked the awkward purification of the Croatian language that followed.

So it's not that much of an accident—certainly not just an ankle injury, though more crippling—that I left the former Yugoslavia. Even while I was there physically, I tried to be away linguistically. After all, at the medical school in Novi Sad, I took down notes in human anatomy—in English.

Politics and words give me a headache, and a jaw-ache. (Switching between Croatian and English I did once hurt my jaw joint! I could barely open my mouth for days afterward. Perhaps it was a form of linguistic hysteria? Psychologically, I preferred no language at all rather than the choice between the two.) Feminists have rightly pointed to the patriarchal aspects of English, and I understand their purges even when they result in "or" expressions, such as he or she, no matter how awkward. I have been tempted to quit the business of words altogether, but I persevere, partly because I could not concentrate on anything else with sufficient enthusiasm, and partly because if it was enthusiasm I needed, I could not only wistfully recall but safely revert to one experience: grasping for tales through foreign words, as I used to do with those Greek myths. I have tried to learn other languages to recreate the revelatory sensation I once had with English, but after many bouts with German—and some with Greek, Hebrew, Russian, French—exhausted, forgetful, I come back to English, like a shaggy dog in heat, returning home and collapsing in his shanty on the familiar old rug that comfortingly smells of urine. Or better, it smells of goat turds. Having had chevre cheese in France, I can't help but think there's something ineluctably cosmopolitan—more than tragic—about that goat turd smell. English words to me are goat turds. With them, I don't feel like a linguistic exile. Despite the stink, I sniff in them the freedom to be away from Croatia and Yugoslavia.

## Holocaust Girls/Lemon

*We are the Holocaust Girls*
*The Holocaust Girls, the Holocaust Girls*
*We are the Holocaust Girls,*
*We like to dig in the dark.*
   —to the tune of "Lullaby League and
      Lollypop Guild," from *The Wizard of Oz*

### 1.

You don't have to be Jewish to be a Holocaust Girl. But it helps. It helps to have been born in the U.S.A. to parents born here, without accents. But it's not necessary. And you don't have to be a girl, either. What matters most is you must love suffering. You have to pick at wounds. Or you can be fat, or otherwise encumbered by what is considered an affliction. Or beaten, or beaten down, or despised. You have to see your pain as a dark hole you could fall into. You practice falling into the darkness. You immerse yourself in descriptions of horror. You stand in the library aisle in the World War II–Europe section and thumb through familiar pages. You stare at the photographs of the skeletons, compositions you've memorized. You watch your tears make little dents, like tiny upturned rose petals, on the pages.

### 2.

Sometimes, what you have to do is jump.

In Lvov, Poland, which was also known as Lemberg, and which became Lviv, Ukraine, the Jews were trapped with no place to go. It was 1943, the time of daily roundups and shootings. *Aktions.* The Jews of the town were cornered. There was no escape, only the possibility of hiding, disappearing. A number of daring, desperate souls stepped down into the sewers and lived there. Eleven of them survived, among the rats and slime and damp, without sun, for fourteen months. They paid jewelry and gold and devalued zlotys to the sewer workers who found them and kept them alive. When the Germans retreated, when the Russians reclaimed the city, the

Jews emerged from the sewer. They were pale as larvae. Covered in filth, backs hunched. Dripping. Their pupils had shrunk, too small to hold daylight. Everything looked blood-red to them, or black and white. A crowd formed and stared at them; they seemed like cavemen. The group found its way to an empty apartment, climbed the stairs. The young mother among them, Paulina Chiger, took her two children to a window and opened it. "Breathe the air," she told them; they breathed, looking down at the street through a blood-red haze. "Breathe deeply the fresh air."

The Aryan side of Warsaw, it has been said, looked the same as it always had except there were no Jews. The ghetto revolt began in April 1943. In early May, before the ghetto burned completely, after particularly wrenching battles, a Jewish resistance fighter named Tuvia Borzykowski, along with seven of his comrades, slipped down to the sewers to pass to the Aryan side. It was dangerous; all day the Germans had been sending gas and grenades into the sewers. After walking and crawling underground for several hours, the eight men saw a huge light. It could only be Germans looking for fugitives. Borzykowski and his friends froze, resigned to discovery and death.

But instead: two friends and a sewer worker, looking for survivors of the revolt. They carried candy and lemons. Borzykowski took a lemon. "It was the first fresh food we had tasted in months," he remembered. He bit into the lemon, ate it, peel and all.

That is what the Holocaust Girls yearn for—to want and appreciate something as intently, as specifically, as that whole lemon, to love the air and sun as much as the family crouched fourteen months in the sewers of Lvov.

They want to greet lovers with that lemon, night after night. They want to see the dark hunger, the preternatural need. They want to *be* that lemon, consumed by one survivor after the other.

That they can't explain this to anyone is part of their tragedy.

3.

The Holocaust Girls want to haunt people, from far away, from another childhood. They want everyone to know they have unreachable souls. They want people to understand that their beings can't be easily grasped or understood, the way it's hard to make the link between the half-century-old photo of prisoners in a bunk, the face of young Elie Wiesel circled, and the glossy photo of the now–Nobel Laureate. It's hard to make the cognitive leap from the one stick among other sticks to the American man in a suit, wearing matching socks, silk or otherwise tie, shoes with names, perhaps (wingtips, oxfords), with his hair cut profession-ally—in short, civilized. In short, named.

4.

Whenever the Holocaust Girls have a task to do, when they're standing in the fifteen-items-or-fewer line at the supermarket, and the other customers are looking at *People* or turning the pages of the *Weekly World News,* the Girls are looking deep into the darkness of Liz Taylor's newsprint eyes, they're imagining roll-call, when prisoners in the camps lined up—fifteen degrees, wooden clogs, thin filthy clothing, empty stomachs—standing hour upon hour. They're wondering if they would have collapsed. They're wondering if they would have formed alliances with strangers with similarly shaven heads, if anyone would have loved them hard enough or life fiercely enough to have saved them crusts of bread and to have slipped them filched potatoes. "Do you have a preferred card?" asks the young cashier at the Jewel, and the person in front of the Holocaust Girl hands over her card. The Girl waits, sighing, while the cashier summons an older employee to ring up the six-pack of beer. The Girl always finds it odd that teenagers aren't allowed to push the register buttons for liquor, but the Girl feels strangely reassured in the shelter of let-ter-of-the-law rules. A few minutes later she's trudging down the street, one plastic bag dangling from each arm, on her way home. Home, home, says the Holocaust Girl under her breath. She knows how lucky she is to have always had a home, keys, heat. She looks at her wooden floors and doesn't allow herself to wish for a big rug, Oriental, magenta with a golden mandala-like design, flamboyantly fringed, deep pile. Comfort, it would sing to her, comfort.

## Belongings

At twenty, he has square feet and wide bones and thick coarse hair; a smile that, while slow, is generous. You want to pet him.

From all the bulk and fur of him you wouldn't expect his hands, magician hands. Quick. He draws caricatures in charcoal, plays Bach on guitar, juggles bean-bags, and folds colored papers into deer and mice, cuts perfect stars with scissors in one snip, hiding, always hiding the effort.

"Ancient Oriental secret," he tells you when you ask. Understand that he drills himself in skills, wrests them painfully from nothingness, trains his hands as if they are wild animals.

Maybe it was night and cold. (According to almanacs, it snows in Seoul.) Concealed by darkness she took him to the orphanage, laid him on a table cunningly designed to revolve, outside to in, accepting infants without revealing mothers. She walked home, still tender from the birthing.

He is seven months old when they send him to us on an airplane. We wait at the terminal to receive him, our son. Thirty babies are carried from the jumbo jet by men and women with dark hair, dark eyes. He is among them, asleep, full head of black hair sticking straight up, skin warm as a fever, voice deep when he murmurs. He doesn't cry. They pass him to me. I cry. I undress him in the airport bathroom like a gift I can't wait to open. His diaper is dry. My hands are shaking.

Maybe it was daylight and, unashamed, she strode to the orphanage to deposit him. She had meant the conception to be a tool with which she would pry open a distinguished place for herself. Too late, she saw it was her censure. She wiped her hands on her clothing going home.

His brother is inside my belly, a quick little fetus seven months old, conceived on the day we decided to adopt. Magic decision. He turns in my womb, taps at me from inside as if curious. I laugh. The Korean men smile for politeness when I laugh, not knowing the joke that is passing between my children.

Maybe she was charmed by a stranger, felt his love like the sun's light and opened herself, morning flower that broke laws with its tenderness. That night when she walked to the orphanage, there were stars above her, stars whose light had begun many hundreds of years before. She knew about stars, she understood that many hundreds of years hence, this moment would be seen by the stars she saw now. Pure light.

They hand him to me, asleep, then bow. Two men. I look at them covertly. This is how my son will look someday, this tall, this dark, this broad of face.

Bewildered, he opens his eyes, dark eyes, so dark I can't see pupils in them. He comes to me nuzzling his forehead in my neck, moving his head back and forth, back and forth, as if saying "No, no, no, no, no." He lays his head against me then sleeps again. Once more, the men bow. They don't know my tongue. We smile. We compare the name-bands on our wrists. Mine. His. Theirs. Yes, they match. We smile.

Maybe this was the punishment she meted out to her lover: to dispose of the object created by his passion and thus make all his passion negligible. Maybe on the way home she ate chocolate.

He is five and in school. He hates school. He says he fears he will fall out of line. On his first day, he asks me to pray to God to see if God can change his eyes. A child told him God could.

I pray a curse on the child who inaugurated this hope in him. I rake leaves in the yard for a week, turn soil, prune branches, master anger. I brush aside pebbles and branches and sticks to discover an ant hill from which emerge a thousand ants. Within seconds they have filed themselves into lines. I shift a stone to divert them. I uncover, with a start, a lemon-colored toy car in a square hole, a small pebbled driveway for its entrance, a pine-cone roof. I kneel and look, intrigued, my heart opened like a flower to the sunlight.

Maybe she was a New Woman, one who stepped away from the governing social order in which, ant-like, individuals served as cells of a greater organism. She was warned that when isolated, one died; when shamed, one lost her place. But she stood brave against it, loved a man despite it, bore a child because of it. In anger she conceived, in triumph gave birth; in hope she gave away her son to live where she believed he would be free.

He is a mewling infant with moist, soft skin, infected navel, self-containment. I do not know him yet. A foster family keeps him. Five sons. They carry him on their backs and feed him rice milk. They sleep with him on their heated floors and tease him so he moves his head back and forth, back and forth, as if saying "No, no, no, no, no." Outdoors, the country smells of minerals and earth, inside, of boiled rice and tea and garlic.

Maybe she hid herself, magician girl, appeared always to be obedient, all the while breaking with the order that sustained her. She bowed as if she obeyed, but broke, then feared the law. She hid the hot fetus within her, the fetus that would cut her, like a sword, from her mother and her father and her husband-to-be. Isolated, she would die. She crept, terrified, to the orphanage's turntable, hoping to abandon there, fear. But fear went home with her, and with it, grief.

He hoards things. I call him a pack rat, though he knows I'm intrigued by the things he keeps. He refuses to cut his thick horse-mane of hair. "Are you saving it for something?" I try to show reason.

"It's only peach fuzz," he answers. "Ancient Oriental peach fuzz."

His room is a labyrinth of beautiful things: guitar, girlfriend's pillow, drawing board, the I Ching, broken clock parts, Holy Bible, plastic jars, blue glass bits, stuffed dogs, burnt-edge corks, wooden boxes, rolls of tape, his baby blanket.

I kneel and look. This, I say, is because, at seven months, he knew that a person could lose everything, his people, his belongings, the smell of his ground, the hot floor where he sleeps, the white robes of ceremony, even the sound of his language. He does not know he remembers these things, or remember that he lost them. I do not remind him, but I let him hoard; I let him explain.

"What happened to your real mother?" asks Clark, blond four-year-old living next door.

"She died," he says.

"So," I say. And maybe she did. I would have.

## Brother

The house on a dirt road, a stream running by it.

In the dream I am always fighting to stay. Someone tries to move me out, an ex-love, someone who thinks my things should remain in boxes, someone who would knock down a wall, make guest rooms, "brighten the place up a bit."

Of course, I would never want to live there again.

Dogs, cats, us children, we had white ducks. The mother duck was nasty and once stuck her bill into Aunt Greta's skinny back while Aunt Greta was sitting on the wooden footbridge. Sent her screaming into the creek.

Pearl and Allan, sister and brother. We call her Pearl, sometimes Pearlie-pie, which she hates, loves, hates it. Too much giddiness in the house. We call him Bub, Bubby, and by the time I reach my teens, Bro, Brother. Brother, come here.

We are driving this time, 1988, in my car. You are accompanying me on my current move, five days from San Francisco to Houston, and I am relieved to have you with me. Outside Fresno I pull up to a gas station and make a quick call back to S.F., some last thing I have forgotten. It's nine a.m. and August in the dun-colored valley, and while the phone rings on the other end, I toe the asphalt to see if it will give, not hot enough yet, and glance at you waiting patiently in the passenger seat. You've done this before, waited for me while I was stringing out a series of last-ditch reasons why I should stay in touch, not leave, hold the fort.

—There's so much we...

—Yeah, there's...

—A lot we could talk about.

—Uh-huh.

The house on a dirt road, a stream running by it, nestled at the base of a valley a mile or so long. The stream is named Log Run, after the logging industry that flourished in these hills in the eighteenth century, a point of history I use at school to construct a personal mythology for myself. We are, I think, rugged country people. In July 1967, we are moving out. Dad is two years dead. Mom and I can no longer take care of the house and grounds. You are a college student, only home summers, and Pearl is off in New York. You and I have rolled up the rug in the living room and we can't stop laughing. I can't. You're making me laugh so hard I'm crying and I tell myself I am doing the same for you, but when I look, you are busying yourself, tending to the lamps. What are you doing? I can never remember your jokes. Where's Mom? Running an errand, perhaps cleaning the kitchen floor in the new red house in town. That's why we're running the hi-fi full blast, bellowing out "The Bells of Rhymney" on the Judy Collins album you gave me last Christmas. I sing loud because the living room looks so peculiar without the rug.

This is not unlike sex, I think to myself, letting up on the accelerator. A figure in dark clothes cutting across a snow-blanketed field, getting closer and closer. Who is it?

Often, when I am with you, I see us in that house stomping around on the bare floors, giddy with loss. We are ragging each other with puns, well, uh-uh, not quite. You are five years older than I, and it seems to me you've always led in wordplay, generously inviting me in, in fact, creating—as I suspect most older brothers don't—enormous room for me to dance and spin around you. You talk. I repeat what you say as if it were my own, you roll on the floor, I jump on you, you laugh at my jokes but they're your jokes, my, your, my body. Yours.

*My towel, your towel.* A game he played with you that I don't remember. Nor could you, until it came up for you in a gathering of men who were trying to understand their rather complex relation to their own bodies. I don't remember but I can see it as you tell me. Our handsome, healthy, robust father on his knees leaning over to bathe your—well, I can see him but I can't quite see you at three, four, five? Your soft flesh. Not mine. The game starts with the sound of the water gurgling into the drain, you are standing up, unsteady on your chubby legs, and Daddy has the towel. Soft, luxurious, the anticipation of being wrapped and wiped, his strong hands sweeping across your body with the towel, rubbing between your legs and around your buttocks where the dripping water is just now beginning to cool. "Is this— my towel? Or your towel?" He holds it up, pulls it to his chest, thrusts it toward you, and pulls it back. You look at the towel, and look at him. His face is rosy, his blue eyes sparkle with the pleasure he takes in you. "My towel? Your towel?" You teeter a little, your lips damp and slightly open, eyes darting from the towel to his face and back again. You're ready to burst. When you do, you are like a little pot boiling over. He sweeps you up from the tub and rubs you silly.

Didn't he? Isn't this a game he played with me?

You roll up the rug in the living room and we arrange it next to the neatly stacked boxes, making sure all is ready for the movers. There must have been movers, but I can't remember them. We are being good children, sober in our responsibilities, though you seem much more an adult now, not yet twenty-one.

We decide to take the last hike, up the trail into the woods, past the place where we always cut a tree for Christmas Eve, on up to the fresh spring, a stopping place on the way up and up. I always drink from this spring, no matter how little water there is, because I thrill to my story of our land: that we have a place so wild and untouched it does not have to be mediated by questions about its purity, unlike the sullen creek it falls to that sometimes gives us earaches when we swim it in the summer. The spring bubbles at the base of a ravine. I love to tear down the slope through the gnarling pines, to leap with accumulating speed over downed branches, twisted and rotting trunks, always seeing myself in a race, a pack leader, the best of my girlfriends, a challenge to my brother, or me and the dog out prowling, wild and loosely ripping up the forest floor on our way to a head-first dive into that crack of damp and puddling earth.

We embrace this last hike soberly. We are two good soldiers about to be relieved of duty, making a last tribute to our father, who ritually took this trip with us during a full moon. The route forms a great circle that takes us bushwhacking through to a trail that leads up one side of the hills to the very top of the valley, and on back down following Log Run to the road and home. By day we walk carefully, stopping often to check the view behind us. Still there. Lycoming Creek drifts along the cliffs out below the grove of pines he planted long before I was born. Up the other side of the ravine we follow old electrical wires along the path of tree stumps.

I used to jump on each stump, turn toward my father, and sing out in a mad prepubescent chant, "Ladies and gentlemen, take my advice: I now pronounce you man and wife. You may now kiss the bride!" By the fourth stump I was besotted with myself; my rendition of a televangelist-cum–commercial announcer opened the way for whatever laughable thing was meant by the coming together of men and women. Swinging up the path, my father, his plaid flannel shirt settling loosely across his broad chest, would whistle and clap.

Goodbye, we say. Goodbye, goodbye. Trees, old shack deep into the forest of the next hill. Who built it? The boarded-up window hides a hairy monster behind the broken plate glass inside. Agh, no, it's only the reflection of my eye, my lashes peering back at me through the crack. Safe here. I am safe here. Goodbye, the opening into the cornfield at the very top of the valley. The pulling out of the woods, the great gallop across open space toward the single tree at the center where we have arrived, breathless, on top of the world looking down.

Going the speed limit, I look over. A buzz of landscape profiles the haggard beauty of your face. I know your body without looking. I have just left behind a man in Oakland whom I think I love, whose broad body I held through the night, pursuing its sweep, swimming out to meet the curving, lolling wave of his embrace. I don't know when I'll see him again. You and I joke about how as adults we've only been able to be close when one of us helps the other move. Two years living across the Bay from you and we saw each other ten times? Maybe twenty? But haven't we always been close?

Sometimes, when I think of you: Congenital immunological deficiency, let him rest now, Janie.

Mommy, is Bubby going to be all right?

Yes, of course, she says brightly. Or she says—does she?—Oh, he's doing the best he can. Her worried face. I can hear her talking, she murmurs to Dad in their bedroom, and, every once in a while, he murmurs back.

Once, looking over her shoulder. You are sitting in a chair in your bedroom, wearing boxer shorts and a robe opened and falling away from your body. She sits holding your leg in her lap and doesn't know I am right behind her, but you do. You look up at me and look back down, noncommittal, your chin on your chest, your hands perhaps loosely clasped across your stomach. There is a basin of hot water, a clean towel, gauze, tape. She wraps her fingers around a lump with a tiny hole in it on the inside of your thigh. She squeezes. I must gasp when the pus erupts from the hole because she turns her head sharply, not removing her hands. "No, Janie! Get away!" which is neither a hiss nor a shout, but—do you remember this?—a kind of warding off. I retreat, and carry with me the way the hole and the red swelling seem to float within your flesh, foreign and invasive, making your leg something different, something other than you.

"My brother gets abscesses," I solemnly learn to say. Otherwise, a mystery. Delicate. Two steps forward, two steps back. Once, that sledding accident: a raucous sweep down the hill slams you into a tree. A cut on the forehead and stitches turn to blood poisoning and the air of the house thickens with worry. Somewhere below me a mother and a father move about. I am in bed upstairs, morning light streaming through the frosty window. Pearl's there? You are in the hospital and we wait for you to come back home. I never go there to see you because healthy children aren't allowed.

Warding me off. Do you remember?

I know your body without looking. Mostly unlike mine, except for the ways we carry ourselves, a certain set of the shoulders when walking, the way we gesture with our large hands when we speak, an occasional inclination to mutter during intimate conversations through a hand clamped over mouth and chin.

Some doctor in a hospital years later will come up with a name: Job's Syndrome. Perfect, you'll say. The man plagued with rashes and boils who sits in a corner, cursing his fate, and you'll laugh.

A car, enclosed space, cutting across territory. My home in boxes you helped me pack. Take these books. Leave these. Let's stop
for coffee, Bakersfield, cut east through Tehachapi, let's have some
country music. Fine. That's fine. What were those things Dad
made, we don't have a name for them. The stained-wood rectangles
he made to fit around the backs of the couch legs, that kept the
couch from slamming into the wall when we'd throw ourselves on
it? Who else in the world would know, or care, about that?

I know your body. You showed it to me over the period of a
year. Two? I was eight, you were fourteen, thereabouts. A mother
and a father move about somewhere. We are upstairs in your
room, behind the closed door. How does it start? You're making
me laugh so hard I'm crying. You make your penis jump like a
puppet, and you make it talk. "Hey, you, little girl!" it says.
"What's your name?" Penis, is that what we call it? You invite me
to touch it and I do touch it. It bobs up and down and I am
delighted. Your penis is always erect whenever you show it to me.
I think this must be its natural state until I catch you sleeping
naked one afternoon and see it curled in a small heap. I am startled but say nothing, don't wake you. Later, you seem to be fine.

Later, you come to know my body. You begin to touch and
probe. I know it's a game, like being tickled only better. I don't
have to scream to make you stop. I enjoy myself. You have been
my brother and my friend all my life. You have read all of *Johnny
Tremain* to me and stopped to explain the part where Johnny
injures his hand. You yourself have big hands and you showed me
just how the wound kept Johnny from using all his fingers, kept
him from practicing his trade so that he had to find another way
to survive and, because of injury, become heroic. That's how I
remember it.

We take turns applying our hands to each other's bodies. Much
laughter. Perhaps, occasional silence. Uncertainty? A moment of
uneasiness, looking at you while you finger me. What comes
later? There must be stories we made up to go with this, too, but I
can't remember them. I don't know the word "sexual," and this
has nothing to do with the climax and release that I will learn
through practice years down the road. You are jocular, intent. We
never finish what we've started, but remain circling.

After a while, the parents figure it out.

You come into your room, or I come into your room, always your room, and one of us closes the door. You sit me down and tell me in a sober voice that we can't play this way anymore. Mom and Dad have taken you aside and explained to you that what you are doing is a very bad thing. I laugh that off, suggest a way to fool them. "Let's just pretend we're playing a game called 'Rip' where we rip each other's clothes. And, uh, the person who rips off the most clothes wins!"

"No," you say. No, we can't.

We do. Don't we? Not that game, and not a game any longer. Outside now, without regularity, almost random. When we catch each other. Once in the barn, where the Crosley has been put to rest. You have become more instructive, and more obscure. I am less certain of your face, the hurried way you tell me what to do. We take our clothes all the way off and you tell me to lie down on the Crosley's back seat. You get in and slowly lower yourself over me until your penis barely, just barely touches the lips of my vagina. We are trembling. I see your body up there, hovering over me, the pink flush and the pallidness of it all mixed. I'm excited and appalled. Your body and my own stretch away as if we both now belong to something else, as if our names are being stripped from us, and the dust-moted air and the roof of the car and the dark wooden beams beyond the open car door breaking the slants of light pouring through the barn walls—all, all of it wheeling away from us before we stop, we stop there.

A figure in dark clothes cutting across a snow-blanketed field. Who is it?

Sometimes I have thought unkindly: Well. He's certainly made a career out of that story.

In the late seventies we are both drawn to the movement against violence against women. I stay there for several years, then move on to U.S. foreign policy. You commit, become an activist, build an organization of men who raise consciousness about the male proclivity for dominance, and the resolution of gender conflict through aggression and violence. You counsel sex offenders, have developed programs for working with teenagers meant to allow them the sense of their own bodily integrity, their own voices, and also meant to teach them how to tangle with the abuses of the adult world. In adult public workshops you sometimes refer to your own experiences, how you lived in the country, a special—a "bright"— boy from the middle class among the working-class families strung up and down our road, how you were isolated from your class- mates because you were too smart and perhaps too sickly on occa- sion. How you had in late adolescence a few trysts with girls across class lines, girls you would not be seen with about town, girls to whom you told yourself you were benevolent, unthreatening, that you were different from other men in the way you intended to get sex. Sometimes you talk about me.

You tell me about a peculiar thing that happened to you as a consequence of your work. An irate mother, a psychologist, has called you up. She thinks you have been manipulating her daugh- ter. You were making a videotape with high school students who were writing and acting out scripts meant to teach them how to protect themselves against sexual violence. Her daughter scripted and acted a story about being molested by a "cousin," who turned out to be her brother. The psychologist, to whom this was news, denies it and has threatened legal action. On the phone she has accused you of being a known child molester. She says you are guilty of once, over a period of time, abusing your own sister.

I laugh that off.

Sometimes, when your friends meet me: Oh, you're Allan's *sis- ter.* I've heard so much about you.

A house on a dirt road. Two cars, trees, dogs, cats, the angry duck. A mother and a father move about somewhere. I know so much about you. Once, 1974, I am out of college and working as a landscaper on a construction crew in your town, Colorado. I have been reading *Lesbian Nation* and sharing it with another woman on the crew because I think, *Maybe,* and, *Well, what if?* You are miserable in graduate school and living with a woman whom you suppose you love and who supposes she loves you, but all that will change. You and I have been to see Bergman's *Cries and Whispers* and have gone for several pitchers of beer because we are so wrought up. How I remember: Three sisters, one of them dying, and a maidservant. The two healthy sisters cannot minister to the third, will not touch her. They circle in separate agonies, falling back from the deathbed, always upright and fiercely cold in each other's presence, but once alone, disintegrating. A glass shard and blood, a sexual wound, self-inflicted.

We drink glass after glass.

Circling in the snow-white landscape, the deep reds and black of the interior.

I am obsessed with the maidservant, how she climbs into bed with the dying woman, opens her breasts to her, gets behind her and holds her with all of her body. How the woman dies that way, a full embrace.

You are my brother across the table. I think you know everything about me. We are drunk when I walk with you back to your house, a circuitous route toward mine. Years I've spent tailing you on woody trails, or out following the weave and kick of your body threading creek water. The informing and surreptitious pleasures of your room. Would you have known me, tracing my hand across your sheets when you weren't there, repelled for an instant by the spots of blood crusting the fabric? How ashamed I was and didn't tell anyone, afraid I couldn't love you enough for the solitary days and nights you spent, your body in torment? You lean against a tree in front of your house and I lean into you, take you in my arms and kiss you, keep kissing you, losing myself in your mouth. There is so much personal pain. Some of it has made me special. You stop me. We stop there.

You referred to this once as "that time you wanted to screw."

Warding me off. Do you remember?

You tell me she was always so "chipper." Everything's going to be all right. So that, when you were feverish, in terrible pain, you felt you had to pretend for her, you had to protect her from how badly you were hurting. "I remember doing that when I was five years old," you tell me, when you are forty-two. What you say to me the times I've come worried but cheerful to visit you in the hospital: "I'm fine." I never know what to do. When have I strayed too far or come too close, trying to fill you up with myself?

Always, as these things happened between us, it was the both of us. Never just you, and never just me. A mother and a father somewhere.

On top of the world looking down. Enclosed space. Cutting across territory. You were the last to see her alive. One minute talking to her in the hospital bed. The nurse, you said, called her E-*liz*-abeth, musically, as if she were a little girl. She could barely speak and you were there to watch over her, be cheerful. Then she seized up, her body arched in the bed. I try to see it, be there. The last thing, as they push you back, pulling the curtains around her. They tear off her shirt, eclipse her head, face. The large failing breasts. Pump frantically at her heart.

Going the speed limit.

The haggard beauty of your face.

## Poetry and Manners

*"Ages with a highly developed decorum find verse a
relatively easy medium. Recent ages have clearly
a low decorum and have run toward prose."*
—R. P. Blackmur, 1951

Imagine what Blackmur would have said about our age, circa 1994. Toward what does an age run with almost no decorum? Toward self-indulgence and the collapse of civility, he might have said. To Hell, I would be tempted to add, which is even south of prose. But I wonder what he might have said about verse, that now somewhat quaint word. Would he have discovered that when there is very little decorum, a strong need for it arises, as it has in current poetry?

Even though I know that Blackmur was using "verse" to include the greatest of poetry, I should note that these days the word suggests the equivalent of impeccable manners and a light touch, like someone who might be a good dinner guest, but with whom you wouldn't want to drink late into the night. Poetry is quite another thing, criminally beautiful at its best; at its least, we expect it to be surprising, idiosyncratic, perhaps, like a visitor who drops by unnanounced full of compelling news. A poem must create its own decorum, by which I mean that the poet— through the admixture of style, content, diction, form—makes the poem behave in ways which we as readers are persuaded that it should behave. The poet establishes a set of proprieties that need not be proper, but which become the poem's norms. Thus, the repetition of "fuck" in Etheridge Knight's poem "Feeling Fucked/Up" is as normative as the recurrent use of "flew round" in Wallace Stevens's "The Pleasures of Merely Circulating." From my standpoint, both poems behave rather well.

Poets sometimes write as cultural outsiders, boldly, aggressively. They let us hear the shout, the cry; their burden, poetically speaking, is to find a decorum even for rage. Other poets are more connected to their particular tribe, are insiders, if you will;

they act as its ears and eyes. They aren't necessarily against any-thing. They are the artificers, the makers, who *add to* the real by recording the less than visible world. Their burden—because their voices will be quieter—is to find a decorum for their poems while avoiding the merely decorous. Most poets, of course, are some combination of outsider and insider. By registering what it feels like to be alive and attentive to the pulses of their lives and to the world itself, by attempting to be radically accurate, their man-ners are likely to be as various as those at a dance where rival gangs with different tastes in music have been invited. Mostly, though, as history shows, even outsiders consent to be graceful and balanced because they have a stake in time-honored ways of being beautiful. Yet one need not be conventional while obeying poetic conventions. Versifiers are those who obey conventions without criminal intent.

My worries lately have to do with limits—both in poetry and in the culture. There's been a need to correct the lack of rigor in free verse. While I understand where this need comes from, it seems to me that the best practitioners of free verse have always been rigor-ous; it's not a large concern. But we do see a great deal of sloppy poetry and it exists more than ever in a sloppy world, which seem-ingly has gotten crazier, out of control. I need not list the horrors. But the horrors make all of us want to pull back, rein in. It may be why I wish for a greater civility in my small world. If I don't know what to do, say, about how murderous our streets have become, maybe I can effectively complain that people speak in movie the-aters while the movie is on. Pathetic, I know, the scope of my sense of reform. Abuses which arise out of anger and deprivation are, in many ways, more understandable to me than simple bad manners. All of it, though, is intolerable. And this is the climate in which we write our poems, words on paper which will correct nothing in our own time.

Outsider poems once were wilder than their historical moment, like "Howl" in the fifties, or extravagantly resistant like "The Waste Land" in the twenties. I'm not sure what a great outsider poem might be now. My guess is that its tenor would need to be subtler and more delicate than its historical moment, that it would be most astonishing in what it addresses yet refuses to give in to. It would surely not be the poem of outspoken complaint or rage; that poem would sound too much like the voices we regularly hear on the news. The conflation of social ills and the behavior of poems: a dangerous yoking. In an age without decorum, I need to be careful of my powerful inclination for order, if not law. I might get too much of what I desire.

Repression, as we know, can be good for language. It is often an advantage not to be able to say what we mean. We might have to resort to fable or parable, to indirection of some sort. We might have to be ingenious. For those of us who came significantly of age during the late sixties in America, repression was the dirtiest word we knew. Off with the shackles! Down with authority! Sides were clearly drawn. We knew who was right, and it wasn't them. Righteousness is certainly not very good for language. The slogan can easily start to replace the well-turned phrase. Most of us had to be wary of that. Not surprisingly in retrospect, some of the best poetry in America at this time was written by poets skilled in traditional meters and rhyme who turned to free verse. Berryman, Wright, Merwin, Kinnell, to name just a few. They had a set of noble manners from which to depart.

Meanwhile in the streets, many were finding, in the name of justice, good reasons not to be civil. As the civil rights movement itself evolved we learned not to expect angry people to be polite. Vietnam, linguistically speaking, produced passionate rhetoric and the language of confrontation, not quarrels with oneself. The sexual revolution arrived and many of us learned what beggars during the Golden Age must have observed: it wasn't happening to us. But then, amazingly, it was, or did, or could. Chivalry, thank someone, was dead, but so was courtship, which was a further blow to language; we needn't be very imaginative or charming to achieve our goals. And, in concordance with all of these phenomena, the psychological community was urging people to get in touch with their feelings, as if this might be desirable. For perhaps the first time in history, people went around baldly saying what they thought. On another front, Muhammed Ali, with style and humor, made public what we now call trash talking, thus invigorating the language while diminishing its value. Sportsmanship, a form of civility, was on its way out, too. Howard Cosell proved how obnoxious, yet contagious one can be by "telling it like it is." No one wanted Emily Post back, but we were developing a subterranean, growing wish for Miss Manners. A few of us needed our wrists slapped, our mouths washed out with wit.

To write a sonnet at this time was at best the act of a literary Republican. And I seem to remember the word fascist being applied to a metricist once or twice.

In the early seventies, when I was teaching Marcuse and Norman O. Brown, I was fond of defining civilization to my classes as an agreement by the many to give up, for the general good, what we really wished to do. Didn't we all wish to be polymorphously perverse? The answer seemed clear. But that was when civilization seemed to be someone else's tired idea. We'd forgotten, or chose to forget, the barbarians at the gates. We forgot because we needed to be the barbarians for a while. The civilized folks were dropping the bombs, and offering rational explanations. We railed and rallied against them. And, in private, we were sure—because it felt so self-evidently good—there was a connection between prolonged foreplay and the end of violence.

In fact we were convinced that rationality was the smokescreen of the powerful. The surreal, to many of us, seemed the only way to approximate the real. Robert Bly's impassioned "The Teeth Mother Naked at Last," in its bold associativeness and leaps of logic, was emblematic of the decorum of the time. His "Counting the Small Boned Bodies" ridiculed the euphemism "body count" by exaggerating it, and addressed the growing debasement of language. These were outsider poems that spoke intimately to the counterculture, thus becoming insider poems for much of the poetry-reading public. Adrienne Rich, to cite another influential voice of the period, was a soul in the process of seeking her own society, which she founded and helped create. Her *Diving into the Wreck*, for example, was an outsider book that arose because she correctly saw the dominant culture, as well as the language of that culture, as antithetical to who she was and might be. We could say that her book was, along with others, evidence of another kind of decorum—revisionist in its goals, direct and confrontational in its diction. While lesser poets employed the surreal as a language-game and were little more than inventively silly, and political poets less able than Rich wrote the equivalent of editorials, the best poets, as usual, remembered that in order to gain our deepest assent they had to engage us with language that went beyond wild invention and correct sentiment. (It could be argued that much of the current attenuation of free verse has its origins in the practice of surrealism without vision and right-mindedness without discovery.) Few of the poems of protest had the radical decorum of, say, Berryman's *Dream Songs*, Merwin's coolly radiant enigmas in *The Lice*, or Kinnell's "The Bear" and *The Book of Nightmares*, to name just a few. Whatever source these poems came from was not immediately evident; one might say that they had surpassing manners, manners that transcended their occasions.

In the seventies, when I lived in a small town in Minnesota, I found myself more capable of generosity than ever in my life. I could *afford* to be generous. If someone needed help, I could assume that this was a singular occurrence, that similar demands on my time and emotional resources wouldn't again be made very soon. Also, everyone in my Scandinavian-American town seemed to have a profound sense of boundaries, which meant that invitations to cross them had measurable poignancy. I suspect that people in small-town America, especially in the Midwest, do not feel the same loss of civility that I've been lamenting. They fear economics more than they do each other. A knock on the door is almost always neighborly. Generosity is a necessary good in sparsely populated, rural areas, and it seems that those of us in more urban environments need to recover a sense that we are dependent on one another.

At the same time I should point out—to make sure I don't romanticize small-town life—that otherness is the great problem in such towns. How to survive as an *other*? The small town may be a paradigm of how boundaries can permit latitudes, but it is also a place where people on the fringe, say homosexuals or intellectuals or African-Americans, develop a hunger for larger and more hospitable boundaries, those offered by cities, or, in another sense, by poems. There may be implications here for open and closed forms. That aside, true community—beyond physical parameters—often arises when you realize that everything you've thought peculiar to yourself has been thought or even lived by someone else. This is how poetry, not to mention literature in general, manifests some of its most exquisite manners; in the course of being true to itself it makes a gesture to others.

From a writer's perspective, I like what Flaubert said—I assume about the balance between repression and freedom—"Be regular and orderly in your daily life, so you can be violent and original in your work." And Donald Justice's admonition that a good poem should exhibit "the maximum amount of wildness that the form can bear" is also relevant, though again it's equally useful to think of expanding the notion of form to accommodate even more of the wild. In the last several years, the long poem and inclusiveness in general seem to be making a comeback.

I have to strain to remember the eighties, but if a new set of manners developed then in mainstream America, it was the manners of indifference. Technology and Reaganism had much to do with this; together they were powerful determinants toward insularity and selfishness. I think of the Walkman as the symbol of the decade. A solitary person in public, say on skates, listening to what no one else could hear. And I think of Reagan being called the Great Communicator and am awash in alienation, as I often was at the time, since he never communicated to me or to anyone I cared about. Oddly, perhaps not so oddly, I think it was a lively, if not good time for poetry in America. More people than ever seemed to be writing poetry, though it's not so clear that they were reading it. Still, intense pockets of interest existed throughout the country, people hungry for language and soul-work, for what technology and the marketplace couldn't provide. Their numbers were comparatively small, but I was heartened by their existence. And yet, with the exception of, say, a C. K. Williams or a Louise Glück book, there was little of the anticipation that my friends and I felt in the sixties and seventies for the next collection of poems by our favorite poet. Or had I become more a captive of my prejudices and sophistication?

The New Formalists came about because free verse had lost its radical verve. Many of its practitioners had begun to misunderstand its freedoms. Its worst practitioners forgot or never knew that free verse needed to be formal, a new set of formalities for every poem. Is it merely coincidental that comparable failures of limits began to exist in the culture? On *Oprah* and *Donahue,* people speak about the awful things they did to one another in front of one another, and in front of *us.* What induces them to do this? Money? An insufficient sense of shame? It's unfair, of course, to liken such people to even bad free verse poets, but we can assume something similar is missing from each: The positive aspects of a compelling tradition haven't been assimilated. Nothing is making them wince. Good writers wince when they fail themselves and their craft. Good *people* wince when they behave badly.

At a dinner party recently, a woman—after a few drinks—asked what was wrong with her criticizing her husband's paintings in public? Didn't she have the right, she wanted to know, to express how she felt? Her husband was present in the room. I think she thought she was speaking as a feminist, and it's possible her desire to criticize his paintings was occasioned by some real and private grievance, though her style made it very difficult to be sympathetic to her. Now, in the history of boorishness this was a small thing. No doubt all of us, at one sad time or another, have believed our private disquiets or hurts so important that they merited the discomfort of others, including innocent bystanders. Or, more likely, we were simply overwhelmed, and were not "believing" anything at all; we found ourselves out of control. Such singular occurrences are almost always forgivable. The woman *did* call the next morning to apologize. It was an act of revision, a little cleaning up after a sloppy night. We welcomed it, and her. Who doesn't—in both writing and life—need second chances? Hers was an act of revision, but what would have been more difficult, and therefore more praiseworthy, would have been an act of grace—a seldom used word for obvious reasons.

While she was criticizing her husband's paintings, I kept thinking of Frost's wonderful line, "We shall be known by the delicacy of where we stop short." I've also thought of that line at countless poetry readings where the poets—without the felicities of language or form—told me more than I could possibly want to know about their private lives. In a culture with little or no decorum, and a comparable lack of personal responsibility, sometimes what we choose not to do may be how we will be best known. It certainly will be a hallmark of grace. Too often, as William

Meredith reminds us in a poem, we consent to be our worst selves whether we're drunk or not.

Is civility, if not grace, always what people in power have a vested interest in maintaining? What stake, if any, do or should the powerless have in civility? And is this relevant at all to the world of poetry and poets? Blackmur once said of Wallace Stevens: "...erudite, by which I mean intensely careful of effects." I would like to think that the angry, the disenfranchised, would wish to be intensely careful of effects, though in ways perhaps that are ruder than those in power might like. But that's probably my wishful thinking. The disenfranchised, acting individually, often just want to break down the door, regardless of the consequences. They don't want to be criminally beautiful, nor do they want to be particularly efficacious. As writers, whether we're outsiders or insiders, we try to control how our words behave in conjunction with one another, or we allow them their legendary promiscuity. In the case of protesters, revolt is either in the control of people profoundly erudite (in Blackmur's definition), or the merely furious will act alone and cause havoc, and not be useful to the cause. Successful rebellion and successful poetry writing are finally the provinces of experts, who learn as they go. Rebellion and poetry writing may begin in grief and rancor, but they must be brought to conclusion by passionate tacticians. Coleridge's notion of poetry as something with "more than usual emotion and more than usual order" may apply here. The civility I want from poems harnesses all sorts of unruliness. The civility I want in the culture is fraught with the fact that people are even more unruly than words, sometimes for good reason, and that I believe in democracy and its annoyances. I of course don't believe in democracy when it comes to poetry. Poets try to exercise a sweet tyranny over their words. That their words often seem willful is one of the difficulties and, I should add, pleasures of composition. On the other hand, the willfulness of have-nots, and of competing claimants for fairness and justice, increasingly suggest the irreconcilability of inequality and anyone's vain desire for an orderly life. I acknowledge this and acknowledge at the same time that most of the culture, only part of which includes people with legitimate gripes, has become murderous, shameless, insensitive to language and the daily lives of others.

It's the small things that irk me most, probably because they're the most likely to repeat themselves. The salesman on the phone addressing you by your first name, the sullen clerk responding with a shrug. Which is why it seems to me there are more opportunities for grace than ever before. I love James Wright, for example, who knew that "the hearts of men are merciless" and therefore was able in a poem not to vilify or caricaturize, but in fact sympathize with President Harding, that easy target. And I love the kindnesses of people who have no reason to be kind to you, but are. Such kindnesses happen every day amid all the other occasions for despair. Once we would have called them normal kindnesses, but when they occur in a climate in which fear and self-protectedness are daily givens, they are noteworthy. If I said earlier that we shall be known by the delicacy of where we stop short, I would like—without invalidating that sentiment—to amend it. We shall be known by our uncommon gestures, our surpassing gestures. Perhaps here is where poetry and manners most truly converge. Both, at their highest levels, involve doing gracefully what is *not* expected of us.

## The World and All Its Teeth

I'm very worried when I see the boy from my writing workshop, gloomy Chico Lopez, strolling down St. Mary's Street with Julio, who used to live next door. This looks like a bad connection. They're talking busily with their heads together, carrying sacks. I've never seen Chico look so animated before. Is it just that we don't ever expect to see people from our classes out in the world? I'm still troubled when I order a taco at El Valle and Irene from Smith Elementary School brings it to me. Wasn't she the girl who was going to go to the moon?

Then I run into Julio's grandpa, Pablo Tamayo, in the grocery store ten minutes later and we fall upon one another, kissing both cheeks, and his face which smells like sweat and dogs even smells sweet to me.

"Guess who I just saw," I say, but he answers, "Kiss her, too," thumbing towards Elena, and I bump heads with Elena, who is lifting the bags of groceries into their two-wheeled cart which they will drag home through the blazing streets. They both look thinner, as if their strands have been stretched. A big black bruise marks his left cheek and he strokes it. He says he fell down the steps by the river. He says it doesn't hurt. "But I been lookin' for you. That day I fell down, I was gonna come over to your house. I need some—help."

I tell Elena in my mixed-up Spanish that her lady friends keep knocking on our door, looking for her. They want the woman who reads the cards and I point them back toward City Street. Elena nods, but that doesn't mean anything—she always nods. We did not know she had a reputation as a *curandera* and reader of cards until they moved two blocks away and her clients in their long white cars started coming to our house looking for her. Michael used to think those cars were social workers, but I didn't believe it. A social worker would have done something for them long ago. I found a sack of faded Loteria cards thrown on the heap of trash left in their backyard after they moved.

La Chalupa, the woman in the rosy canoe. El Venado, the poised deer. I took them home and spread them on our front porch to air out the smell of dog.

Today I say, "Stick around five minutes in front of the store and I'll drive you." He shakes his head at me like Naw, naw, but I know they'll be out there. I race around the store grabbing cilantro, tomatillos, a single poblano pepper. In the car he will peek into my bag and laugh. "You know what to do with all that?"

We used to close the windows on one side of our house to keep the smell of their house, the powerful doggy waves, from drifting over. Their house smelled stronger even than pork chops cooking. You wouldn't think people could stand it. Maybe living inside, they grew immune. Once Pablo left his cracked jacket lying on our couch and it took two days to get the smell out. Maybe if you loved dogs you wouldn't notice. Later our windows had nails in the corners to pin them tight against burglars and the stench seemed farther away.

It was said Pablo sold dogs that were not his own. Some mornings a dog might be tied to a tree and by afternoon it would be gone. I asked him once, "Where did you get that fluffy gray dog?" and he said, "From someone who didn't need it."

"But Pablo, that's not right!" and he wagged his finger at me.

"Right, right, since when have things been right?"

I was just as curious about his customers. With all the loose dogs wandering around downtown, who needed to buy one?

We missed so many little things after they moved. We missed the way Pablo stood in his front yard pointing the hose toward his one big tree, whistling. He stood and stood, water coming out in a tiny stream. When I asked why he didn't turn the hose on harder, he stared at me. "For what?" He said trees didn't like to drink too fast. He had the patience of a porch swing, just hanging there, waiting.

I missed his lit-up face when I'd take over bowls of chili or soup. He couldn't believe our chili tasted so good without any meat in it. "I heard of chili without beans, but no meat?" He held his spoon of chili up to the light and shook his head. He said we were strange. I even missed the three red flannel shirts he wore on top of one another when the first northers blew through.

You would think, because of the criminal Julio, who lived with Pablo and Elena, we could not have been such good friends. At first Julio just seemed like a bum who sat on the porch and drank beer with his shirt off and his tattoos blaring and his ponytail down to his waist. Later our lawn mower and bicycles vanished and the muddy footprints led straight from our garage to Pablo's back steps. Then our VCR and jumble of video tapes disappeared from our bedroom and we offered Julio a reward to get them back for us. He said, "I'll do what I can," without blinking. A few days later he returned to say sorry, they were too far gone already.

Another day I glanced casually into his messy bedroom to see one of my very own Portuguese coffee cups sitting on his dresser. Where did he get it?

For years I thought he was their grandson. I argued with people in the neighborhood. Alma Vasquez said, "Grandson, my foot." Finally when Pablo came to us waving his census form, asking for assistance, he had to explain. If he had adopted the criminal as a baby years ago, the criminal would still be his son, yes? He wished it weren't true.

After they married, Elena wanted somebody to put little white clothes on. They hoped and hoped, but no baby came. Then Pablo met a pregnant teenager who gave them her baby. Even as he spoke so many years later, the element of invention remained distinct. You could almost feel him pulling tiny threads out of the air.

"I thought"—and here Pablo put his head in his hands and stared down at the wood of the table—"I thought it would all be different."

Sometimes he mentioned that Julio was on his back. Once he came and cried in our living room. He kept asking, "Can't you get him in jail?" He always thought that because we had been to college and read books, we might have some power.

I called the police department and spoke with a detective. "We have someone—uh—in our neighborhood whom everyone including his father—uh—knows is doing bad things. He doesn't work but he always has money. He sits on his front porch drinking beer from a large bottle in a paper sack at ten a.m. watching everybody come and go. By the time we get home our screens have been slit and our doors chiseled open. He has been seen selling VCRs at La Paloma Lounge. The owner says she's afraid to call the police. Personally I think she's making a little off the side. The Paletta women at the end of the block say he used to peep through the windows at them when he was just a little boy. To see them in their underwear. We are talking bad news here, sir, major bad news, and no one knows what to do."

I wish I could have taken the Richter scale measurement of that detective's sigh.

He said the usual. He said, "We have to catch him doing it."

A hundred pieces of Sunday newspaper blew down the street.

We never caught him, but when he felt we were looking harder, things stopped happening. Maybe they happened in neighborhoods we couldn't see. Then Pablo came to say they all had to move out because their landlord was going to fix the house up and sell it. We were sad to lose Pablo and Elena, but glad about Julio. They'd found a little garage house behind a bigger house on the next street. It was the color of a peach. He didn't know if he liked the idea of a house the color of a peach.

"But you'll have the river right at your back window."

"What did the river ever do for me?"


They're waiting in front of the grocery store. I drive them home and Elena keeps shuffling her legs in the front seat and snorting. "You have a *lot* of friends," I say to her in Spanish. "The big car ladies." Pablo says he hates their house, it's too hot. Everywhere is hot. Ten years ago I stopped saying the word, at least during the summer. It felt redundant. Pablo says, "I'm coming over to talk to you." He asks about Michael and the baby and where is the baby, anyhow? I say he's at the house with Michael because it's too— hot—to bring him out.


Then I reluctantly attend my own writing workshop at the West Side Food Bank. Somehow these people received funding to slap a poetry group in between their slices of white bread and bologna and their bean and cheese tacos. I was so shocked when they called to invite me to conduct it, I said yes. Now I'm stuck. We have six weeks to go.

So Chico arrives with his Spurs hat on backwards and Felice in a see-through blouse with a stiff lacy push-up bra underneath. I think she's fourteen. And Arturo won't ever sit at the picnic table outside with us, but has to sit way off by himself on a ledge by the trash can. Because of Arturo, thank you very much, I have to speak at a high-decibel level at all times. He doesn't want anyone to look at his paper. And Sergio without any paper or pencil ever and Ricky Gray Eagle who turned his face away when I said I liked his name and Marisela who really *loves* poetry and wrote a stark narrative about borrowing a clove of garlic from her neighbor for her mother. And Leo with his limpid dark eyes and smooth brown jaw. I would probably have dreamed of kissing him in high school. And three elementary kids who somehow got jumbled in with the rest of them.

I say to Chico, "I saw you with my ex-neighbor Julio the other day, are you friends with him?" and he says, "Aw, miss, don't go messing in my private business, okay?"

So I say nothing more. About that. Directly. But later when I'm talking about dignity as regards somebody's grandfather in somebody's poem, I'm looking at Chico out the corner of my eye hoping he applies it to the people he's hanging with. It's easy to see how anyone can go down the tubes.

This Tuesday they ask me to sign some schooly-looking documents vouching that I've really seen them. I say, "What are these?" It turns out my class was offered in the beginning as a trade-off for lingering detentions. I feel like mayonnaise. I feel like Little Debbie twinkie cakes.

But their hard-won sweaty sentences make up for it. I show them how to break their lines. Their hearts are already broken.

> *My grandfather loved me*
> *he really liked me too.*
> *He gave me a ring of silver*
> *to wrap around my dream.*
> *He gave me a story*
> *the size of six horses and three sheep.*
> *He kissed me when I went to sleep.*
> *I felt the smell of roses*
> *circling my pillow.*

*He said he would always be here*
*but he's not.*
*He got shot.*

Then they all want to write about someone being shot. And the worst thing is, they all know somebody.

Later I'm reading their papers on the couch at home and writing little hopeful notes in the margins when the big knocking comes at the front door, boom, boom, boom, the way Pablo always does it, and Michael answers. Pablo staggers into our front hallway and falls against the wall. This is wrong. This man used to be a boxer. He carried trays of fresh doughnuts high above his head.

"Help me move," he whispers, "into the housing where old people live."

We help him to the couch.

I bring lemonade. His sweat is dripping.

Michael says, "Someone hit you. Someone beat you up. Where did they hit you?" and Pablo points everywhere, head, shoulders, arms, stomach, legs.

"It was Julio, wasn't it?"

Pablo closes his eyes.

"You can turn him in, you know. How old is he? Thirty-five? Forty? He's been living off you forever! Kick him out! Are you waiting till he kills you or what?"

A whisper. "She won't let me. She still thinks of him—like that baby—he was. That she took care of. I told you. But it's worse."

"Worse?"

"Remember that time I fell down on the middle of the floor in the night and Elena come to get you, she couldn't remember how to call the Emergency, and you called the ambulance and they took me to hospital and I was in hospital with that diabetes for a few weeks and then I came home? Well, in that time I was gone I think something happened to make her—think of him more like a husband than a son."

"What?"

"She acted different when I got back. Like—the love changed.

She stood behind him different. She fold his clothes better. She took him food in bed."

A long silence in which I am thinking of Elena in her baggy faded aprons and what else he could possibly mean.

Michael, as usual, is brisk and businesslike. Michael never acts shocked. "Well, I've told you for years, as long as you let him live off you, he'll do it. As long as you buy his food and pay his rent—what more could he need? If you kicked him out, Pablo, he might have to work! Hardly a tragedy! If you can't kick him because you're afraid of him, then you get help, like social workers or police. You could get a restraining order if he's beating you up. Kick him out of your house and onto his own two feet! Pablo, he's got feet! All it would take is a little follow-through. And come on, you want to go apply at the elderly housing place? I'll take you."

If Pablo moved there, Julio couldn't come with him.

Pablo, as usual, isn't listening. He's staring up at the curtain rods from which I've hung old quilt tops. He's staring at light filtering softly in through lost patterns of blue boys on blue rocking horses and calico bow ties. He won't really apply for elderly housing because it would make him feel—elderly. I remember the nude Kewpie doll tattooed on his forearm and lean over to make sure it's still there.

Michael touches his shoulder gently. "Pablo—we care about you. You're getting hurt."

"But if I kick him out, she'll die."

"Why?

"Because taking care of him keeps her alive. I just know it. And if she dies, then it will be just me and the dog and the boy probably come back by then to get even." He's talking about the one worst-looking scrap of a dog that he always keeps, not the ones he sells. He's talking about a bad mess of a man as a boy. He's talking about the way problems tangle people up so hard we're ruined for years. Tied in knots. You pull the string but it knots. You open your mouth to say something new, but the world opens its mouth faster and bites you.

"Pablo," I finally speak again. "This thing you said about Elena and Julio. You didn't mean you thought—while you were gone—do you think?"

"Yeah yeah yeah, I think it. I think maybe he was drunk and maybe she was already sleeping. Maybe she got confused or something. Maybe she thought it was me. I think it happened more than once, too, because he's acting real—close with her. God! She seems more shy, girly."

Elena, at eighty-four, is eight years older than Pablo. She's an old eighty-four, too. I've seen ninety-four-year-olds that looked and acted younger. She wears those heavy knit stockings and clunky shoes like grandmothers in Bulgaria. Sometimes a scarf wrapped around her head. She never picks her feet up more than one inch when she walks.

By now the juice has sweetened him. He's stopped breathing so hard. "You need to do it," Michael says. "No one else can do it. If you don't do it, the story will just continue and you'll be in it."

Outside, the street-sweeping machine rumbles by with its giant squeaky brushes. Pablo nods. "I'm—in it. How did I get in it? I was just—baking doughnuts. Sugar. I was just standing there with sugar on my hands and this soft lady come in and I have to lean way over the counter to hear her. She takes twelve doughnuts that first day and another day come back and take eighteen. I say to myself she must have a big family, no? But it turns out she's working for them nuns, them sisters at the church who like doughnuts one day a week. She was cleaning. She told me later. She had nobody. I'm still married to my first wife then, but she go off with this guy named Rico pretty soon when the kids get big and boom! It's like they all went off together. I'm by myself for a while before I marry Elena and lemme tell you that time by myself was the worst thing that ever happened to me. Ever. Nobody waiting. No rice in the pot."

"But peaceful?"

He looks at me sharply. "Whadda you know? Who cares, peaceful? It's *sad*."

And I know he won't do it. He won't kick the criminal out because it might happen again. No two ragged white socks pinned up on the line by somebody else to console him. He'd have to do it himself.

I hear the strangest low-decibel dirge rise up out of the couch and the wooden floor and the fringes of the rug. It seems to come from the stack of papers I threw down. It sounds like heat hanging on for months and months. It sounds like the deep shy voice of Erica, one of the elementary girls in the workshop, who finally gave me a paper yesterday. Bent and scraped and smudged. A story about what it's like to sleep in the car. Every night her father sends her to the driveway. She says there aren't enough beds in the house. The wind presses against the car on cold nights and makes her hug her sheet, the one she keeps balled up in the back seat. But hot nights are worse because she has to leave the windows open.

"I like the car," she writes. "I can't drive it but I know it real well. I know that little hole where the ashtray used to be but it got lost. I poke my fingers in it. I have good dreams sometimes and other times scary. What if a bad person came to the car and tried to get in. One door won't lock. I sleep with my feet to that door. If you're walking down the street in the dark you can't see if someone's sleeping on the seat. My daddy told me that. I love my daddy."

# Dora Rewriting Freud: Desiring to Heal

His erection startled me. At first, it seemed merely to point me out, acknowledging my part in nothing more than the simple and various human desires in our encounter: the desire to be loved and to be healed, the desire to be naked before another and thus to be understood utterly and to be wordlessly explained, the desire for a life beyond this one, the desire to represent what is the truth. What could be more natural, that I was there, a witness to another man's ailing body. For a fleeting moment, I, too, wished to be naked, to be as available to him in his suffering as he had made himself to me. The sheer exclamation of the pleasure in one person touching the body of another—I have been a doctor long enough to know what joy and power there is in the laying on of hands—must have frightened me, so explicit and insistent it was in this form. Gradually, I let myself become aware of my stethoscope, my white coat, my cold hands in their latex gloves, as they all continuously emitted their signals. The entire milieu of my chilly, fluorescently lit office seemed to be warning us both of my very great distance. I excused myself abruptly, saying in an oddly flat voice that I needed to get more liquid nitrogen to finish burning off the wart. I let the door slam shut loudly behind me.

In considering later what had occurred between this patient of mine and me, I found myself recalling to mind what had drawn me to medicine in the first place. Before I was completely aware of it, I had begun to write at my cluttered desk, allowing myself to feel the presence of his body again, to touch his fragrant skin (I suddenly recalled his cologne) without the barrier of my latex gloves. Whether it was another poem, or a long love letter, or the beginning of this essay, I cannot be sure. What I do know is that in the act of writing I encountered again the shocking, empowering energy of a great desire. A desire that belongs, the way I see it now, to all of us.

My earliest conscious recollections of disturbances within my own body are those of the minor bumps and bruises whose pain was alleviated by my parents' kisses. Kissing was the most potent and intoxicating of all elixirs. Pure physical contact had the power to cure. My body, before I was capable of truly hurting myself, could be reconstituted with my mother's moist breath in my ear as she sang me a comforting song. The pleasures I felt, more intelligible to the child's mind than my parents likely suspected, are in great part what led me later in life to the healing arts. I desired to be made well in their eyes, to be acceptable, to be beautiful, to be kissed. My desiring of my parents had a good deal of its expression in the ritual of the tearfully extended, oftentimes exaggerated "boo-boo," presented for their fastidious attention. To be well meant to be loved.

Music and magic, and particularly their expression and absorption in the physical body, were the primary modalities for healing in the bits and shreds of Latino culture that I encountered as a child. My grandmother's dark bedroom, windows covered by thick red-velvet draperies, as if to keep out the weak winter light and the sad images of scrawny trees, seemed more a shrine dedicated to the various saints before whom she lit candles as offerings. I would hear her praying or singing quietly in Spanish, believing, perhaps, that she was restoring health to an infirm relative back in Cuba whom she would never see again. Though I could not understand most of what she said, I let my heart be carried by her evident hope that her words could reach across the oceans. My mind was transported in her songs, all the way from the sickly Elizabeth, New Jersey, landscape, sailing triumphantly above the grim refineries and landfills, to the verdant, lush Cuban countryside where I imagined she had lived. Healing had a voice and seemed rooted in a most potent physical longing, a longing to be with the ones you loved. Later in childhood, my family's Venezuelan maid, Bonifacia, would make me and my brothers special potions from tropical juices and other secret ingredients. Some potions caused laughter, others could restore friendship, or ease the pain of a lost pet. I still believe in the inherent magical properties of her concoctions, just as I understand the placebo effect: she, too, taught me that healing is also a consequence in some measure of what the mind desires.

As I grew older, doctoring and desire became more interconnected. Playing doctor, the almost universal childhood experience in American culture, began for me, my brothers, and my cousins at around the age of eight. The enactment of adulthood was all the permission we needed to examine our own and each other's genitals freely and without shame. Though the myriad implications of our sex acts was not yet within the realms of our conscious imaginations, we did guess capably at what might fit where. Fingers to vagina, penis to anus, mouth to nipple, each combination we employed, shedding more light on the body's functions and sources of pleasure. Listening to the heart, ear pressed to bare chest of a playmate, was the opening of a vast interior world. What did another person contain? The ingredients listed in our nursery rhymes—sugar, snails, spice, and puppy dog tails—seemed unlikely, even impossible. Whatever it really was, it felt very, very good.

At around the same time, I began to learn to fear what another's heart might contain. I recall the particular experience of playing doctor with my best friend at the time, and the discovery his mother made of us with our pants down in a hall closet, flashlights pointed at each other's dicks. Our happy curiosity and arousal were suddenly transformed and redefined as shameful in a moment's judgment. Our queerness was apparent, revolting and indisputable. Her angry screams, and even more the beating my friend received before my eyes with one of the flashlights—the very instrument of our mutual and brief enlightenment—terrified me. The bandages we wrapped him in afterwards were blindingly white, the blood stains that soaked through them were grotesquely real, and the iodine made him wince and cry visible tears. The body could now bear the imprint of pain, the bruises and welts written upon the skin like a language that was once terribly familiar. Desire had its consequences.

Just as the body could be made legible by violence, I also came to learn that the body itself could write upon the world. It could remake its very form, I observed, as my own body changed under the influence of puberty and weight lifting. On the soccer field, my movements became more purposeful and effective, and my approach to the sport took on the quality of narrative, as if through a game a story could be told, a deeper meaning expressed. Hair and muscle sprang up on me, connoting sex ever more urgently. I walked differently, advertising myself to the other teenagers around me. My penis enlarged, and demanded much more of my attention. I grasped it like a megaphone, ready to shout at the top of my lungs as I came how unimaginably wonderful it felt. Naturally, I masturbated with my friends, boastfully comparing the sizes of our dicks but never daring to touch one another.

Not surprising, then, as my body began to speak more boldly its language of desire to the outside world, that adolescence was also the time when I began to understand medicine as a "desirable" profession and as a force in shaping (or in cleaning up) the culture. My parents, dedicated as they were to ensuring their children's security and success, urged me to consider a career as a physician. As the child of immigrants, I imagined that my white coat just might make up for, even purify, my nonwhite skin; learning the medical jargon might be the ultimate refutation of any questions about what my first language had been. Meanwhile, government-sponsored public health messages about smoking, exercise, and drugs filtered into my consciousness. Dr. Ruth became wildly popular, her strong German accent communicating a scientific detachment and coolness equal to that of the Matterhorn. Gym and sex education classes took on a distinctly clinical tone, intent on sanitizing our minds and bodies. Physicians who practiced in our upper middle-class community came to school and gave solemn talks to assemblies in the multi-purpose room about the dangers of smoking pot and VD.

Perhaps, I fretted as I memorized biology homework assignments full of meiosis, gametocytes, zygotes, and reproduction, science could pin down the definition of desire. In Sunday school lessons I had learned about Adam and Eve, and read Genesis; their secular counterparts were laden with an equally insidious morality. We dissected frogs and cats beneath the sterile fluorescent lights, and all our instruments were autoclaved at the end of the day. I remember laying open the reproductive organs—how tidy, glistening, and clean the pickled genitals seemed. The body was, I was taught, the very cleanest of machines. When a beautiful young woman in my class with long hair got body lice, a sort of panic ensued in our high school. It was as though a witch had been discovered, and when her parents burned her favorite jeans and black concert T-shirts, and then had her head shaved, the teachers seemed both pleased and relieved. The message seemed to be that the purpose of the body was reproduction, and a relentless self-control over its processes and smallest environments was the only business of life. The pathologization of not only tobacco and alcohol, but also out-of-control, "dirty," and "addictive" consumption of sexual pleasure and food, became the other side of the medical coin.

By my junior year, my favorite teacher in high school was Mr. H., a middle-aged man with graying temples and an evident passion for his subject matter. He taught AP Bio, and was building an electron microscope himself. He was not exactly handsome; I recall other teachers commenting once that he was "smarmy." His hands and, after rolling up his sleeves, his veined arms would get covered in chalk dust. After school, he dirtied himself with black grease assembling his microscope. When he taught us, he engaged us with his entire formidable body, running frantically up and down the aisles, heaving his chest as he bellowed out questions, coaxing answers out from even the shyest of mouths. His lectures were more invigorating and draining than the calisthenics of gym class. No one failed to notice his tremendous bulging crotch, his tight polyester pants stretched almost painfully over his obvious hard-on. He injected a kind of sexual energy into the classroom, to which I was unaccustomed and attracted. Most importantly, we learned insatiably from him. He transfused the lifeblood of his risky enthusiasm into our anemic textbooks.

In a community where most parents likely dreamed that their daughters might someday marry physicians, the reaction to what occurred between Mr. H. and a female classmate of mine might be considered surprising—though Mr. H. never was the hygienic physician clad in a spotless white coat that Marcus Welby was portrayed to be. The affair was made public by them both, to the young woman's parents and to Mr. H.'s wife (from whom we all later learned he had been long separated). Mr. H. was asked to resign the next day, despite strident protests from the students in his class. The humiliation and dejection in his eyes were apparent

as he made his chaste announcement. Science became a frightening arena, indeed, where matters of the heart, excepting, of
course, its laborious physiology, were disallowed entirely and if
pursued led to the sternest of punishments. The message to us
was that passion could indeed be regulated, especially the excited
intercourse between teacher and student, scientist and layperson,
and, by extension, I would now argue, between physician and
patient.

So it was in this environment that I, too, became enraged and
indignant upon reading the increasingly frequent and prurient
reports in the media at large of chemistry teachers molesting their
impressionable students, psychiatrists seducing their hypnotized
subjects, and dentists fondling their anesthetized patients. (All
the while, as one glance at today's headlines will reveal, the parallel stories of priests and other assorted evangelists raping their
faithful followers, from altar boy to secretary, went somehow
untold until much more recently.) A facile self-righteousness
arose in me, paralleling my growing awareness of my different-
ness from those around me. I constructed a possible medical
identity where desire was forbidden and in fact repellant, which
served to defend me from my growing and undeniable sexual
interest in other men. I thought I could be cured of my own
emerging identities, just as I imagined drinking too much guava
nectar and listening too intently to merengues had caused me to
become Cuban, or masturbating too much had made me gay. I
had nearly come full circle in my beliefs. In my fear of what I
might become, and in accordance with what I had been taught, I
reinterpreted the body as designed for reproduction and not love
or pleasure, for harboring low cholesterol and triglycerides, not
the rich voice of the soul. My grandmother, my parents, Bonifacia, and my queer playmates disintegrated in the bright glare of
my self-examination.

I lost twenty pounds as a pre-med during my sophomore year
of college; the more I desired anything, especially the man who
has since become my lover of the past ten years, the less I permitted myself to eat. At the same time, I exercised obsessively, so that
I was utterly exhausted at the end of each day. Though I frantically studied my pre-medical course materials, I loathed the thought

of visiting a doctor for the worsening pain in my left upper abdomen. After a prolonged period of time around midterms when my intake of Diet Coke and Marlboros precluded that of food—my base appetites were almost completely suppressed—I felt a pain in my left side so sharp I dialed Campus Emergency. Minutes later, lying naked except for a flimsy gown on one of the Student Health Services examining-room tables, I had a fantasy that was almost overpowering in its vividness. My attending physician was an older Mr. H., and though his strong physical presence seemed undiminished, his voice and his manner had grown much gentler. When he spoke, the pain ceased. He examined me without stethoscopes, reflex hammers, or electrocardiogram leads. When he rested his head on my chest, I could feel him listening to my heart and lungs, understanding all that which I had for so long found impossible to say. He then ran his hands over my body, extracting each gossamer toxin that was a shadow of my form and dissolving it in a pool of sunlight. That is when I realized he was naked, too, and that I was not ashamed of my urgent erection. Indeed, inexplicably to me at the time, I felt a certain power.

The door opened unexpectedly, putting an end to my dream. Then there was the clatter of a clipboard on a metal countertop, the cold stethoscope, the clumsy lubricated finger. I was given some intravenous fluid, and when I came to my senses, was given the diagnosis of a pulled intercostal muscle. Reassurance, it appeared, was the only medicine I needed. I returned to my dorm dumbfounded, and feeling more than a little bit silly. It was much later that I realized what had occurred in those few hours when I feared I was dying, even wished that I might die: I had located an intersection between my own mortality and the world around me, which was named desire. I wanted to live and to be loved, and at the same time I yearned to erase myself from the face of the earth. I wanted the morgue-like steel and chill of the doctor's office, and the warm hands of another upon my body telling me by his touch that I would endure.

Not long after this incident, I made love to my best friend for the first time, confirming what we had known for almost two years. What barrier it was that had been removed by my experience of illness I could not have articulated then. I can report now, however, the healing I felt in each kiss, each touch, each murmured word. My body belonged to me again, as soon as I had owned its desire. The crossing of some threshold, whether from bodily illness to mental health, or from repressed misanthrope to unabashed queer, was suddenly a critical process to investigate. So I changed my scientific methodology from neurophysiology to prosody, my tools from physics equations to rhyme, my materials from atoms to phonemes. If straight science could not provide the vocabulary I needed, perhaps the mysterious and complex human body could explain itself to me in its own terms.

It is through language, then, that I have found a way to love my patients, to desire them and thus put to work one of the most powerful elements of the therapeutic relationship. Present in my poetry is both the rhythm of my grandmother's praying and the thudding of a flashlight striking flesh. I am healing myself when I write, allowing my mouth to find another's mouth, because writing itself is the meeting of two expressive surfaces, that of the mind and the page. I can press my ear to their chests in each lyric, and lie down for the night beside them in each narrative. The pleasure in touching their skin I experience again in the pleasure my hand creates as it brushes against the smooth page. The love I feel is in the beating iambic heart of my lyrics.

The image of the page as yet unwritten upon conjures up powerfully my patient Mary, smoothly bald and pale white from chemotherapy. On the bone marrow transplant unit, because patients stay for such long periods of time, their hospital rooms are transformed even more undeniably into bedrooms; each morning I would visit Mary in hers during my rounds. Our encounters were always preceded by an almost ritualistic handwashing, necessitated by strict rules to prevent infection as the bone-marrow ablation therapy left her without the cells responsible for immune function. She could not have been more naked, more available, and inaccessible to others, more beautifully free. As I let the warm water run over my hands, I would begin to forget that the soap I was using was bactericidal; the killing of even the smallest of organisms seemed to have no place in our growing intimacy. I imagined at times that I was visiting a secret love, so much urgency did I feel in her desire to live. We spoke in hushed tones, hardly a word about the progress of her cell counts, more and more about silly, temporary things like our favorite Chinese restaurants, how much we each owed in parking tickets, the nurse's new butch haircut. On and on, like teenagers in a booth at a soda fountain. When I'd leave, I feared during the long hours I was away from her that I might never see her again. When I'd cry, she'd tell me to shut up. Wondering whether she felt the same way I did, I'd feel my heart quicken at the slightest intercourse: my clumsy otoscope whispering light in her ears, my stethoscope hearing her heart's demand to live, the inexplicably delicious constriction of her pupils.

Many doctors must fall in love with their patients, though far, far fewer would likely dare admit it. What else were we to do, one of us dying more quickly than the other, the other less capable of preventing death than the first. So we loved each other in the ways that we could. We listened to each other attentively, and held hands. I write about her now, and she is alive. Constrained as we were by our respective roles, as doctor and patient, gay Latino man and straight white woman, still we found the space to make a very particular kind of love—a love that concerned itself less with gender than it did with transcendence, with going beyond thresholds. Highly erotic and deeply pleasuring without ever having slept together, as commonplace and yet unexpected as life crossing over to death, immortal as each retelling or the act of writing. Both Mary and I left our loving friendship, I think, healthier, closer to being cured. She waved to me as she left the hospital, still bald, beautiful, but more alive.

However, I remain fearful for the future of this sort of honesty. The so-called personal lives of physicians and patients—as if lives could be so carefully divided up in such an acute relationship— are already the subject of a scrutiny that seeks to eradicate the possibility of human connections. One needs to look no further than the cover of a major newsmagazine which appeared not too long ago to see the face of a physician so many now fear; ironically, though it was an image meant to sensationalize, it is a face as beautiful to me as those of so many of my patients. The story was about a dentist with AIDS who allegedly infected several of his patients with the virus, and who had died leaving behind a "furor": how did he give it to them? the text of the article insistently asks.

I am certain that the hysteria around the issues of doctors with AIDS reflects the deep anxieties around the desire inherent in the patient-doctor relationship that remains pervasive in the culture at large, specifically with regard to the queerness inherent in a profession that in its practice crosses so many boundaries. Suddenly every lurking suspicion could be true. The bespectacled, nerdy older man sticking his colonoscope up your ass actually likes it; worse yet, so might you. The image of sick physician as queer is brought more sharply into focus through the equation of AIDS = gay man. So it is not surprising that the same old sanitizing tactics once again have become implemented, with rules having been laid down as to what procedures are safe for HIV-positive physicians to perform and which are not—without a single shred of scientific evidence to suggest that the virus could even be transmitted through such contact.

People with AIDS, of course, were the subject of similar if not more aggressive attempts at quarantine before the public at large began to fear ever more outwardly its physicians. Many times during medical school I had encountered interns, residents, and attendings trying to guess which patients were most likely to give them AIDS through some vividly imagined mishap. In some cases, those patients known to have AIDS would receive no care at all because of such fears. To this day, some surgeons outright refuse to operate on patients with AIDS, even those they suspect might harbor the virus. Other physicians simply insist on proof of seronegativity before undertaking any invasive procedure.

My own fears of AIDS at one time in my life influenced my own practice of medicine. As a new intern on the wards in San Francisco, each emaciated body I encountered seemed a potential version of me. I saw my own face over and over again in their faces, the dark complexions, the mustaches, the self-deprecation. Incapable as I was then of loving my patients, my well-rehearsed, internalized self-loathing dominated my emotional response to them. I hated them for reminding me that I was no different, that I was not immortal despite my medical knowledge. I wished actively that they would die, all of them in one fell swoop, and the blackness of my thoughts carried with it a certain weight which I felt in my chest. My heart was gradually pressed out of me, and I blamed my inability to cry on the long dehydrating hours I spent in the hospital. Instead of making love with my partner of many years on the nights we shared a bed together, I slept fitfully, dwelling in nightmares about AIDS.

In some ways, I know I have been dying of AIDS since the moment I first learned about the virus. What I had not been doing during those first few months of internship was loving despite the virus, or because of the virus. My healing powers, as rudimentary as they were then, were hindered by a facile willingness to know death purely and simply as an enemy. When I met Aurora, she changed everything. At first, she did not speak at all, except with her huge, moist eyes. I had admitted her to the hospital at two a.m. one grueling on-call night, with the emergency-room diagnosis of "AIDS failure to thrive." It was not until two weeks later that Aurora told me that she was dying of love, of too much love.

Aurora was a pre-operative male-to-female transsexual, according to the terms of some of my colleagues; to others, she was a freak. My jittery and bumbling attending, with a nervous laugh, wondered the next day on our formal rounds at her bedside what "it" had between "its" legs. Aurora just stared at him with her incredible eyes. She had been placed in isolation, because her chest x-ray was suspicious for tuberculosis. "Consumption," she would murmur to me later, "yes, I am being consumed by my having loved too deeply." I was too busy to notice then the campy melodrama in her tone of voice; I could barely breathe through my mask, and thought only of getting out of her room as soon as it was possible.

One day she began to flirt with me. "I know you're in there," she purred into my ear one morning as I mechanically examined her. I paused only briefly before I plugged my ears with my stethoscope, with the intention of listening to her heart sounds. Without saying anything, I raised her hospital gown up to her nipples, this time noticing the fullness of her breasts, the deep brown color of her nipples, the deep grooves between her delicate ribs. "Do you think I am beautiful?" She brought a crimson silk scarf up to her eyes, and she peered seductively over it at me. Her eyes were made up in three shades of green, the eyeliner and eye shadow thickly applied. I had seen her at her mirror only once, hands trembling slightly, as she applied her cosmetics. At that moment, I had thought her beautiful, not at all pathetic or threatening or "failing to thrive." She seemed hopeful and human, full of the love she kept so rapturously spilling out to those around her. But I was too busy to give much thought to what I had felt; my job was not to feel, but to palpate. Not to love, but to diagnose.

During the course of about eight weeks, Aurora gradually deteriorated, despite the intravenous fluids and antibiotics. Her cough became more insistent, as though it were finally winning a long drawn-out argument. She appeared less frequently in her flowing emerald-green kimono, and stopped putting on her eye makeup. She gossiped less about the other patients, and no longer held court in the patient lounge, where she had often been seen pointing out the cute male passersby with her nail file as she manicured herself. I pretended not to see her; I still listened only to her heart sounds, and not to her heart. "You know you're gonna be mine," she sang out to me on another day in her naughtiest Spanish Harlem accent, parodying one of the week's popular dance club songs. I rolled my eyes as I left her room. I never said more than a few words to her on my visits. I busied myself with collecting the data of her decline: the falling weight, the diminishing oxygen saturation readings, the recurring fevers. "I'm burning for you, honey," she said with arched eyebrows by way of goodbye on the last day she spoke. Again, I said nothing.

Expecting her usual chatter more than I ever could have admitted it, I strode into her room the next morning without knocking as was my habit. No salacious remark greeted me, however, no invitation to sit on her bed, no perfume. The silence registered. She seemed to be lying sideways in her bed, with her face half-buried in a pillow. The room's curtains had not been drawn open yet; she remained motionless as I jolted them apart, flooding the bed with sunlight. Still, she did not move. When I rolled her over, seeing her face stripped of all her makeup, expressing not recognition but a deeply subterraneous pain, a primitive and wordless pain, finally I was moved. As I groped for her, finding her body half-paralyzed and oddly limp and angular like a bird that has flown into a windowpane, I began to feel broken myself. I was witnessing the loss of love from the world. Finally I was hearing her voice, and when I frantically listened to her heart and to her lungs, I finally heard the love in them. I heard my own desire surface for air in my long sobs.

Aurora died that day, and when she died she left behind an element of herself in me. I find her voice in mine, like a lover's fingers running through my hair; my voice sounds warmer, more comfortable to me now. I discover her hands on my own body when I examine a person with AIDS, searching for the same familiar human landmarks that bespeak physical longing and intimacy. Her glorious eyes return to me when I finally see someone, or when my own bring forth tears. Her friendship and her love of life return to the world in these words, in the poems that I hope might ascend to reach her in whatever realm in which she may now exist. Instead of giving me AIDS as I had feared, she gave me hope. Science failed to understand her, though it altered her body. Medicine did not love her, though it penetrated her with needles and x-rays. Only writing can find her, because it is the same journey she has made, from the imagined to the actual, from the transitory to the persistent. From the unspoken to this physical and loving lament.

# MICHELLE CLIFF

## *History as Fiction, Fiction as History*

I am reading *The New York Times* on Sunday, January 4, 1994. There is the following headline: RECOMPENSE BEING SOUGHT FOR MASSACRE. The article underneath the headline describes events of seventy-one years ago when a white mob terrorized a black town in Florida. The town was named Rosewood. During the rampage of the white mob at least eight people were killed; every house, every place of business, church, school, was burned to the ground. Today, the town consists of a single house and a sign bearing the town's name.

Rosewood is an American ghost town. Not born of the romantic, mythic violence of the Old West, but created of something else—banal, commonplace.

American history has been tamed. The books record no evidence of Rosewood or what happened there, or elsewhere.

How do we capture the history that remains only to be imagined? That which has gone to bush, lies under the sea, is buried in the vacant lots of big cities.

In my mind I erect a scaffolding; I attempt to describe what has not been described. I try to build a story on the most delicate of remains.

I traverse the American landscape as someone foreign-born, as a writer, a novelist, as a woman who has fallen in love with this country—certain that this love demands accountability. This love impels my search into America's past.

Some months ago I was driving to the University of Virginia. There was to be a panel on women and multiculturalism. I am weary of the shorthand which passes for cultural commentary, political awareness in these times. Why can't we use more words? Why can't we take the time to say what we mean? Why do we settle for a term like multiculturalism, as if it means the same to us all? Why must the complexity of America always be reduced to simplicity?

On my way to the university I cross the Hudson River at the Fishkill Correctional Facility, which I mistake for Sing Sing. When you drive this country you become aware of places where people are kept, you begin to tell them by sight, from a distance, the state-of-the-art and the ancient.

Huge rolls of razor wire, like baled hay, like the kind strung on the fences in Johannesburg's suburbs. One of these places reminds me of another.

I remember when I saw San Quentin by night. A wrong turn on the way to the Pacific Ocean, and then the lit-up Oz, but yellow, not green like the Emerald City. It was a Friday night; scores of dressed-up women were leaving the prison. I parked and went inside to ask directions, and noticed a sign saying San Quentin Gift Shop hanging above the guard's head. The entire prison was washed in yellow light. I thought about George Jackson and his life and death.

I thought about his prison letters as a testament to his intellectual survival. About all of us communicating from what may seem like prison. Where the guards wear the uniform of what will be released as American history.

I am driving past the coal mines of eastern Pennsylvania. Like the salt mines of Detroit, the refineries of New Jersey, there are small houses, gardens, clotheslines hung with laundry bang up against them.

Slag heaps stand like monuments.

From the height of the Alleghenies I descend into the terrain of farmland, battlefield. I am preparing to write a book about the black-centered struggle for emancipation, a struggle which for the most part has been excised from the official record, and from the volumes which cascade from library shelves, the various miniseries and Hollywood movies smitten with the period of enslavement and the Civil War. Whenever I mention the heroine of my novel—the entrepreneur and radical Mary Ellen Pleasant—to scholars of this period, they say they have never heard of her, or they ask me, in a non-questioning way, "Didn't she run whorehouses in San Francisco?"

I have done research in libraries in search of Mary Ellen Pleasant. I have read an interview she gave to an African-American newspaper, *The San Francisco Elevator.* I am getting a picture of her in my mind, this woman who funded what we know as John Brown's raid on Harpers Ferry, who went south with a wagonload of guns to arm the slaves. Now, on this journey across the American landscape, I am also in search of the past she inhabited. And it is all around me. The past coexists with the present in this amnesiac country in this forgetful century. It is as Toni Morrison says in *Beloved.* "Everything is now. It is all now."

If eyes can be inherited, dimples, tendencies, why not memories; why can't our DNA contain inklings of the past?

I am nearing Antietam battlefield. On the car radio they are playing gospel music from our nation's capital. Blessed Assurance, Jesus is mine! Oh, what a foretaste of glory divine! The D.J. cuts in, apologizes for playing Pat Boone, saying she wanted to give the boy a chance, but "enough is enough."

I drive through the battlefield. It is early morning. A mist hangs over the cornfield. Cows are grazing. The same farmhouses, barns that were witnesses in 1862. I pick up a stone, also a witness. The past closes in. I have seen photos of that day and recognize the ditch where the bodies were piled like cordwood when the day was over. I walk through the ditch. Blackbirds pick over last year's cornstalks. Pick through the ground. There is the sound of a mockingbird calling for its mate. An old sound. And behind that plaint the hum of cars in the early morning, Saturday, on a secondary road in the Maryland countryside.

I drive on to Sharpsburg where the graves lie. Row upon row of tiny white stones. The word *unknown* repeats and repeats. So many times that to read it may become meaningless. The stones resemble nothing so much as babies' teeth. I store this image away, to use later. Everything is grist for the mill of the imagination.

I recall a play by the African-American playwright May Miller, *The Straggler.* A one-act play which dwells on the ironic thought: What if the Unknown Soldier were black?

I drive through the gorge which is Harpers Ferry. John Brown is noted here and there. What did I expect? I hold nothing against John Brown. He cannot help what history has made of him.

I arrive at the University of Virginia where I am informed by the graduate student who is my escort that Thomas Jefferson didn't own slaves, which is news to me. Villagers, as they're officially known, built the university, Monticello, every rotunda the great man dreamed of. They liked him so much they just pitched in. She tells me this with a straight face.

She continues my orientation: Sally Hemings, the slavewoman who bore Jefferson several children, either didn't exist or she was white.

I ask her if she's ever met a white person named Jefferson, or Washington, for that matter.

I suggest that she read Barbara Chase-Riboud's novel *Sally Hemings,* which, like my proposed book, like Maryse Conde's *Tituba* and Morrison's *Beloved,* attempts to rescue an African-American woman from the myth of American history.

She does not seem interested.

It is through fiction that some of us rescue the American past. As artists, Morrison has said, it is our job to imagine the unimaginable. The interior of the slave ship, for example. The rush to suicide of the cargo, for example. But also: the resisters, female and male. Those who organized and armed themselves and fought back. The history of armed and organized African-American resistance has been made unimaginable by the official histories of this country. One or two incidents are allowed in these sanctioned pages, but these more often than not end with the hanging of the hero. The extraordinary extent of ordinary people involved in a centuries' long struggle goes unacknowledged.

I am driving along a secondary road beside Lake Erie on a Sunday afternoon in early summer. There are high soft clouds on the horizon. My eye catches a sign, hand-painted, in earth colors, by the side of the road. WELCOME TO TOUSSAINT COUNTRY. Nothing else. Or does it say TOUSSAINT COUNTY?

Either way my heart jumps. Did some of the Black Jacobins, as C. L. R. James called them, end up here? Why would many people consider this a bizarre thought, and me some sort of extremist for having it?

Jamaican slaves, recalcitrant and troublesome, ended up in Nova Scotia. Why not Haitians in Ohio? The state of *Beloved.* Stop on the Underground Railroad. Why not use our historical imaginations, envisioning the armed and organized network as extending throughout the Western Hemisphere? Wherever the institution of slavery thrived.

I am thrilled by these unimaginable thoughts.

A few days later, I am in Omaha, in an old brick building on the black side of town. Around the building are small tidy houses, vegetable and flower gardens, lilacs are in bud, rhubarb stalks are beginning to redden, tulips are just about over. It is early afternoon. There are housedresses, work clothes, undershirts, and nightgowns flapping in the breezes of the Great Plains, off the Missouri River. On the street are debris of rusting cars, and a beat-up place with the "best barbecue in Omaha" has ceased to exist.

A woman, disheveled, crack-skinny, runs in front of my car screaming, "Bitch!"

She is a casualty of our forgetfulness.

Here again the present collides with the past in this Midwestern city, as it does everywhere in this American landscape. The brick building is the Great Plains Black Museum, in this town where Malcolm X was born.

The rooms of the museum are packed. A son's graduation portrait from West Point. Buffalo soldiers on duty at Fort Robinson. Did they witness the death of Crazy Horse?

A woman in a high-neck collar, her hair upswept with tortoise-shell combs. A man in a high-neck collar with a watch fob across his vest. Named and unnamed, these faces are the past. Tuskeegee airmen. A woman named Liza Suggs who wrote her family's story of their escape from slavery. Records of towns named Brownlee and Brownville, all-black towns in Nebraska: the legend explains why such settlements were necessary, and suggests that towns with the words "free" or "brown" in their names, dotting the American landscape, were African-American communities.

I find here the epitaph of Ben Hodges:

SELF-STYLED

DESPERADO

A COLORFUL PIONEER

1856–1929

Upstairs a pioneer dwelling has been recreated. Quilts, canned goods, recipes, home remedies, iron bedstead. I find myself imagining the families who put this food by, who passed through the phases of human life on this bedstead, under this quilt. I pass my hand across the label on a Mason jar holding strawberry jam, imagining another hand. This, too, is history.

In the basement a figure in an Olympic warm-up suit raises a black-gloved fist. In the basement are newspapers from 1919. They lie on a table next to the black Olympian.

Headlines—

LYNCHING        RIOTS        RACE

RED SUMMER (bold in red ink)

RIOTING

RACE

LYNCHING ELUDED

RIOTING                RACE        RACE

RACE        WAR HERO

LYNCHING

The head-and-shoulders mannequin from the window of a black beauty salon stands to one side. On one bare shoulder is inscribed:

LADY DAY

1915–1959

At the end they chained her to her hospital bed. They said they'd found a white powder around her nostrils. I think back to the woman on the street in the bright sunlight. I think of "Strange Fruit."

My book is coming together in my head.

I make notes and drive on to Grand Island, which promises something called a pioneer museum. I ask the woman at the desk if she has any information on black American homesteaders in Nebraska.

"Oh, there were no black people in Nebraska," she says.

This is comic and tragic at the same time.

I wonder for a moment where her own people came from. Were they among the Irish who fled the great famines? I remember reading a letter written by Frederick Douglass on a visit to Ireland, witnessing the consequences of British racism, recognizing the need to make common cause. I remember reading that when Douglass spoke in Boston, scores of Boston Irish came to listen and to cheer him.

I end my journey in the California wine country in the town of Napa. I am visiting the grave of Mary Ellen Pleasant. At one side of the plot is a huge white oleander bush, at the other a huge blackberry bush. The petals of the oleander and the juice of the blackberries meet on the ground. On the marble slab between is the epitaph she insisted on.

SHE WAS A FRIEND OF JOHN BROWN

Behind those seven words lies an extraordinary life.

# SUZANNE BERNE

## *Looking for a Lost House*

The summer I was six, my parents rented an old gray-shingled house surrounded by tall hedges on a foggy, dissolving spur of Massachusetts shoreline, a house I still consider my most indelible home. We stayed there just three months, long enough for me to grow a quarter inch and to need new sneakers. One of life's ironies demands that we crave most what we have hardly had a chance to know, and so I have gone looking for this house again and again, most often on late summer afternoons right before a thundershower when the air stops moving and the grass turns bright green. Sometimes I think I will never find it. Which doesn't stop me from looking.

What I'm looking for is rapture, a dreamy, seclusive kind of rapture, which the house offered first in the guise of tragedy. The woman who owned the house had inherited it from her parents. Her mother had been killed in a boating accident on Pleasant Bay; her father had been driving the boat, and he died a year later. Of guilt, I understood, without being told. Such a terrible event lent the house a voluptuous poignancy. I used to sit in a peeling wicker rocking chair on the back porch and stare at the floor planks, imagining the dead woman had sat there, too, and stared at the knotholes, the flecks of scattered birdseed, the footprints trailing up from the garden. She had been blond, I decided, and had played the harp, the most morbid instrument I could picture.

As is true of cloistered places, time seemed permanently suspended at that house by Pleasant Bay. The old rugosa bushes, the moss-eaten shingles, the snarling lion's-head door knocker, all felt bypassed the way small towns sometimes feel bypassed, so that the house's melancholy history seemed more solid location than a fact—to enter it was to step neither forward nor back but simply *into* a life where the window shades always seemed half-drawn. Looming privet hedges blocked all but the pitched roof from the street; turning past the hedge into the driveway, one plunged into a darkened, aquatic world beneath ancient locust trees. Sunlight filtered through in shafts, as it did when I dove underwater in the bay and opened my eyes to look up at the surface. Shadowed by the locusts and whale-hump rhododendrons, with ivy drifting like seaweed from the rotting shingles, the front of the house looked strangely sunken, as mysterious and perpetual as a ship-wreck.

Inside was cool and damp and smelled of salt. A hallway led into the living room with its wood-paneled walls and leather-bound books, each with a filigree of mildew. Two glass cases bulked in a corner, crowded with ivory warriors gripping spears, jade dragons, a handful of shark's teeth. The house's departed owners had collected mementos from their travels to Asia, including a curving Japanese sword half-pulled from an ornate scabbard hanging just over the door to the stairs. A sword like that, my father said, could cut the hair from your head as neatly as scissors.

It rained all but four days in June and July, and on most afternoons I would pad barefoot over the sandy rush mats peering into each glass case, spelling out the titles of those faded books, opening a few to hear their spines crack and to surprise the silverfish. I coveted everything in that living room, especially an ottoman made from a wrinkled elephant's foot. Sometimes I would lie down on the rush mats to smell the sweet, musty straw, and to pick at whatever had caught between the matting. Once I found a tiny blue glass bead, which I ate.

My family survived several mishaps that brief summer which, like the elephant's foot ottoman and the Japanese sword suspended by a single nail over the doorway, only seem disquieting to me now. The kitchen had an enormous black cast-iron stove with molded curlicues flowering up its squat legs; one afternoon my younger sister pressed against the stove when it was fired up and carried away an intricately patterned burn. She must have shrieked and there must have followed tears, my mother's worried face, first-aid cream, and surgical gauze. But all I remember is that I thought her burn was beautiful; it looked like a tattoo.

On another afternoon, the baby wandered out of the front door, past the privet hedge, and down the middle of Old Harbor

Road. She had gone searching for cupcakes. Each morning an elderly neighbor we called The Cake Lady baked three dozen cupcakes, then iced them poisonous shades of pink, yellow, and green. She sold them for a nickel apiece. The local board of health eventually found out about her, and her five sibylline cats sleeping by the flour bin, and shut her down. But that summer it seemed only we knew about her fusty, secret bakery. We visited as often as possible, with coins stolen from the change scattered on top of my father's dresser, waiting under our umbrellas for The Cake Lady to stump up to the screen on legs that went straight into her black shoes without stopping for ankles. Once we forgot our nickels and she gave us cupcakes for free. When a bicyclist spotted the baby, she had just staggered past The Cake Lady's mailbox, smiling broadly, stretching out her hands like a supplicant.

Even ghosts followed the strictures of romance in that house. Every other week or so, while we sat in the dining room eating dinner, someone would point at the window and hiss that the rocking chair was moving. And there on the back porch, all by itself without the slightest breeze, the wicker rocker violently rocked. After gawking a moment we would all rush around to the living room and squeeze out to the porch—to discover nothing there. Only I knew it was our landlady's dead and mangled mother, risen at last from the murk of Pleasant Bay, come back properly to haunt us.

Then one windless July night my brother shouted for us to *look*, and while everyone else lost time in setting down their forks, I jumped up still clutching mine and pelted out of the dining room. In my hurry I tripped over a foot stool and skinned my knee tumbling across the porch doorstep. The next instant a soft, grunting thing scrabbled past me, a rank, degenerate-smelling thing, rather like a dead mouse in a broom closet, and in an ecstasy of horrified anticipation, I screamed, then opened my eyes, and screamed again.

It was a raccoon, drunk on all that rocking. The rest of my family arrived in time to watch the raccoon stagger from the porch and into a hydrangea bush. Our mystery ended. We all went back to our fish and potatoes, feeling (at least I felt) that we had lost something grander than we had expected to find. Nowadays I wouldn't be disappointed to see a ghost transform into a raccoon, but I was disappointed then and perhaps that's why I screamed a second time.

Of course, I've never lived anywhere since that felt so immune to malevolent intrusion. Every child has a place she remembers as the most protected in the world and, like this damp old house for me, usually she wasn't allowed to live there very long. It's an intrinsic part of childhood to experience, even for only an hour, the deep seduction of security. This experience becomes our first home, no matter where it is or how tentatively we knew it. Enchantment lies in glimpses, after all. Which is why that first home, like childhood itself, can never be remembered perfectly, but only in startled flares of recognition. A glass vase on a windowsill, a dark place under the stairs. Forever building on echoes, we buy tables and chairs we seem to recognize, choose mysteriously familiar wallpaper, lay down our carpets in a recurring floor plan—searching always for the right pattern to unlock the combination that will let us back inside.

Although, to be truly memorable, this first home must also have its portion of the world's tragic history, its weird and absurd events, occasions to be framed and hung up as stories. We tend to chapter our lives by the houses we've lived in, and thus an interesting life, not surprisingly, can often be read through the interesting houses it inhabited. Romance desires the unusual. So, like souvenirs from Asia, I have saved the tales of my sister's burn, the baby's escape, that spectral raccoon, to help me recall a rickety rented house as especially remarkable. Something to contemplate on clammy nights when I stir up the fire and pull the curtains in another, less-reliable home.

And yet for all its curios and oddly innocuous dangers, perhaps that old house was most singular simply for the scope it offered: its impression of many rooms, secretive corners, dark hallways, and back doors that allowed a child to step outside unnoticed and slip away across the wet grass. If the house hadn't had a garden, and if that garden hadn't given way to a rough mesh of green, which itself gave way to a broad lap of saltwater, I wouldn't have had the span that measures everything, and the impression that it's possible to have everything, however fleeting and false, give rapture its quick-beating heart.

Privacy and possibility intertwined then. I had only to be left alone to have an adventure or, better, sense the prickling immanence of one. Watery summer light flowed right up the stairs and washed into our bedrooms; on those few especially bright mornings I would wake up feeling afloat and drift right through breakfast, sailing past cereal bowls and glasses of milk, past the sound of my own shouted name, into an eddy of the afternoon. When I think of daylight in that house, I recall the baby's room in particular because it was painted the color of oyster shells, with transparent yellow curtains murmuring at the windows. When she took her naps, it seemed she slept inside an egg.

My own room was tucked under a gable at the end of the hall. With a child's love of child-size places, I had chosen this room for myself because it fit me exactly. Under a ceiling no more than five feet high, the room contained a tiny closet and next to it a little handmade pine bureau with three reluctant drawers. I slept on a mattress on the floor, and at night the cat would come and curl around my head like a Russian hat. Nothing was too high for me to reach; I could encompass the entire space by flinging out my arms and taking a single jump. I owned that room as I have never owned anything since, and ownership made me restless. On warm afternoons when I was supposed to be napping, the close white smell of privet sifted through my window, stirring me straight out of bed. Outside sea gulls screamed. Bees glinted in the rhododendrons. Flecks of white paint from the windowsill chafed away between my fingers, spiraling down like snowflakes. I leaned out farther, farther, until midges danced around my ears. At last I would slide back inside to watch shadows lengthen across the ceiling, waiting for my mother to call me back to the cavernous world of downstairs.

So it is that like snails, little children carry home on their backs—sheltered though they wander away, eat from unknown kitchens, play alone by the water, their toes curled neatly against sharp mussel shells. Everything is possible. They are at home everywhere. Until, that is, someone tells them that home is a tight place. Until, all too soon, they grow a quarter inch and must move into another house, and then another and another, each of which fits them less and less securely than the one they first remember.

But in that first-remembered home, wherever the first safe place might be, vistas open wide. A green lawn slopes for acres, all the way to the sea, where the beach is white and the water is blue. Above, the house shines like the moon. At a touch, the door springs open. *Come in, come in.* In that house there is nothing to fear because fear is only interesting. Ghosts of gruesome tragedy glide by, but the house is never haunted. Strange and fragile objects crowd the shelves, but none ever gets broken. A breeze blows in through the windows, fluttering lace curtains, bringing the pewter scent of rain. Someday the child will collect her own tokens of disaster; but for now, she moves from room to room admiring tokens collected by others without knowing where they came from—the shark's tooth that never bit, the sword that never struck, the elephant's foot that never stepped anywhere but into the living room. Outside, the wind shifts and the boats swing suddenly around on their moorings. The bay, of course, is always Pleasant.

Thunder rolls; the child smiles. She may even bear scars from that first-loved home, and for a long time believe them merely markings on the skin.

## Out of Control

My wife and I are waiting for children.

Every morning for three months, Joan's alarm goes off at seven—even if she hasn't climbed into bed until four or five—and she gropes the night table in the dark for her basal thermometer, slips it under her tongue, hits the snooze bar on her clock radio, and sinks back into sleep. A basal thermometer shows finer gradations than a standard fever thermometer; it lets her keep close track of her baseline resting temperature, which she records every morning as a dot on a graph. One morning each month, that graph takes a steep jag upward by one-half of a degree, heralding an egg's departure for her uterus—fertilization day if we're in luck.

The temperature chart is our way of eking out what little control we can have over the process of conceiving a child. We could just make love every day, but the books, the doctor, the nurse practitioner, all say that's not the best approach. Better to skip a day or two in between, allow some time to build the sperm count back up. The seventeenth day in Joan's cycle seems to be *the* day, which means twelve, fourteen, and sixteen are our lucky numbers. Which means we can, maybe, cajole the Fates, just a bit—nudge up our odds, just a notch.

During the eight minutes of snooze-bar somnolence while Joan works her magic on that thread of silver mercury, I lie next to her, wide-eyed in the first intimations of gray daylight. The thermometer may slip loose and slide back into her throat. She may grind her teeth—she does this sometimes while she sleeps—and shatter the instrument, choke on a mouthful of ground glass, blood, and mercury. At 7:08 the radio will flip itself back on in the middle of the local news. Until it does I watch the minutes jump by on the digital display, listening, just in case.

During the years in which I moved into puberty and out the other side, I spent more of my waking hours in my parents' basement than in any other single location. "I'm going downstairs," I would say, flipping the light switch and unlatching the sliding bolt that kept down whatever lurked behind the basement door when the lights were out. Like all good basements, ours was womb-moist and dark, humming with the life of heating oil burning in the furnace and the susurrus of water racing through the copper pipes. To move through that basement was (still is) to navigate the castoff accoutrements of the lives that spun themselves out upstairs. Old 45's that had been played a thousand times in a single year, then never again. Towers of games that traced the receding of Christmases past the way layers of sedimentary rock trace the receding of geologic time in road cuts. Bikes with tires so flat they adhered to the concrete floor. Chests full of old toys that we hadn't fought over in years—blocks grasped by none but cobwebby fingers; stuffed dogs that were missing tails and ears; little Fisher-Price people, undying optimists, each just two knobs of painted wood, still smiling up through the lithified dust as though certain someone was about to pick them up and play with them again. As with all objects I had once invested with affection, I felt sorry for them. So it was with most every item down there. Although the rest of them lacked faces to show it, I could feel their longing; they missed what they once had, which was the warm light of human emotion. Everything in that basement sighed in some inaudible stretch of the spectrum.

In one corner, in front of the only window that wasn't a standard cellar fixture but a four-foot-square factory window that looked out from a corner where the lawn dropped away, was a plywood workbench beneath a hanging fluorescent lamp. That corner bench was the place where all those sighs came together, the spot where the basement acoustics focused them and made them audible, and they harmonized through the fluorescent tube of light overhead. I spent countless hours at that workbench. The halo of light and sound enveloped me, isolated me in a hall of storied darkness, especially at night, and the isolation was broken only rarely—by my mother descending with laundry or by my father coming down to search for a tool. "Cellar dweller," they called me, and I wonder now whether they themselves sighed then the sigh of lost affection, the sigh of love escaping. And of course the symbolism can go the other way also—my descent to the whispering realm of the once-loved. Too easy. And untrue.

What I did at that corner bench was mostly tinker, and what I tinkered with were mostly electronic gadgets. The common quests of taking things apart to see their workings. What a visual thrill this was, looking at the inside of a piece of electrical equipment, at the workings revealed. What a trigger to the imagination. The order and precision evident in a printed circuit board were overwhelming, but so was the aesthetic appeal—the colors vivid, the board itself varnished a jade green and clad in a bright copper map that curled its way in and out of itself, myriad metallic peninsulas terminating in silvery peaks of solder. On the other side, the regularity of tiny supine cylinders that were resistors and diodes. Resistors were labeled not with anything as banal as numbers. Instead they were coded with four bands of color, a hued language indecipherable to all but initiates, voices that spoke to please the eyes—black, brown, red, orange, yellow, green, blue, violet, gray, white (forever embodied in the mnemonic my knuckleheaded shop teacher taught us: Bad Boys Rape Our Young Girls, But Violet Goes Willingly). Interspersed with the rows of resistors were capacitors, which were often little tin cans, storage tanks in miniature, usually sheathed in blue or white shrink-fit plastic. Or they were bipedal tabs dipped in cerulean gloss, dried glassy and bright and good enough to eat. I remember this, I do, craving these hard-candy components as I did chocolate or cookies.

Most of the stuff I took apart was ancient, and much of the beauty of those colorful components has been replaced in today's gadgetry by the perhaps too orderly ranks of integrated circuit chips, boxy black insects with long rows of silvery legs. Gone are the components I could *see* work—the relay armatures that would snap down against a bit of copper-wound iron, casting out tiny sparks when the flats of the contacts broke apart or slapped together; the solenoid actuators that, on electrical command, would suck a bar of iron into a hollow winding to set going some intricate mechanical contraption; and, of course, the vacuum tubes. What fascinated me most about vacuum tubes was what was inside—or rather what *wasn't* inside: the vacuum itself. Fine filaments and emitter plates would glow without burning because there was no oxygen in their rarified environment. I remember trying to scratch together a digital display like those found in old calculators, with glowing wires for number segments. But the hair-thin wires I connected across battery terminals would glow briefly and then, exposed to that dank cellar air, would pop in miniature explosions, leaving behind a fine snowfall of metallic droplets and a faint odor reminiscent of the sweet, smoky odor of melting solder.

The primary thrill in such gadgetry, the gut instinct triggered, was my sense of potency in knowing how such things worked, for such things could be reconfigured, reassembled in new ways to serve my own ends, to perform for me. No one I knew would do that. At least not reliably. What I exercised in that corner of our basement was a need for controlled interaction, for reliable give-and-take that transpired in consistent, predictable fashion. More consistent than the few kids I hung around with. More consistent also than my parents, or my sisters, or my brother (though this was at least as much my fault as theirs). No need to fear around devices that I myself had assembled or rigged together. Something didn't go as planned, I took it apart again, found out why, and *made* it go as planned. Try doing that with friends or family.

There is a single human gene, given the dull moniker "p53," that has been implicated as having a hand in about one-half of all cases of cancer. Or perhaps I should say it has been implicated for *not* having a hand in cancer. When it's working well, p53 serves to disable or destroy cells that have DNA damage before those cells can reproduce and become cancerous. But in about half of all human cancers, something has gone wrong with this p53 gene, this cellular police officer and assassin, and it has stopped doing an efficient job. Mice that have been bred without it grow normally for only four weeks or so before their bodies become cancer-ridden. This makes me wonder whether the greatest threat to the healthy functioning of an animal comes not from body systems that fail to flourish, but from systems that flourish too well, systems out of control.

An animal or a plant is an intricate complex of living systems. There's strong evidence that cells as we know them today originated as colonies of simpler living components. So that chloroplasts, the subcellular dynamos that use sunlight to make sugar, were initially independent operators and at some point were absorbed and colonized as food producers by early plant cells. And our own cells, in their early history, colonized the capsular generators of energy that are known as mitochondria and that today serve to fuel on a cellular level all of our bodily functions, including my composition of this essay and your comprehension of it as a reader. This suggestion of a symbiosis (*endosymbiosis*) at the most basic levels of living things raises the question of internal balance and, in an important way, sets us at odds with ourselves—mitochondria at odds with nuclei, and so on.

If a cell itself can be seen not only as a system of cooperating components all finely tuned to effect the functioning and survival of the whole, but also as a system of competing microorganisms all struggling for individual survival, then the primary difficulty facing the cell is not one of nourishing these systems—this being the responsibility of each system itself—but of controlling these systems, of maintaining the balance so that no single system moves into primacy at the expense of the other systems. In an animal, a tumor is an instance of the failure of such control— wild success for a specific system or type of cell, but at dire expense to its neighbors and symbionts. At all levels, lack of control is pathology. An influenza virus grows out of control until it kills its host. Bacteria replicates unchecked in a wound until it brings on gangrene and amputation. Cambium cells in an elm trunk begin to bloom out of control, creating a large, knobby tumor, or burl, that is sliced up for fine furniture veneers. *Homo sapiens,* having circumvented many of the natural checks on its growth, pushes against the boundaries of earth's life support systems. Perhaps, then, our primary biological imperative, the one we fail to follow at the cost of our very being, is to regulate, to govern, to control.

It may just be that I've become accustomed to writing stories. I sit down again and again with these blocks of texts, these reflections and reminiscences, and I try to develop a line through them, a narrative, an order in which each piece performs its task and delivers the reader, prepared, to the next piece. But each chunk maintains its own opacity, a certain stubbornness, a will that refuses to be broken. So I get up and pace. I print out page after page, feed whole trees, it seems, through the rollers of my printer, and scratch at them with my mechanical pencil—arrows, deletions, additions, notes, comments. Insults and curses. But they will not bend to my will. From somewhere hidden come snatches of laughter.

Switches. Buttons. Relays. Keyboards. Devices for control. But also intercoms. Radios. Walkie-talkies. Telephones. Sometime near my fifteenth birthday I stood up from that bench in the corner and walked across the concrete floor to the telephone, which was fastened with lag bolts to the basement wall near the foot of the stairs. And I made my first call ever to a girl. Her parents wouldn't let her go out with a boy by herself, she told me. Which meant, I suppose, that we could have double-dated, but we had no friends in common. Not surprising—the body count in my extended social circle at that time was three. I have no excuse— we could have gone out with friends of hers. But just the walk across the cellar floor to that phone, the hours of pacing, the extended internal rehearsals, the pushing of those seven magical buttons (I could probably, with a gun to my head, even now dredge up that sequence of seven digits), had all raised my blood pressure, my pulse rate, my body temperature, to dangerous levels. Just talking, at that remove, was further into the void than I had ever before ventured and I was faint with unknowing and self-awareness. I hadn't the resources, the confidence, to make a show of it in the face of *three* independent wills. Secretly, I was relieved.

We never did go out, but for the next four months I spent two or three evenings a week on the phone with her. I always placed the calls, but she seemed happy enough to talk. I have no memory of the words we said. I almost never do remember words, and when I do I distrust the memory as a product of my own imagination. I suspect, though, that she did most of the talking. I saw her most every day in school, in geometry and English class, the two subjects I excelled in and enjoyed the most that year in high school.

Almost every day we talked face-to-face, but I preferred our mediated, evening conversations, the way the telephone removed from
play all those other aspects of self and body that refused to be kept
in check, that tended to wander into uncomfortable and unself-
conscious expressions of truth. The singularity of voice was about
all I could manage to keep hold of. The telephone allowed me to
present who I wanted to present. And my imagination was sufficiently vivid to conjure up the rest of my obsession from her voice
alone. It was all the intimacy I could handle.

Joan and I have taken to buying organic milk, which isn't
always easy to find and is always about twice the cost. Regular
milk contains traces of too many substances that would be anath-
ema to a developing embryo. Growth hormones and antibiotics
given to cows to increase production. Plus whatever is sprayed on
the fodder they are fed. Things embryos can be sensitive to.
We've been eating some organic foods for a few years, but now
we always choose organic when we have the choice. Study after
study is showing that, once inside the body, the organochlorines
in pesticides mimic the functioning of something the body makes
itself—estrogen. Estrogen is the hormone that makes girls
women. It can also make boys sterile. Hormones carry marching
orders for many of the body's soldiers, and embryos are exquisite-
ly sensitive to such orders. The more estrogen in the womb, the
fewer Sertoli cells in the testicles of a baby boy. The fewer Sertoli
cells, the fewer hormones produced at puberty, and the fewer
sperm produced through a lifetime. Some of the animal species
that have shown declining fertility rates over the past fifty years,
species that may be falling victim to the great numbers of toxins
that exhibit estrogenic effects: Florida panthers, sea gulls, and
humans. And the more estrogen, the greater the risk of breast
cancer. Are we being paranoid? Perhaps.

Freshman year in college and I was lying on my narrow mattress reading Hardy's *Jude the Obscure* while I should have been
doing my calculus homework. When I was not yet sixteen, they
had asked me, in effect, what I wanted to be when I grew up.
Monumentally naive, I had answered "an electrical engineer."

We're born into a world, raised in a school system, that spoon-feeds us the myth of the success of the talented, the achievement of the better-brained. What's left out of that recipe is the yeast—the confidence one needs to focus the brain without being mauled to the edge of death by one's fears. Part of the beauty of those days and nights at the basement workbench was the lack of an audience, a lack that gave my fears no foothold. How could I have performance anxiety if I didn't have to perform? I was only pleasing myself, after all.

So there I was lying on my bed in a gray Massachusetts city, avoiding the performances I was supposed to be engaged in so I could lose myself in a performance no one else would ever see, a performance of the imagination, an opportunity to remove myself from myself, to let go of self-awareness within an imagined Wessex that held no real risks for me. So seductive and safe was this imagined world that I decided I would go it one better; I would write my own stories and live in my own visions of Wessex. All through high school I had written poetry, but narrative? I put aside the calculus and physics books. I put aside the major, the school, the whole possibility of a life spent developing new gadgets, and instead I took full-time to literature and to writing. It's a commonplace that the writer is god to his characters, but the writer needs his characters and their world more than they need their god.

We have almost no control over our memories. Experience generally does or doesn't stay put in memory regardless of our will. And what our memories give us back is often unbidden. These involuntary memories can be the best sort, memories brought on by odors or music that suddenly translocate us.

During the year I was supposed to be studying to become an electrical engineer, I worked part-time in the college's electrical shop. Researchers of various stripes came to us to have test equipment built or repaired, and I spent much of my time bent over a soldering iron assembling or disassembling power supplies and oscilloscopes and such.

Soldering is the best way to ensure an electrically sound joint between two conductors. The solder melts and fuses with the two metal surfaces being joined. But exposed metal oxidizes, reacts with the air to form a thin film that's not pure metal. If copper didn't oxidize, the Statue of Liberty would gleam like a tower of newly minted pennies in New York Harbor. Molten solder can't find a foothold on oxidized copper. To make matters worse, applying the hot tip of a soldering iron to a metal surface speeds up the oxidation process. So to deal with the problem of oxidation when soldering, there is flux.

Flux is any substance that will bind with these oxides and flush them away, protecting the surface of the metal, keeping out the savage oxygen, and allowing the flow of solder to fuse with fresh metal. The most commonly used flux is rosin. Rosin is what's left over from resin—pine resin—when turpentine is distilled. Violinists and pitchers use it powdered to absorb moisture from bows and fingers. Plumbers and electronic technicians use it in paste form to carry away oxides. For the technician this is easy, as most solder used in electronics is hollow-core solder, a tube of solder already filled with rosin ready to eat away oxides as soon as it touches a hot iron. So in that electrical shop in Massachusetts I would bend over my bench, my face close to the work, touch solder to iron, and the rosin would smoke with a sweet, evocative fragrance that would take hold of my memories and translocate me in time and space back to my parents' basement, where I had first known the smell. And I would give in to it, gladly.

If writing stories is a venue for exercising dominion over one's creation, it is also an indulgence in the sweetest of thrills, which is the letting go of the control of one's *self.* At times I convince myself that the essence of true happiness is the lack of self-consciousness, the ability to operate without fear of falling short, without fear of being snickered at. Self-awareness coils in on itself in strangulating loops and cuts off all possibility of creativity. Most everything I do, I do for the approbation of others. When others are happy with me, I am happy with myself—valued and valid. Which means I must always be in charge of that person people see. To understate the case, this is wearying.

This joy in letting go is evident in the most physical of pleasures—eating, sleeping, making love—but also in the act of creation, the focusing on the constructions of the imagination rather than the constructions of the id. As with sleep, the loss of the self in the act of creation is a pleasure I'm conscious of only in retrospect.

Any creative act, any movement to something new, any construction of something that never before existed, requires a loss of control, a letting go, a circumventing of norms, rules, restrictions. This is true, I believe, whether the creation is a work of art or science—for example, a new theory of the genetic origins of cancer—or is a new type of organism, a mutation. Either way there is a circumventing of standard controls, standard methods—in one case with thought, in the other with the operation of nucleic acids.

This is one way of looking at it—the rules have been broken, you're up in the air, and god only knows (assuming a conscious god) whether you'll come down on your feet, where you'll land. Creation breaks the rules of predictability—outcomes are always uncertain. Success or failure hangs in the balance, and the balance is usually tilted toward the latter. In a way, any act of creation seeks to lay down new rules, new standards, methods, traditions.

From a different perspective, though, creation *is* the rule. In evolution, for example. Assuming no sort of all-encompassing intelligence is running evolutionary history—and I believe this lack is gospel in evolutionary thought*—then present from the start in the biochemical "rules" that set this system going, indeed set all of life going, must be a rule that says something such as the following: "On a regular basis, small random changes will be injected into this process of life in the form of an alteration of base pairs on a twisted DNA ladder."

Why this rule? Because without creation, no progress is ever possible. The earliest self-replicating organic molecules might have contained the molecular blueprints for making themselves larger and more numerous, but only by repeatedly testing out

---

* Though I wonder: if neurons and glial cells—essentially "stupid" components—can work together in amazingly intricate and coordinated fashion and form a human intelligence, might not millions of essentially stupid life-forms work together in amazingly intricate and coordinated fashion—as they do in any ecosystem—to comprise some thus far indescribable and perhaps ultimately unknowable form of ecosystem or global "intelligence"?

unpredictable variations could they ever become more complex, could they ever expand to become DNA and nuclei and mitochondria and cells, organs, systems, creatures that would one day take flight. By the trillions, these test pilots crashed and burned in the primordial soup. And by the trillions, equally risky ventures in mutation crash and burn today. But out of those trillions, a lucky few find themselves better off than their precursors, better able to flourish and reproduce and take advantage of whatever world they live in. And they do just that. These are the species, the life-forms, that will define the world to come.

Art and science operate in similar fashion—through jumps of the imagination that contravene old rules, old orders. And it is through these jumps of imagination, this repeated transcending of control, that we have created this stupendously complex entity we call civilization.

Joan no longer bothers with her seven a.m. wake-up calls. Three months of charts set the pattern and now it is simply a matter of counting days. We do what we can. She has started to take folic acid supplements, recommended by the National Institutes of Health for all women of childbearing age. Folic acid helps prevent neural tube defects in babies—spina bifida, anencephaly, and other such atrocious insults. Defects that develop in the embryo's first month, a time when many mothers-to-be aren't yet aware they're pregnant. We read books, inquire about prenatal seminars at the medical center. Joan is taking up yoga. Controlling those things we can control makes us feel better—we're doing something, after all. But more than half a year has passed now, and still no success.

One of the speakers in the rear deck of our old Chevy cuts in and out over bumpy roads. In a Michigan winter, all roads are bumpy. A copper lead inside the speaker has separated from a terminal. So I climb into the trunk and drop the speaker, my hands gone numb with the cold. I stick the screws and the screwdriver to the big speaker magnet, which seems to be freezing to my fingers, and carry the whole mess inside. Even in the less-than-zero cold, I've been waiting to get a few free minutes to do this, because it means I can pull out my soldering iron and get those shiny drops of liquid metal curling out their fragrance. I plug in the soldering iron on the kitchen counter, uncoil the solder. Here I am, waiting for the heat to rise, waiting for this stretch of pliable wire solder to melt on the hot iron tip, waiting for those curls of sweet smoke to take me back to a time when the world was still within my grasp, still ready for the push of a button.

# Food: A Memoir

### Greens

Start simply.
Lettuce green (light).
Collard green (dark).
Endive (deep thick white).
Lettuce green (red at the curling edges).
Lettuce green (with a spine of white).
Mustard green (lace-spice).
Cabbages, kales, and Brussels sprouts (yellow past their prime).
And escarole (and oh...).
Endive (the thick white).

Greens are my delight.

Swiss chard is too watery. It used to be just right. Now I prefer a denser green: kale or collards, late at night. And endive once was bitter. Are children's taste buds more refined?

Now in those days our baby-sitter was a girl named Susie Smart. Short green hair, red dress. I mean, the other way around. It was I, I was the boy with the green hair. In those days the first thing I learned to do in cooking (not strictly speaking, since it was raw) was how to dry washed lettuce. I wanted to wring it in a towel, squeeze the water out. Someone taught me not to treat it like my showered hair. Her red hair curled up at the ends (you could see the phantom of the curlers in there still), a short green dress. And pumps, undoubtedly. Smart was her name and smart was her outfit. She was a mere nineteen. A proper college girl. She came to us from the suburbs. And we mocked her.

I learned that elsewhere—and we must carefully follow this custom—salad comes after the meal. Only crass Americans would start that way. True or false? Salad clears the palate. Salad differentiates. Now and then, us and them. And I learned when and I learned how to dress a salad. At the end, and simply: lemon, garlic, olive oil, and salt.

End simply.

So lettuce go then you and I. See, the evening is spread out against the sky, like—just like the salad course on a tablecloth of white, on damask, that's a lie, on paper, years, long meals, or seasons later, in a Roman restaurant. Salad came first there, and the raw fennel in it woke me up. Walk into the courtyard. Look up at the sky and turn around. All those clouds are lettuce leaves, now my mouth is watering.

### Bread

An interest in bread's a lovesome thing. An interest in bread displays a most interesting mind. Crust might. Mind.

Patience is a virtue I don't have. And following directions, I don't like to—so never do much baking. But look: just the right combination of cliché and word and love—is something close to bread.

Right?

### Fish

"New fish! New fish!" the women cry out—on Barbara Stanwyck's first day in San Quentin, in *Ladies They Talk About.*

"Do you like fish?" the pretty waitress asked me. But I became embarrassed and could not answer her.

Further questions concerning fish: What is reticulated? What is articulated? Fish without scales are not kosher. I say what I say; you say what you do.

### Sweets

I have a friend named Candy Schwartz (not her real name) and she's a candy connoisseur. She's a candy expert, candy is her specialty. You could say candy is her middle name, but it's not, it's her first name. As for me, I do not eat much candy. In a word, none whatsoever.

. . .

The madeleines my mother bought and brought back to the car seemed soggy, nothing special. I was only ten and did not know Marcel. Did she hope one day we would remember them and thus be cultured—later making someone else's sweet, his mind, his past, our own?

I'll never do anything like this again, they swore at each other, they wondered why they had ever bothered, they disappeared in bitterness, they crystallized; I melted into the back seat of the car. The supermarket was like any other but not. You could buy crêpes at a stand outside, crêpes with fine white sugar—warm and granular and liquid—crêpes were fast food there.

And this is what she'd say: What a good memory you have! Doesn't she have such a good memory? She has a very, very good memory. She learns things by heart.

I learned things by heart. I memorized them.

### Meat

There was a short time when I hoped to be a butcher. I studied all the charts and names of cuts. The pig, the cow, the lamb, traversed by dotted or dashed lines: shanks, flanks, ribs, loins, and chops. (Yes, this was a child who lusted for some order.) From early on I saw that every butcher was a man. Still I studied them: watched their knives. And when they flashed them there, through the air, in the meat, against the wood, I knew it: This was beauty. This was art.

Say yes to slices of roast loin of pork, with applesauce and mounds of hot white rice. Say no to tripe bubbling in tomato sauce, and beef that's stewing. But order kidneys in a red wine sauce, impress the waiter and the rest (I was still ten). Because innards were sophisticated, order kidneys more than once. And taste them: dark and difficult.

### Complications

The eggs left cooking all day—all weekend?—while we went away, until they exploded and covered the kitchen. Ruined the pot.

The can of tomatoes that fell with so much force—from the wall-mounted can opener onto the kitchen floor—that it all reversed direction and made a mushroom cloud up to the ceiling. Tomato stayed spattered on the ceiling for so long.

The amount of oil it took to fry the eggplant.

The food she ate in the store before we got to pay.

The danger of canned mushrooms. *One* could kill you.

The smell of kasha, fouling up the house.

The fresh tomato with a strangely colored pulp. Was it okay to eat? They fought about it then they got divorced.

It all ends up together in the stomach anyway.

The desperate meal she took me to—I could not eat. Why sit in a restaurant then wait till food is served to say that I'd be well-advised to touch myself for pleasure, rather than succumb to this desire for other women?

You know you'll eat a pail of dirt before you die.

### Spice

All hot and fascinating. Burlap sacks of cayenne, turmeric, and something white, glaring in the sun. All exposed. Your hair is long black curls. And nearby, vats of lemons in an oily brine, olives, other pickles. And nearby, tables full of mangoes, eggplant, cucumbers, a pale green squash. Nearby, chickens waiting to be killed. Then you took me to your special spice store. The store was dark and narrow; the shelves had cannisters of everything, both whole and ground. All pungent and delicious.

Back into the sun.

I hid those spices in my suitcase, taking them past customs in plastic bags tucked into all my shoes.

"It's important to be biased," my grandfather said. "Otherwise you're just a piece of bland sand."

Spice: Piercing gloom—oh perfect day! Melody, words, accompanied. All praise.

Spice: Eyes kiss. Eyes water.

# Bad

In the practice of my trade, as writer and teacher, I lie by omission, I sometimes think, as much as I tell the truth. I note, for an eager, untalented first-year student, that her story is *interesting*, that it *shows terrific energy*, that *there's some marvelous insight here* into waking up hungover on Saturday morning after a debauched night at ATO. At summer writers' conferences, I am not about to tell a seventy-year-old woman that her personal diaries, recorded since World War II and bound in leather, need to be buried or burned before she can think to write what consumes her, the story of her life. In book reviews, it is unusual when you or I say, outright, that a book by one of our colleagues is ordinarily lousy.

Mercy is all to the good, and maybe it's another name for being afraid—often for obvious, sometimes honorable, reasons—of telling what seems to be the truth. But sometimes I find myself, as I read a set of essays for school, or put down a stranger's galleys after not many pages, wanting to stand, and flap my featherless wings, and howl that, goddammit, this is outright bad. I've been thinking about what constitutes badness, and reflecting on the pleasures of announcing its presence in the room.

Bad, I recall, was once good. In novels and poems—and especially at poetry readings—of the fifties and early sixties, to call a musician or writer bad was to say he was excellent beyond words. Because jazz was the music of the revolution, and because the best musicians were black or admirably, like Gerry Mulligan, blackened in their art, the sense of life as protest, the sighing song about being Beat, was punctuated by what used to be called negritude. When one was good at being in a state of protest, at being, through one's art, not only accomplished (conventionally good) but also avant-garde and crazy with this life and showing it, one was bad (*un*conventionally good). Norman Mailer wanted the badness of *The White Negro* but wasn't, he might in his sixties admit of himself in the sixties, good enough.

If you're bad, nowadays, you no longer swing: you dance to rap, you fight the power by wearing angry T-shirts and by doing what, if you're white, you think black people do. If you're black and smart, like Stanley Crouch or Ernest J. Gaines or Toni Morrison or David Bradley, you've been watching the white folk strive to be bad while you've labored to make your work as good as you can.

Bad, in other words, is protest-and-Perrier unless the badness takes place in the real arenas of race—the streets or the voting booth or sometimes the page. People who call themselves or others bad, in that old-fashioned sense, are no longer good enough to get away with it.

Of course, conventional bad remains to us. Richard Nixon did well by doing bad. He was bad, he is bad, he died bad, and we will miss him because his badness helped to define what many of us think is, in public life, good. Vietnam was bad. The invasion of Grenada was bad. The failure of nerve by the West in Bosnia was bad. Desert Storm was done well for bad reasons; to the hundred thousand non-Westerners who died in it, badness abounded. Our confrontation of Haiti began and will end badly. Hollywood's renditions of teachers and writers, no matter how many times they are attempted, are bad. Journeyman baseball players who earn a million dollars a year to hit .243 and play average infield represent something bad. Pop Warner football, with its emphasis on winning at every conceivable cost, before rapaciously howling parents, is bad. Spectators at Little League games tend to the bad. Television commercials for beer are bad. Songs on jukeboxes that take as their subject sundown, long nights, or truck rides are bad. Women who feel constrained to dress for business by looking like men and carrying cordovan attaché cases have been subjected to what's bad. MTV is bad. Press secretaries are bad. Plastic bottles for whiskey are bad. So is most beaujolais nouveau and the fashion for giving it as a gift. So is the airplane announcement about *smoking materials.* So is the seating space on the plane. The old *New Yorker* was bad. The Anglophile new *New Yorker* is bad. People who talk about the old or new *New Yorker* are bad. So are writers who comment on them. Men's vertically moussed haircuts are bad. The cheap shots in *Spy* are bad, especially any referring to me.

Bad is what you call an applicant for a job at a university who describes her method of teaching the writing of fiction "an empowerment of the gender-oppressed and racial minorities." She adds, promptly, that she has also found her method to work in "bringing out silenced white males." Which leaves us with no one to do the *oppression,* she forgot to say. She will be hired, I've no doubt, and will go on, canons firing, to become a star in some department. She will teach her students that they're victims. She will teach them how to prove it.

Also bad are literature professors who think that contemporary writing is, at its best, the cream in the departmental coffee. They tolerate writers although it is their secret, they think, that Geoffrey Chaucer, were he to make application for work, would not be hired because he is a dead white European male and because his degree isn't good enough, and because he doesn't do theory. These people do not understand that literary art is not only the cream in their coffee, but the hillside on which the coffee is planted, the earth in which it is grown, the sweat on the skin of the men and women who pick the beans, the water in which the ground beans steep, the mouth that, savoring it, speaks by expelling words in shapes of breath it scents.

It is bad that black writers do being black, Chicano writers do being Hispanic, lesbians do being homosexual, and feminists do being feminist—instead of each doing art, or professing English, or writing about the nature of the world that has the temerity to exist outside them. It is bad for their souls and our minds that careerism so drives their critical faculties and their prose. A young artist or professor knows that you achieve success now by writing, painting, composing, or critiquing by way of your genes and the color of your skin. Authors once strove to get good by being more than the total of their birth weight multiplied by their genetic code. It's bad that they now claim credibility (and royalty checks) on the basis of the accident of their birth.

In a burst of badness, Peter Brooks, in a review in the *Times Literary Supplement,* yawns that "We have known for some time that fictional characters are linguistic constructs, that the impression of mimesis of real persons that they may give is a mirage, and that to ask how many children Lady Macbeth had is the wrong way to interrogate literature." Professor Brooks bends backward into the professorial critical wars to recall the feud between A. C. Bradley and L. C. Knights, whose *How Many Children Had Lady Macbeth?* is evoked by his question. Brooks reminds us that Shakespeare's characters aren't, you know, real; they're, you know, language; when you speculate about the biology of a linguistic construct, you're believing in the language instead of prodding at it, disproving it. You aren't cool.

I am of the body heat school, the school uncool. I think that to ask ourselves—so long as we don't require a specific number in reply—how many children Lady Macbeth might have had is to believe in her as a person-on-the-page, a figure-on-the-stage, and is to ask questions in *a* right way. Has she not sexed her husband past all inner and social restraint—meager as they might have been—and into dark, maddened criminality? What was she like in bed, we well might wonder: Was she cold and withholding? All nakedness and surrender? Did she claw at his flesh? Startle him with his own appetites? Do we not imagine about what's not made explicit? Is that not one reason for a writer to withhold instead of delineate? Does the writer not, him- or herself, speculate or intuit or *feel*—there, I've said the F-word—about the secrets of his or her self as well as these metaphors for self, these people, pulled up from the page?

And note: such thinking "is the wrong way to interrogate literature." Literature, then, is not studied or read, it is not considered or enjoyed: it is interrogated. Tie it in a chair beneath hot lights. Pump it full of chemicals. Apply electrodes to its most delicate parts. Beat it, steal its family, *disappear* it. The aggression in the word is noteworthy, and it is bloated with self-delight, with arrogance. We know the right way, that sure locution says. And it is bad, and a symptom of bad education in the graduate schools, and a guarantee of bad education by graduate students turned college professor and high school teacher, and an assurance, for years to come, of literary papers and essays and books that hum with contentment and cover the field—a living blanket of flies on the body of literature.

Mr. Brooks reminds us that "we really haven't found a vocabulary, or a conceptual framework, that takes us much beyond the formative cultural work done by Dickens, Tolstoy, George Eliot and the rest." Don't you love that "the rest"? Thackeray and Emily Brontë, Gaskell and Chekhov: the rest.

Why not think a moment of those Victorians, of those "the rest": Thomas Hardy, for example, clumsy and obsessed and brilliant in spite of a self-professed disdain for his own prose. He writes *Tess of the d'Urbervilles*, in 1891, intending, according to his subtitle, "A Pure Woman," to assert that purity has less to do with having borne an illegitimate child and having committed adultery and having murdered the child's father and her adulterous partner than his readers might think.

Hardy presupposes Tess. He doesn't only write her: he believes in her. He doesn't see her as "an illusory ideological formation, another product of Western logocentric metaphysics," which is how Brooks defines character. "The concept of character," Brooks goes on, "is the reification of a figure, in which the sign itself ('character' as an engraved mark) is substituted for what it signifies ('character' as the traits constituting selfhood)."

Hardy didn't know that. He wrote about a woman he conceived as flesh and blood in his imagination and whom he tried to make tangible and persuasive on the page. He believed in her enough, the dolt who was "one of the rest," so that in the posthumously published, putative biography of Hardy by his wife, Florence—it was actually his own grindingly discreet autobiography—he twice describes women to whom he was attracted in these terms: one had "quite a 'Tess' mouth and eyes: with these two beauties she can afford to be indifferent about the remainder of her face"; of the other he says, "In appearance she is something like my idea of 'Tess,' though I did not know her when the novel was written." Thomas Hardy is in love—with, I guess, "an illusory ideological formation."

I think, sometimes, that many postmodern critics do not love anything except the control they exercise in alleging the artist's uncontrol. They are well-fed revolutionaries, bourgeoisie in guerilla costumes. Their field is power, and some it of resides in their knowing what they say and your not knowing what they say because they use bird whistles, eyebrow twitches, invisible ink codes, furtive-fingered recognition gestures, and secret handshakes understood mostly by them. I'd like to call that smug codification bad.

But I know as well as you that what's bad is also found in language perpetrated by writers in the name of love and of loving their characters. I am thinking of a first novel I won't name. It's done; the author can't be helped with this one, and there's always hope that someone—editors have been paid, in the past, for such work, and some have even done it—will warn him or her about such writing. In that novel, the birth of a child is exhaustingly awaited and then the child dies. The mother is crushed, but plods on through her life. At the end, at a reception, a handsome restaurant owner asks her to dance. She "folded herself into" his arms, and they "sailed across the room." Those terms are of course bad: they are constructed of received language, and they are not speaking to us; they show that the writer believes he or she *is*, but we know he or she cannot be. For how does the human body fold itself into someone else's embrace without breaking or at least bending very painfully? How does it sail across a room unless someone has pitched it? The character ceases to be particular when expressed in such language; she here becomes an echo of ten thousand writers and ten thousand characters who enjoyed being held by a man while dancing. Each time a writer fails to particularize such a moment, a character dies, and we are left with television: the general idea of, the electronic signal about, a woman who dances. It's the jokester's convention, and the master of ceremonies calls out "Number Eleven," and everyone knows to laugh.

Suddenly this character knows—but only because the author has decided that the book is going to end here—that "she had survived, it was all that mattered, to survive and endure and let go." She knows that "the future belonged to her." The handsome man dips her and she laughs. "Looking at the ceiling, she thought she heard soft applause, the sound of baby hands clapping."

Those are the last words of the novel. They are bad. They are failed feeling—the failure of a writer to find the right words about emotion: sentimentality, that is to say, and the careless use of language as a rhetorical weapon—to, in this case, bludgeon the reader into acceding to the novelist's postulations about emotional life. We know that we long to speak to the dead and to be consoled by them. And good writers have made this common knowledge uncommon. Here, the author has made this impulse embarrassing and the protagonist infantile. By asking the reader to be infantile, too, the author invites the sort of antagonism we reserve for baby talk between lovers we're not. Bad.

Also bad: *The Bridges of Madison County,* a *New York Times* best seller for, it seems, most of my adult life. This paragon of dead prose is about a Marlboro Man photographer and the woman whom he makes beautiful with his great art. It was at first reviewed almost nowhere. Word of mouth made it sell so many copies, its author installed an 800 telephone number on which his enchanted readers could leave messages about their powerful response. In turn, book-chat people have begun to write as if they take the book seriously. The earning of money unfailingly has this effect.

The woman made beautiful says, "If you took me in your arms and carried me to your truck and forced me to go with you, I wouldn't murmur a complaint. You could do the same thing just by talking to me. But I don't think you will. You're too sensitive, too aware of my feelings, for that.... My life...lacks romance, eroticism, dancing in the kitchen to candlelight, and the wonderful feel of a man who knows how to love a woman...."

The next morning, as cowboys who know how to satisfy a woman always do after satisfying her, he leaves. "Her mind was gone, empty, turning. 'Don't leave, Robert Kincaid,' she could hear herself crying out from somewhere inside."

Why is this bad? The entire phenomenon is bad—the work itself, and its enormous popularity, which tells us that we, as a reading populace, are in love with what's bad. What we love, apparently, is talk that doesn't sound like people, but that does sound like speeches made by a person-on-the-page written by someone who doesn't listen to the rest of the world or know how to make plausible an imitation of the world. If you agree with me, you are asking for homage to the world in what you read, not homage to theory about " 'character' as an engraved mark."

If you agree with me, you know that the dialogue I quoted from the novel is a summary of points—he's sensitive, she's needful, and he is a dervish in her cold bed—and not the statement of a soul with whom your soul, you feel, needs communion. Indeed, then, you probably believe in something like souls and something like communion which is available, without brain death, to readers.

If you agree with me, you marvel (to say the least) at a woman whose mind is not only "gone," but is in its absence still present enough to record that it is "empty" and that, while vanished and hollow, it is "turning." While turning stomachs are appropriate, perhaps, a turning mind suggests something like those whirling plastic barrels from which women in tights pluck lottery winners on cable TV. Note further, please, that while her mind is both gone *and* enough on the scene to record its empty *tour jeté*, it can assist her to "hear herself crying out from somewhere inside." You can only cry "out" from someplace that's in, of course; so logic is not what the statement's about, but emotion. She hears herself with a mind that's not there, yet, turning, cries out when she does not, in fact, cry out. It's a silent cry, then, and yet the author feels the need to tell us that it's "from somewhere inside." From where else?

This is the language of television, of bodice rippers, of the Harlequin Romance. It is incapable and irresponsible writing, unmediated by thought or the gift of artifice, or by the author's belief in a character sufficient to move him. It's what the majority of readers seem to want. That's bad.

What's good, then? Am I not defending the old-fashioned and ignoring the hard-edged new? Well, the hard-edged new is old, I'm saying. No one has yet written a more profoundly moving, vast, and encompassing novel in America than Melville did in his *Moby-Dick* of 1851. Surely, it is the template by which we judge both our jokes about and our attempts to write—or, as readers, to find—The Great American Novel. William Gaddis's *The Recognitions*, Ralph Ellison's *Invisible Man*, Thomas Pynchon's *Gravity's Rainbow*, Eudora Welty's *Losing Battles*, Maureen Howard's *Natural History*: these come to mind as candidates; each is vast, encyclopedic, steeped in American history and in the lives of characters about whose fate we care. Only in the Pynchon are the characters flat, two-dimensional—commentary, in effect, on the difficulty of dealing in contemporary terms with emotion. The others, including the Melville, deal with *feeling* as well as intellection. Remember that *Moby-Dick* begins with an 1851 rendition of the blues ("Whenever I find myself growing grim about the mouth; whenever it is a

damp, drizzly November in my soul; whenever I find myself invol-
untarily pausing before coffin warehouses, and bringing up the rear
of every funeral I meet").

Contemporary fiction of the unemotional sort plays off the
emotions it seems to forswear; the narrator—these are usually
first-person novels—manifests the pain he or she then insists he
or she doesn't care about and that the prose, it's insisted, doesn't
reflect. And then the author factors the pain into his or her passages, so that you feel them on the author's behalf. At its clumsi-
est, we have the author turning you into a parent or lover and
you're feeling just terrible on his or her behalf. At its best, we have
*L'Etranger* with a chaser. "Mother died," Meursault announces,
and then he boasts that he can't recall when. We respond by sup-
plying the emotion our protagonist claims not to feel. Our partic-
ipation in that transaction consists of this: we have endured a
parent's death, or we fear it, or fear our own, and fear for the
strength of our love, or fear to be *unloved*. We are loyal to those
tawdry elements of life, that is to say, which a professional post-
modernist pretends to believe one can afford to put, as they like
to term it, under erasure. But they are human, and we are, too,
and the fiction we read for our souls' sake—and not for the sake
of advancing our career—is what responds to our humanness.
Find out which detective stories about passion and trespass your
neighborhood theorist reads during the campus vacation.

If you don't agree with me, give up: you will. You will remember the death of a parent, the loss of a friend, the terror or illness
of a child you tried to protect. It is those moments—they are lived
at body temperature, there is nothing cool about them—that
define a life. In the art about which you're serious, you seek,
willy-nilly, examinations of, metaphors about, the heat of your
existence. Even if your blood has run cold, you don't want any-
body else being cool about such times. They are your times, and
you were on the face of this earth and in trouble or love, and
while you are perfectly willing to be attractively disenchanted and
invulnerable in public when you need to, you know that the
warmth of flesh, the muddiness of earth, the terror of madness
and death, the hugeness of institutions, and the brevity of your
life and the lives of those you need are what your seriousness

involves. Such moments help you to define your morality. You seek them and it in the art you make or surrender to.

What resorts to trend and gossip, to evasion and gloss, to the cutely second-rate, or what drops its bucket all the little inches down into the mud and gravel of jargon and career, is the opposite of what your soul requires, and it's bad. And maybe what is worst is the noise of some tired writer who, preaching and confessing, flaps his unfeathered wings in your face. Doesn't he know better?

*Ploughshares · Fall 1994*

Rosellen Brown is full of contradictions. She appears friendly and voluble, and admits she loves to perform in front of an audience, but she considers herself shy, and claims she is crippled with discomfort at parties. About writing novels, she says, "I have to struggle with my almost total inability to tell a story," although in *The New York Times Book Review,* Michael Dorris—after commending its literary merit—called her last book, the critically lauded and best-selling *Before and After,* "an unabashed, read-until-dawn page turner." After publishing four novels, two collections of stories and essays, and two volumes of poetry, with another forthcoming, Brown still wishes she had become a musician, able to deliver a "crystallized feeling that connects on a visceral level," complaining, "I get tired of trying to be smart." And Brown, a New Yorker–turned–New Englander, a pure-bred Yankee, somehow became an avid Houston Rockets fan, faithfully following the perennial chokers over twelve years until finally, with Brown in the stands at the Summit, the Rockets beat the Knicks to clinch the NBA Championship this summer.

But these sorts of discrepancies of character are what interest Brown about people, and she has made it her life's work to explore the complexities of the human heart, the intricate and unpredictable ways that ordinary women and men react to circumstances of fate. "There's no single truth," she says, and would never presume to offer one. "I take very seriously the idea that novelists raise questions and don't necessarily answer them." Rather, she only attempts to provide a measure of comprehension for her characters' actions, whether such insights are sympathetic or not. "Novels are where we learn what it feels like to be someone else, where we learn to be patient with ways of looking at things that are not our own."

Much of this attitude comes from Brown's peripatetic childhood. She was born in Philadelphia in 1939, but only spent ten weeks there. As her father pursued jobs in textile sales, her family relocated to various cities in Pennsylvania and New York and California, and Brown was profoundly affected by the rootless upbringing: "It's always been a kind of obsession in my writing that I haven't felt like I belonged anywhere."

To this day, she is convinced that if she had not moved so much, she would not have started writing at all. In 1948, she arrived in Los Angeles, and all summer, she laboriously made new friends. But by chance, because of an arbitrary zone line, she ended up going to a different school from them. "I was very lonely and unhappy," she recalls. "I started writing really as an attempt to keep myself company." During playground recesses, she began jotting poems and stories in a notebook, and arrogantly announced at the age of nine that she was going to be a writer (one of her first efforts was a mystery story called "Murder Stalks at Midnight").

Her parents encouraged her. They weren't educated, did not even go to high school, but they were liberal-minded and had vague intellectual aspirations. They kept a bookcase of great books called "the five-foot shelf," and Brown remembers reading Turgenev and Dostoevsky at an early age. Exhausting that resource, she pled for her adult library card. The librarians were reluctant, though, insisting she hadn't taken full advantage of the children's section. "I used to take home ten books a week, or however many I could fit in my bike basket, read them all, and bring them back. I had to convince them that I had read every goddamned book about a girl who opens a tearoom in the summer and finds her career and also her love."

Brown spent her high school years in Queens and concentrated for a time on journalism, driven by a demanding and attentive teacher. "This sounds like Colette or something," she laughs, "but he used to lock me up in the newspaper room to finish my pieces. I wrote very flowery essays about individualism and apathy for a column called 'Vanity Fair.' They were downright Emersonian in their moral thrust."

She won a New York state scholarship to Barnard College, where she took three poetry workshops with Robert Pack, who had a tremendous influence on her, teaching her the fruits of revision. She soon became the star of the college literary community, editing

PHOTO: JANICE RUBIN

the literary magazine and publishing a sestina in *Poetry* when she was twenty. Confident, a little brash, she enrolled in the Ph.D. program at Brandeis University, and was promptly humbled by a literature professor who regularly reduced students to tears. "He felt that we had all learned a lot of romantic mush in college and he wanted to undo all that and make us scholars," Brown says somewhat bitterly. "There were a lot of students who wanted to write, and one by one, we bailed out."

After she received her master's, she left school, married her boyfriend, Marvin Hoffman, and moved to San Francisco. Brown credits her husband for being a vital source of support, inspiring her to keep writing, then and now. "It's not coincidental, I think, that part of his first attraction to me was that I was an aspiring writer. In fact, our first conversation on the telephone had to do with *The Kenyon Review* and Norman Mailer. He kept me from going through some of those really guilty moments that women have when they put their kids in day care centers or get baby-sitting help. He worked, this was my work, and God knows, it got no smaller shred of attention than his." A testament to their equal partnership was their decision to go to Tougaloo College in 1964, immediately after Hoffman received his doctorate in clinical psychology. Brown was invited by the Woodrow Wilson Foundation to teach at the black college, which was ten miles outside of Jackson, Mississippi. Since Tougaloo happened to have an opening in psychology as well, Brown and Hoffman accepted, largely—although apprehensively—for political reasons. "We didn't conceive of ourselves in any heroic terms," she concedes, "and we weren't quite ready to see ourselves as activists and demonstrate, because frankly we were scared, but we went there thinking that we could do our bit for civil rights at a very hot time." It turned out that the presence of whites on campus was reason enough for vilification by the community, which referred to Tougaloo as Cancer College. Riding in integrated cars or mailing anti–Vietnam War letters was even more provocative. "It didn't take too much to get sugar put in your gas tank," Brown says.

The experience, as expected, forever changed them, and gave Brown the subject matter for several of her books, including her first collection of poetry, *Some Deaths in the Delta*, which was published in 1970. The poems contrast the racism and violence of the South with the despair of urban life in Brooklyn, where Brown lived for three years after Mississippi. Several years passed before she turned to fiction. "I felt at the time that my talents could be best served by dealing purely with words, not narratives. It was only when I began to realize that I wanted to write about other people besides myself, and to look outward rather than inward, that I started thinking I needed to write stories." She released a collection of fourteen stories, *Street Games*, in 1974, depicting the everyday lives of the residents on a single block in Brooklyn and their confrontations with class, sex, and race.

From that point on, as Brown and her husband raised their two daughters in New Hampshire, a deeper, more abstract, and consistent theme emerged in her fiction: the tension between public and private duties, the tugs of familial and marital responsibilities in the face of ideological and personal claims. In *The Autobiography of My Mother*, Brown's first novel, Gerda Stein, a celebrated civil rights attorney in Manhattan, is visited after an eight-year absence by her daughter, Renata, a former Haight-Ashbury hippie who has had a baby out of wedlock; Gerda and Renata, criticizing the hypocrisy of each other's generation, struggle over the custody of the child. In *Cora Fry,* Brown's favorite of all her books, a woman narrates a cycle of eighty-four poems; she yearns for freedom from her provincial life as a rural New Hampshire housewife, but feels just as trapped by the prospect of escape. In *Tender Mercies,* her second novel, Dan Courser accidentally steers a boat over his swimming wife, Laura, paralyzing her, and the family is tested by enormous wells of blame and guilt during her rehabilitation. In *Civil Wars,* Teddy and Jessie Carll, former civil rights activists whose marriage is faltering, live as virtually the only whites in a black development in Jackson; when Teddy's sister and husband, virulent segregationists, are killed in a car accident, the Carlls become guardians of their two racist children. And in *Before and After,* which had its start as a one-act play, Ben and Carolyn Reiser, New Yorkers who have settled comfortably in New Hampshire, are torn apart when their seventeen-year-old son kills his girlfriend; Ben decides to conceal evidence, while Carolyn, a pediatrician who has seen the girl's corpse, insists on full disclosure.

In many of the novels, the chapters shift in style and points of view, sometimes going from conventional third-person to stream-of-consciousness first-person, and almost always, the precipitous moment of action takes place offstage. "One reason for this avoidance," Brown acknowledges, "is that I can't write action without a funny kind of embarrassment. Mainly, I think of myself as a meditative writer. The scenes that interest me the most are the ones in which people are thinking about what's going on around them."

She regards poetry, on the other hand, as a "purer vehicle for celebration and elegy," similar to music. "It's sufficient in poetry, I think, to be able to represent the world in a heightened way. This is why portraying events and action is so difficult for me, because I truly believe that just to give witness and call attention to things, to make familiar things new, is enough. Of course, you can't do that in fiction, you can't merely call attention to the world for two hundred pages." Hence, Brown was eager to return to poetry, and Farrar, Straus & Giroux will be publishing a sequel to *Cora Fry,* entitled *Cora Fry's Pillow Book,* this fall with the original work. She's back to work now on a new novel about an author researching her great-grandmother, a Jewish émigré from Russia who lived in an 1882 New Hampshire farming community.

Brown still doesn't feel she belongs in New Hampshire, where she continues to spend her summers, or in Houston, where she has lived since 1982, teaching fiction and essay writing at the University of Houston, but she has accepted her role as an outsider. As she plumbs the hard moral questions of contemporary and historical life in her writing, she feels this sort of mobility, which she regards as particularly American, gives her "endless chances to start again. Maybe I'm not putting down roots anywhere, but at least I'm putting down something."

—*Don Lee*

# BOOKSHELF

*Recommended Books · Fall 1994*

**SHARK DIALOGUES** *A novel by Kiana Davenport. Atheneum, $22.00 cloth. Reviewed by Katherine Min.*

Hawaiian-born writer Kiana Davenport's new novel, *Shark Dialogues,* resembles a myriad of dreams, each of them urgent and vivid, some dark with destruction and heartbreak, others bright with triumph, all shimmering with sensual beauty. Davenport manages to create a world that seems both real and mythological, a place of concrete history and pure magic.

The novel concerns an extraordinary family, descendants of a nineteenth-century shipwrecked Yankee sailor and the runaway daughter of a Tahitian chieftain. Their great-granddaughter, Pono, one of the most powerful female characters in recent fiction, is the story's compelling center. A beautiful, pure-blooded Polynesian Hawaiian, Pono is a *kahuna,* or seer, who dreams the future and walks with a cane made from the spine of a man she murdered. Her fierce strength and almost terrible dignity dominate the book and bind its characters. "She was *kahuna,* creating more life around her than was actually there, heightening the momentousness of each living thing by simply gazing upon it."

When she is eighty years old, Pono summons her four granddaughters, Ming, Vanya, Rachel, and Jess, each of "mix blood" parentage, to her coffee plantation on the Big Island. Having driven their mothers from her life almost willfully, Pono is ready now to tell her granddaughters the incredible secrets of their family history, secrets that include her all-consuming love affair with a man kept hidden from the world.

Pono's story is the story of Hawaii, and the islands become the novel's real central characters. The prose is as lush and sensual as the land it conjures—from the dense jungles and rain forests that retain the natural wildness of Hawaii to the greasy alleyways of the opium dens in Honolulu, from the desolate peninsula of the leper colony at Moloka'i to the black moonscape of hardened lava below

Mauna Loa. And always, everywhere, is the ocean, the water which surrounds them.

Land and water abide, land and water heal. "In physically rejuvenating the land, he renewed something spiritual and intellectual within himself," Davenport writes of Pono's lover—a process of renewal shared by all of her characters.

It would be impossible to sum up the many stories *Shark Dialogues* contains, but the history of this family, of this island, burgeons with life: whale hunts, shipwrecks, volcanic eruptions, wars, terrorist bombings, murders, rapes, suicides, the slow, sickening waste of diseases. People die in horrible agony, in body and in spirit; they fall in love and lose one another, couple in fierceness and desperation. And many, against all the odds, survive.

*Shark Dialogues* is also the story of a paradise lost, of a once strong and proud people overrun by outside exploitation, by development and its attendant ills, the West literally rotting native flesh, sapping its will and strength. The excesses of the novel are the excesses of the epic—the prose sometimes purple, the plot galloping from tidal wave to Pearl Harbor—but it is the nature of Davenport's achievement that we admire her sheer ambition, her determination to work on as large a canvas as possible, to include everything, and to spend it all.

*Katherine Min's fiction has appeared in* Ploughshares, TriQuarterly, *and other magazines. A new story is forthcoming in* Prairie Schooner.

**AUTOBIOGRAPHY OF A FACE** *A memoir by Lucy Grealy. Houghton Mifflin, $19.95 cloth. Release date: Sept. 27, 1994. Reviewed by Don Lee.*

At the age of nine, following a playground collision with another child, Lucy Grealy was plagued by a persistent pain in her jaw. After several misdiagnoses, it was determined that she had Ewing's sarcoma—cancer. In *Autobiography of a Face*, Grealy, who is now a poet, recounts the next eighteen years of her life, during which she endured nearly thirty operations, with poignant grace.

Initially, Grealy was innocent to the implications of her disease and its treatment, not realizing that victims of Ewing's sarcoma are given only a five-percent chance for survival, not understanding that the operations and chemotherapy and radiation would leave her disfigured. Instead, she was almost insouciant, enjoying the attention at the hospital and wanting to show off her scars at school. But in due course, with half her jaw missing, she was teased mercilessly by her classmates. "The cruelty of children is immense," Grealy writes, "almost startling in its precision." Adult strangers, particularly men, began taunting her as well, and Grealy grew to feel ashamed about her looks.

Strangely, the hospital became a refuge for her, despite the pain of chemotherapy ("Pain, if nothing else, was honest and open—you knew exactly what you were dealing with"), whereas school continued to be intolerable and home was increasingly unstable: her father was not doing well professionally, and her mother, who was always disappointed when Grealy succumbed to tears, suffered from depression. The hospital was the only place she didn't feel self-conscious, and there, she tried to come to terms with her disfigurement. She could not fathom why patients who were having cosmetic surgery didn't appreciate how lucky they were to be merely healthy, normal, and she strove, with remarkable equanimity, to transcend petty desires for beauty.

Yet as each operation brought more disappointment, bone grafts deteriorating time and time again, Grealy surrendered on many occasions to self-pity and loathing. Respite came when she worked at a ranch during high school and when she wrote poetry at Sarah Lawrence and the University of Iowa, and she was eventually able to land a number of friends and lovers, but still, she could not avoid defining herself by the way she looked. Her face remained both a locus of despair and an excuse for being "unlovable," as she often called herself: "This singularity of meaning—I *was* my face, I *was* ugliness—though sometimes unbearable, also offered a possible point of escape. It became the launching pad from which to lift off, the one immediately recognizable place to point to when asked what was wrong with my life. Everything led to it, everything receded from it—my face as personal vanishing point." Of course, then, Grealy was utterly lost when considering a life with a successfully reconstructed face, a prospect she must reconcile at the end of the book.

*Autobiography of a Face* is a memoir of disquieting candor and power. Grealy gives her adult years somewhat shorter shrift than they deserve, but the account of her arduous coming of age is both haunting and inspirational, and she makes a lyrical statement about the complex relationship between beauty and self-worth in our society, about the ruthless "importance in this world of having a beautiful face."

**THE SIXTEEN PLEASURES** *A novel by Robert Hellenga. Soho Press, $22.00 cloth. Reviewed by Joan Wickersham.*

A character in *The Sixteen Pleasures* tells of a shop in Rome where petitioners in marital annulment cases can buy old postcards, old inks, and old uncanceled stamps, for the purpose of fabricating evidence from the past. This desire to rewrite the past, to make it turn out differently, is a theme that resonates throughout Robert Hellenga's elegant and original first novel.

Margot Harrington, a young American book conservator, travels to Florence to help rescue artworks damaged in the great flood of 1966. She is journeying into her own past as well, searching for the audacious life she might have led if she had not been forced by her mother's fatal illness to leave Italy years before. At the same time, she recognizes that the notion of a "road not taken" is naive fantasy. "Mama always maintained that anyone who'd heard Frost read 'The Road Not Taken'... would know that the last line was ironic, a joke, but I'd never understood what she meant till now. There is no 'road not taken,' there's only this road."

She falls in love with Sandro Postiglione, a worldly and affectionate Italian art restorer who lives for the daily pleasures of food, love, and conversation, "content to let his little boat drift wherever it would." And while living within an order of historically independent and intelligent nuns, she comes upon the only extant copy of the notorious *Sonetti lussuriosi*—sixteen bawdy sonnets by Aretino, with joyously explicit engravings after Giulio Romano's drawings. She receives from the abbess a subtle and difficult commission: to circumnavigate the bishop of Florence, who wants to control the destinies of both book and convent, and to sell the Aretino for the benefit of the nuns.

As the story unfolds in surprising and wholly satisfying ways, the novel becomes a meditation on erotic love, on the bonds between parents and children, on the definition of "home," and, most importantly and insistently, on the shape of human lives.

Do we control our own destinies, or are we at the mercy of other people and events? Or, as the abbess suggests, perhaps "we can't make any sense out of life until we give up our deepest hopes, until we stop trying to arrange everything to suit us."

Yet for all the ambitiousness of his themes, Hellenga is a refreshingly understated stylist. The novel is carefully structured, but it has the feeling of a leisurely, almost meandering journey, with dozens of fascinating side trips. The narrative roams from the posturing and politicking of academics to the tortuous paradoxes of canon law, to the arcane challenges of stripping water-damaged frescoes from plaster walls, to a blow-by-blow description of bookbinding that is as gripping as any thriller, to a wonderfully funny scene in which Sandro's mother confronts Margot with the erotic engravings: "You do these things with my son?... And this?... And this?"

Longing for the past and at the same time longing to have done it differently, haunted by her dead mother's voice and by her absence, in love with Italy but nobody's fool, Margot is a complex and sympathetic character. Her cool, precise narration helps to make this a novel of self-discovery in which the pilgrim is as interesting as the pilgrimage.

*Joan Wickersham's fiction has appeared in* The Hudson Review, Story, Best American Short Stories 1990, *and* The Graywolf Annual Eight. *Her first novel,* The Paper Anniversary, *was published by Viking last year.*

**BONE BY BONE** *Stories by Gary Krist. Harcourt Brace, $19.95 cloth. Reviewed by Jessica Treadway.*

The best stories are often the ones that surprise us, either because we aren't expecting what happens, or because they take us farther than the destination we had in mind.

In his second collection, *Bone By Bone,* Gary Krist gives us thirteen compelling variations on the "What if?" theme, pushing plot and character beyond conventional comfort zones and into the realm of discovery which comes only through risk.

What if a man decides to leave the woman he lives with, because her multiple sclerosis is getting worse? She stays in the bedroom, in her wheelchair, as their friends help the narrator load his belongings into a moving van. "This is what it feels like to be despicable," he tells himself. "But even now, as I'm leaving, I can't quite believe it. I just wasn't strong enough for this....It's as simple as that." The narrator's willingness to see and acknowledge his limitations, and his realization that the people who are helping him move are likely performing "a last duty" of friendship, make "Baggage" a story not about what *should* be, in a perfect world, but about what *is,* in ours.

In "Bludgeon," a story about spiritual and physical power, two men on the lam from an alcohol rehab run over a deer in the road, maiming but not killing it. Trying to find something with which to put the animal out of its misery, they stumble into the house of a man in a wheelchair, who offers them the use of a pistol he keeps in a coffee can. What happens then reminds us, with a shiver, of how compassion sometimes lies down with cowardice, and how a good intention can still come to a bad end.

Most of Krist's characters are not in wheelchairs. Like most of ours, their pain is invisible, and it disables them to different degrees. They seek safety and solace in the usual places—drugs and alcohol, religion, insanity, geographical moves—but with Krist as creator, their searches feel fresh. "Hungry" begins this way: "When Mr. Medwik at the Hart Memorial Funeral Home refused to upgrade my title from Assistant to Associate Embalmer, I knew that it was time for me to go to Alaska." The narrator and his mother, who also works at Hart Memorial as "a part-time greeter/mourner," decide to change their luck and lift their spirits by relocating from upstate New York. Problems arise when, one by one, their friends ask to be included in the cross-country move to the place chosen from the atlas because of its name: Hungry, Alaska. "As in Hungry for Something Better out of Life," the narrator notes.

In a trilogy of stories about the Eriksons, narrated by a son, Krist deftly depicts the way families are defined and sustained by love, betrayal, jealousy, laughter, loss, and, most of all, the yearning that is seldom fulfilled, at least not where we look for it to be. "She and I understood each other that day," Cliff tells us, describing a clandestine visit he and his mother made to a Catholic church when he was a child. "We shared a like need for the waxy scents, the blood-rich colors, and the exotic, comforting darkness held within that church's walls....But now...I saw a different woman, one who had interests of her own, separate from mine, one whose secrets were no longer my secrets."

Krist, whose story collection *The Garden State* received the Sue Kaufman Prize for First Fiction, writes with humor, insight, and grace about the human condition, in all its triumph and folly. *Bone by Bone* deserves to be not only read but savored, page by page.

*Jessica Treadway's collection of short stories,* Absent Without Leave, *received the John C. Zacharis First Book Award from* Ploughshares *and Emerson College in 1993. She is working on a novel.*

**TIPPING POINT** *Poems by Fred Marchant. The Word Works, $10.00 paper. Reviewed by Sam Cornish.*

Fred Marchant's first collection of poetry is autobiographical, yet intellectual and poetic enough to avoid the clichés of confessional poetry. There is honest emotion when he writes of his father abusing his mother, or of the same man dying of prostate cancer: "the home of maleness, / the fountain of youth, the spring of come, / the walnut, however / you want it, has, in my father's own words, / 'turned bad.' " Marchant is able to write about his father's anger and suffering with both immediacy and distance, and an emotional clarity emerges in these poems, as well as in those about the body and the poet's own aging, his youth, and his service in Vietnam, where he was a lieutenant in the Marine Corps (he was later honorably discharged as a conscientious objector).

*Tipping Point* is about a whole life without self-pity. Rather, it is about a life of compassion. A family is revealed in profoundly moral and realistic terms by a son who writes about them as common people, living as best they can: "Now the wind sounds out clearly / and says this is the mountain / of forgiveness, and that the work / will be to traverse the empty spaces / with meaning."

*Tipping Point* is clearly one of the best first books of poetry to come out in some time—a moving reflection of a society and generation that came of age during the Vietnam War and of a white American male writer's odyssey, which is anything but self-serving in its relentless, brutal honesty.

*Sam Cornish's most recent book of poetry is* Folks Like Me, *published by Zoland Books. He is also the author of* 1935: A Memoir, *published by Ploughshares Books.*

**COHEN AWARDS** Each year, we honor the best poem, short story, and essay published in *Ploughshares* with the Cohen Awards, which are wholly sponsored by our longtime patrons Denise and Mel Cohen. Finalists are nominated by staff editors, and the winners are selected by our advisory editors. This year, we combined the fiction and nonfiction categories, since only one essay was printed in 1993; each winner receives a cash prize of $600. The 1994 Cohen Awards for work published in *Ploughshares* Vol. 19 go to:

BILL PHILLIPS

**CLEOPATRA MATHIS** *for her poem "The Story" in Winter 1993–94, edited by Russell Banks and Chase Twichell.*

Born in the small college town of Ruston, Louisiana, Cleopatra Mathis was raised by her Greek mother's family, along with several members of the black community who worked at the family's café. Mathis says that their influence—combined with that of her grandfather, who spoke no English, and her grandmother, who ran the business—far outweighed that of her father, who was half-Cherokee and left when Mathis was six years old.

After studying at a variety of colleges, she began teaching English in Texas and received her bachelor's degree from Southwest Texas State University in 1970. It was during seven years of public high school teaching that Mathis became interested in poetry. When she moved to New Jersey, she enrolled in a workshop at the New School for Social Research, then went to Columbia University for her M.F.A., graduating in 1978.

Her work has appeared in many magazines and journals, including *The New Yorker, The New Republic, Antaeus, The Southern Review, The Georgia Review,* and *The Iowa Review.* She has published three books of poems, *Aerial View of Louisiana* in 1980, *The Bottom Land* in 1983, and *The Center for Cold Weather* in 1989, all from Sheep Meadow Press. Recent anthologies with selections of her work include *The Morrow Anthology of Younger American Poets* and *The Made Thing: An Anthology of Contemporary Southern Poetry.* She has received a fellowship from the Fine Arts Work Center in Provincetown, the Robert Frost Award, an exchange fellowship to the Tyrone Guthrie Centre for the Arts in Ireland, a National Endowment for the Arts grant, and the Lavin Award for Younger Poets from the Academy of American Poets. She lives with her family in Hanover, New Hampshire, where she is Professor of English and Director of the creative writing program at Dartmouth College.

Mathis writes, "Three aspects combined to make 'The Story': my fascination with the Cupid-Psyche myth, the notion that faith is intrinsic to the survival of love; my Greek grandmother's belief that the soul lives somewhere deep in the back of the head and the devil's route is through the eyes in his endless pursuit; and lastly, the event of my husband's benign brain tumor, located next to the pineal gland, which the ancients claimed housed the soul. Our neurosurgeon, a man with a Ph.D. in English literature, removed the tumor in a dangerous nine-hour operation. In that mysterious, roundabout process that writing allows, the poem is dedicated to the surgeon."

**FRED G. LEEBRON** *for his story "Lovelock" in Fall 1993, edited by Sue Miller.*

Fred Leebron was born outside Philadelphia in 1961, grew up in Narberth, Pennsylvania, and attended a Quaker school in Germantown. As the youngest of five children, he was drawn to writing as "the best chance to get all the words out before anyone interrupted." He was once a program vendor for the Philadelphia Phillies and Eagles, and for six months he worked in the locked unit of the Philadelphia Psychiatric Center. He received a B.A. from the Woodrow Wilson School of Public and International Affairs at Princeton University, an M.A. from the Writing Seminars at Johns Hopkins University, and an M.F.A. from the Iowa Writers' Workshop.

His stories have appeared or are forthcoming in *The Gettysburg Review, Grand Street, The North American Review, The Quarterly,*

*The Threepenny Review, The Iowa Review,* and elsewhere. His work has also been anthologized in *The New Generation* and *Flash Fiction,* and he is the co-author of *Creating Fiction: A Writer's Companion,* due out from Harcourt Brace in 1995. Awards for his writing include a Fulbright Scholarship, a Pennsylvania Council on the Arts Literature Fellowship, a Henfield Foundation Transatlantic Review Award, a Wallace Stegner Fellowship, a James Michener Award, and a fellowship at the Fine Arts Work Center in Provincetown. Until recently, he taught writing at the University of San Francisco and served as a strategic planning and development consultant for nonprofit organizations. He now lives with his wife and two-year-old daughter in Provincetown, where he is Acting Executive Director of the Fine Arts Work Center.

Leebron explains that the inspiration for "Lovelock," which will be reprinted in *Voices of the Exiled,* a Doubleday anthology, "comes from a brief encounter I had in New Orleans in 1985 and an overnight stay I made in Nevada four years later. A number of weekends from high school spent at Atlantic City roulette tables also played a role. I began writing a novel that contains 'Lovelock' as a chapter in the spring of 1992, during a daily train commute between San Francisco and Hayward."

**EDITORS' CORNER** Some notable new books by former guest editors: *Winter Numbers* and *Selected Poems 1965–1990,* poems by Marilyn Hacker (W.W. Norton, forthcoming in Oct.); *Women, Animals, and Vegetables,* essays and stories by Maxine Kumin (W.W. Norton); *Split Horizon,* poems by Thomas Lux (Houghton Mifflin); *Shelter,* a novel by Jayne Anne Phillips (Houghton Mifflin/Seymour Lawrence); and *The Inferno of Dante,* a new verse translation by Robert Pinsky (Farrar, Straux & Giroux).

**ANNUALS** This turned out to be a banner year for awards given to works in *Ploughshares.* Three out of the twenty stories in *Best American Short Stories 1994,* edited by Tobias Wolff, were picked from *Ploughshares,* the most selections from a single literary journal in the current history of the series: Carolyn Ferrell's "Proper Library" (Spring 1993, edited by Al Young), Laura Glen Louis's "Fur" (Fall 1993), and Jonathan Wilson's "From Shanghai" (Fall

1993). In addition, Thomas Rabbitt's poem "Over All" (Winter 1993–94) will be appearing in *Pushcart Prize XIX: Best of the Small Presses;* Jeffrey McDaniel's poem "Following Her to Sleep" (Winter 1992–93, edited by Marie Howe and Christopher Tilghman) will be in *Best American Poetry 1994;* and Helen Fremont's story "Where She Was" (Winter 1992–93) will be published in *Prize Stories 1994: The O. Henry Awards.*

MORE PRIZES Congratulations to this year's Pulitzer Prize winners, three of whom have been contributors to *Ploughshares:* Yusef Komunyakaa for his poetry collection *Neon Vernacular;* E. Annie Proulx for her novel *The Shipping News;* and poet Lloyd Schwartz for music criticism in *The Boston Phoenix.* Also a toast to Chase Twichell, a poetry recipient of an Academy Award in Literature from the American Academy of Arts and Letters.

GIFT IDEA Knopf has launched the Everyman's Library Pocket Poets, a series of volumes of classic poets. The books are beautifully hardbound and priced reasonably at $10.95 each. Thus far, the series includes volumes of Baudelaire, Dickinson, Rossetti, Shelley, Stevens, and Keats, with plans for more.

S.O.S. Share Our Strength's third annual "Writers Harvest: The National Reading" will take place on Wednesday, November 2. Over eight hundred writers will read in two hundred locales across North America to benefit hunger relief organizations.

—*Don Lee*

# CONTRIBUTORS' NOTES

*Ploughshares · Fall 1994*

**FAITH ADIELE**'s work has appeared or is forthcoming in *Ms., Life Notes: Personal Writings by Contemporary Black Women* (W.W. Norton, 1994), *SAGE: A Scholarly Journal on Black Women*, and *Testimony* (Beacon Press, 1995). She works as an administrator at Radcliffe College, and is currently writing a memoir that explores Nigerian/Scandinavian identity.

**CHARLES BAXTER** is the author of three books of stories, most recently *A Relative Stranger* (W.W. Norton), and two novels, *First Light* (Viking/Penguin) and *Shadow Play* (Norton). He teaches at the University of Michigan and lives in Ann Arbor.

**SUZANNE BERNE** is the recipient of a National Endowment for the Arts fellowship for fiction. Her stories and essays have appeared in many publications, including *The Threepenny Review, Ms.*, and *The New York Times Magazine*. She is working on a novel.

**FREDERICK BUSCH**'s latest book is *The Children in the Woods: New & Selected Stories*, published by Ticknor & Fields. His recent novels are *Long Way from Home* and *Closing Arguments*. He is the Fairchild Professor of Literature at Colgate University.

**RAFAEL CAMPO**, who was named *The Kenyon Review*'s Emerging Writer of the Year, is a resident in medicine at the University of California, San Francisco. His first book of poems, *The Other Man Was Me*, won the 1993 National Poetry Series open competition and was recently released by Arte Público Press. He is currently at work on a collection of essays and a second book of poems.

**MICHELLE CLIFF** is Allan K. Smith Professor of English Language and Literature at Trinity College. She is the author most recently of the novel *Free Enterprise*, published by Dutton.

**LISA COHEN** lives in New York City. She has written about film for *The Village Voice* and about books for the *Voice Literary Supplement*.

**JANE CREIGHTON** has published essays in *The American Voice, Gulf Coast, Mother Jones*, and the anthology *Unwinding the Vietnam War*. Her collection of poems, *Ceres in an Open Field*, was published by Out & Out Books. "Brother" is from her new manuscript, *My Home in the Country*.

**FRANK DESANTO** spent seven years in educational publishing in New York. He now teaches at the University of Michigan, where he completed the M.F.A. program as a Javits Fellow, and where "Out of Control" was granted a Hopwood prize in 1994. It is his first published essay.

**STEPHEN DUNN**'s *New & Selected Poems: 1974–1994* was recently published by W.W. Norton, which also released his *Walking Light: Essays & Memoirs* in 1993. He teaches at Richard Stockton College in New Jersey.

**JOSEPH FEATHERSTONE** is in charge of a new urban teacher education program at Michigan State University. He has been a school reformer, a political activist, and a literary critic, as well as an editor of *The New Republic*. His recent writing includes poetry, as well as essays.

**SUSAN JANE GILMAN**, a fiction and nonfiction writer, has published previously in *Ploughshares, Story, The Village Voice, The New York Times,* and *Newsday*. She earned her M.F.A. at the University of Michigan, where she won three Hopwood Awards, including one for the essay published in this issue. She is at work on a novel.

**ALBERT GOLDBARTH**, a recent recipient of the National Book Critics Circle Award, will be publishing a new book of essays this fall: *Great Topics of the World* (David R. Godine). In 1993, *Across the Layers: Poems Old and New* was issued by the University of Georgia Press.

**RODGER KAMENETZ** is a poet and writer who teaches at Louisiana State University. His books include *The Missing Jew: New and Selected Poems* and *Terra Infirma*, an autobiographical meditation. Harper San Francisco recently published *The Jew in the Lotus*, a personal account of Jewish Buddhist dialogue.

**SUSAN LESTER** makes her home in Tallahassee, Florida, with her husband, near her two grown sons. She is a graduate student in Florida State University's writing program and teaches English to the foreign-born. Her stories have appeared in several small magazines, including the *University of Windsor Review*.

**FRANCES MAYES**'s essays have been published in *The Virginia Quarterly Review, The American Poetry Review, The American Scholar, The Southern Review,* and *The Gettysburg Review*. The essay in this issue will be included in a memoir of Italy, due out from Chronicle Books in 1995. She is the author of four poetry collections and the textbook *The Discovery of Poetry* (Harcourt Brace).

**EDITH MILTON** has written reviews and critical essays for a variety of periodicals, including *The New Republic* and *The New York Times Book Review*. Her fiction and essays have appeared in *The Yale Review, The Kenyon Review, Tikkun,* and *Witness*, among other magazines, and in *The Best American Short Stories* for 1982 and 1988.

**VALERIE MINER**'s latest novel is *A Walking Fire* (State Univ. Press of New York, 1994). Her other novels include *All Good Women, Winter's Edge, Blood Sisters, Movement,* and *Murder in the English Department.* She is also the author of *Trespassing and Other Stories* and *Rumors from the Cauldron: Selected Essays, Reviews, and Reportage.* She is Associate Professor of English and Creative Writing at the University of Minnesota.

**KATHLEEN NORRIS** is the author of *Dakota: A Spiritual Geography* (Ticknor & Fields, 1993). Her next book of poems, *Little Girls in Church,* will be published by the University of Pittsburgh Press in 1995. She lives in South Dakota.

**JOSIP NOVAKOVICH**'s prose has appeared in *Antaeus, The Paris Review, The Threepenny Review, Ploughshares, Pushcart Prizes XV & XIX,* and *The New York Times Magazine.* Next spring, Graywolf Press will publish his essay collection and his story collection, and Story Press his *Fiction Writer's Workshop.* He teaches at the University of Cincinnati.

**NAOMI SHIHAB NYE** is the editor of *This Same Sky, A Collection of Poems from Around the World.* Her first picture book for children, *Sitti's Secrets,* illustrated by Nancy Carpenter, appeared from Four Winds Press in 1994. Later this year, she will publish *Red Suitcase,* a new book of poems (BOA Editions), and *Words Under the Words: Selected Poems* (Far Corner Books and Eighth Mountain Press). She lives in San Antonio, Texas.

**DEBRA SPARK**'s novel, *Coconuts for the Saint,* will be published in the fall by Faber and Faber. Most recently, her stories have appeared in *Passages North, Epoch,* and *Agni.*

**CHARLES WIESE** is an artist living in Houston, Texas. Formerly employed as a research scientist and aerospace engineer, he recently completed his M.F.A. in photography at the University of Houston. He has a particular interest in the histories of flight and technology and their roles in Western cultural formations. He has published one artist's book, *Deportment,* and is currently working on his second, *The Fully Abridged Dictionary of the English Language.*

**S. L. WISENBERG** has published in several genres in *The New Yorker, The Kenyon Review, Tikkun, The Miami Herald,* and many anthologies. She teaches at the Medill School of Journalism at Northwestern University. "Holocaust Girls/ Lemon" is from a book-in-progress made up of pieces of fiction and nonfiction.

# MFA

## Writing Program
## at Vermont College

**Intensive 11-Day Residencies**
July and January on the beautiful Vermont campus.
Workshops, classes, readings, conferences, followed
by **Non-Resident 6-Month Writing Projects** in
poetry and fiction individually designed during residency.
In-depth criticism of manuscripts. Sustained dialogue with faculty.

**Post-Graduate Writing Semester**
for those who have already finished a graduate degree
with a concentration in creative writing.

Vermont College admits students
regardless of race, creed, sex or ethnic origin.
Scholarships and financial aid available.

### Faculty

| | |
|---|---|
| Tony Ardizzone | Phyllis Barber |
| Robin Behn | Francois Camoin |
| Mark Cox | Mark Doty |
| Jonathan Holden | Cynthia Huntington |
| Richard Jackson | Sydney Lea |
| Diane Lefer | Ellen Lesser |
| Bret Lott | Jack Myers |
| Sena Jeter Naslund | Christopher Noel |
| Pamela Painter | David Rivard |
| Mary Ruefle | Betsy Sholl |
| Darrell Spencer | Sharon Sheehe Stark |
| Gladys Swan | Leslie Ullman |
| Roger Weingarten | W.D. Wetherell |
| David Wojahn | |

**Visiting Writers Include:**

| | |
|---|---|
| Agha Shahid Ali | Hortense Calisher |
| Alison Deming | Valerie Wohlfeld |

### For more information:
Roger Weingarten, MFA Writing Program, Box 889,
Vermont College of Norwich University, Montpelier, VT  05602
802–828–8840
Low-residency B.A. and M.A. programs also available.

# SHORT
# STORY
# CONTEST

The **Boston Review** is pleased to announce its second annual Short Story Contest. The winning entry will be published in the December 1994 issue of the **Boston Review** and will receive a cash prize of $300. The stories are not restricted by subject matter, should not exceed 4,000 words, and should be previously unpublished. There is a $10 processing fee, payable to the **Boston Review** in the form of a check or money order. All entrants receive a one-year subscription to the **Boston Review** beginning with the December issue. Submissions must be postmarked by October 1, 1994. Stories will not be returned. The winner will be notified by mail. Send your entry to: Short Story Contest, **Boston Review,** 33 Harrison Avenue, Boston, MA 02111.

# *The Missouri Review*
# Editors' Prize Contest 1994

## $1,000—Short Fiction
## $1,000—Essay
## $500—Poetry

### Deadline: Postmarked by October 15, 1994

One winner and three finalists will be chosen in each category. Winners will be published and finalists announced in the following spring's issue of *The Missouri Review*. Entries must be previously unpublished, and will not be returned. Enclose a SASE for notification of winners.

## Complete Guidelines

- **Page restrictions:** 25 typed, double-spaced, for fiction and essays, 10 pages for poetry.

- **Entry fee:** $15 for each entry (checks payable to *The Missouri Review*). Each fee entitles entrant to a one-year subscription to *MR*, an extension of a current subscription, or a gift subscription. Please indicate your choice and enclose a complete address for subscriptions.

- Entries must be clearly addressed to: Missouri Review Editors' Prize, 1507 Hillcrest Hall, UMC, Columbia, MO 65211. Outside of the envelope must be marked "Fiction," "Essay" or "Poetry."

- Enclose an index card with the author's name, address, and telephone number in the left corner and the work's title in the center of the card if fiction or essay.

**1992 Winners:** Fiction—*David Borofka*, Essay—*Tom Whalen*, Poetry—*Jeff Friedman*

**1993 Winners:** Fiction—*Michael Byers*, Essay—*Michael Steinberg*, Poetry—*Maureen Seaton*

**Subscription Rates:** 3 years–$36 2 years–$27 1 year–$15

# SUBMISSION POLICIES

*Ploughshares · Fall 1994*

*Ploughshares* considers submissions postmarked between August 1 and March 31. All manuscripts sent from April to July are returned unread (we adhere very strictly to the postmark restrictions). Our address is: *Ploughshares*, Emerson College, 100 Beacon St., Boston, MA 02116-1596. *Ploughshares* is published three times a year: usually mixed issues of poetry and fiction in the Winter and Spring and a fiction issue in the Fall. Each is guest-edited by a different writer, who will often be interested in a specific theme. More often than not, however, these themes are designed to be as inclusive as possible. From August to November this year, we will be accepting submissions for the Spring 1995 poetry and fiction issue, edited by Gary Soto. Mr. Soto is open to a variety of subjects, but at the moment, he is thinking of centering his issue on the themes of everyday events of evil or sexuality. From November to February, we will be reading for the Fall 1995 fiction issue, edited by Ann Beattie, who will not have a particular theme for her selections. You may submit for a specific editor, but please be timely, as we accumulate quite a backlog. You should also understand that staff editors have the responsibility of determining for which issue or editor a work is most appropriate. If an issue closes, the work is often considered for the next one. Overall, we look for submissions of serious literary value. For fiction: one story, thirty-page maximum length, typed double-spaced on one side of the page. No criticism or book reviews. For poetry: up to five poems, individually typed either single- or double-spaced on one side. (Sorry, but "Phone-a-Poem," 617-578-8754, is by invitation only.) Always submit fiction and poetry separately. Only one submission each of fiction and/or poetry at a time. Please do not send multiple submissions of the same genre for different issues/editors, and do not send another manuscript until you hear about the first. Mail your manuscript in a page-sized manila envelope, your full name and address written on the outside, to the Fiction or Poetry Editor at the *Ploughshares* office. (Unsolicited work sent directly to a guest editor's home or office will be discarded.) All manuscripts and correspondence regarding submissions should be accompanied by a self-addressed, stamped envelope (s.a.s.e.) for reply or return of the manuscript, or we will not respond. Expect three to five months for a decision. Please do not query us on the status of a submission until five months have passed, and if you do, we prefer that you write to us, indicating the postmark date of submission, instead of calling. *We cannot accommodate revisions, changes of return address, or forgotten s.a.s.e.'s after the fact.* We do not reprint previously published work. Translations are welcome if permission has been granted. We cannot be responsible for delay, loss, or damage (usually postal-related). Never send originals or your only copy. Payment is upon publication: $10/printed page for prose, $20/page for poetry, $40 minimum per title, $200 maximum per author, with two copies of the issue and a one-year subscription.